BABY SCOUT

Gunslinging and Whoring During the Chopper War in Southeast Asia

By

Michael W. Mason

© 2001 by Michael W. Mason. All rights reserved.

No part of this book may be reproduced, stored in a retrieval system, or transmitted by any means, electronic, mechanical, photocopying, recording, or otherwise, without written permission from the author.

ISBN: 0-7596-8103-1

This book is printed on acid free paper.

1stBooks - rev. 01/09/02

CONTENTS

Introduction vii
Prologue xi

Chapters

1. In-Country 1
2. Sandbags And Feces 13
3. Baby Scouts 21
4. Virgin Flight 31
5. Kool-Aid And Bunker Rats 49
6. Busted Cherry 61
7. Grease Guns And Gunslingers 73
8. Blown Out Of The Sky 91
9. Killing The Dead 107
10. Bullets And Butt Plates 115
11. The Exotic Whores Of Saigon 123
12. The Last Flight Of #395 153
13. Dead Scout Walking 181
14. The Sex Factory Of China Beach 201
15. The Silver Bird 219

Epilogue 225
Excerpt From The Sequel 229

ACKNOWLEDGMENTS

Col. Russell W. Thresher, U.S.A.F. (RET.), for his savy and technical advice which was sorely needed and gratefully appreciated.

Harry Horn: one of Journalism's best, for his insightful critiques.

Suh Si Neuhbauer for her beauty and artistic inspiration.

Samantha Marshall for being the *sounding board* on my concepts concerning women.

Wanda Hamilton for her realistic illustrations.

Kadi Hendricks: friend and helpful grammar critic.

Rev. Bruce Carlson: Vietnam pilot, advisor, editor, friend, and author of *Redbird Down.*

INTRODUCTION

This is my soul on paper, a personal narrative based on real people, places, and factual events. It's a story from thirty year old remembrances...recollections from a time when boys either matured quickly or died before manhood. I will personalize my year, *in-country*, and introduce you to to the other Baby Scouts I flew with, killed with, and went wilding with.

These writings are not a history lesson. Military jargon and technics will be minimal. This simply, and frankly, is the story of a naive teen who goes to war.

You will become the gunslinging character. You will think his thoughts, see what he sees, and feel his emotions. You won't like some of it. Most likely, you'll hate most of what you're about to do as a young, gunslinging Baby Scout. But, don't be surprised if you find that being a Baby Scout outweighs the horrors you must face on a daily basis.

You might be enticed by the CONTENTS page to read the *blood*, *guts*, and *sex* chapters first. Don't! The chapters progress off each other. It is best to live the adventure as it unfolds.

The experience with the Baby Scouts will be the palette that gives color to the gunslinging teenager. I was that boy. You will become him and go on the suicidal, thrillride of your life.

Most names have been changed, but the people are real. They lived, fought, came home, or died. The extreme violence, erotica, the bizarre, and the loony, were daily faire. A Baby Scout's life expectancy, when in battle, was estimated at seven seconds. Is it any wonder the young Scouts fought and played hard. Every mission was considered the last. Few Scouts ever believed they would go home, other than in a flag draped, aluminum box.

It all happened a long time ago in a sweatbox netherworld known as South Vietnam. 1968 was the year of *Tet*, the North Vietnam offensive. It was also the year that brought about an end to the Hanoi bombing, saw the demise of L.B.J., and the rise of Richard Milhouse Nixon. The *My Lai Massacre* was being covered up, and a new American conscience was making me an enemy in my own country.

I dedicate this story to the legendary Baby Scouts of the 25th Infantry Division, nicknamed *Tropic Lightning*. Outside of military lore, and legend, there are no chronicled reports of this helicopter, aeroscout outfit.

Until now, the saga of the Baby Scouts was only verse on the lips of soldiers. I am proud to document for the first time, anywhere, the existence of this mostly, teenaged fighting force that terrorized the enemy in two war zones, including the infamous *Iron Triangle.*

I didn't much question my role in the war. Some of us relished it more than others. Toward the end of my tour in Vietnam, I became *short*. It meant I only had a month to go before boarding the shiny, *Silver Bird*, or *Freedom Flight*, home. New arrivals were called *greens, fresh meat, cherry,* or simply, *FNG,* or *Fucking New Guy. FNG* was the most popular acronym, but *meat* was the most prophetic.

It was January 30, 1968 and my legs were tingling, half-asleep, and wobbly as I walked down the exit ramp. My eyes were blinded by the white light of the Asian sun. It was a long and tiring flight on the converted Air Force cargo jet. My watery eyes slowly focused and through the heat waves rising from the hot, concrete tarmac, I saw troops marching toward a gleaming, silvery jet. They marched two by two and each suntanned face had a smile. Cargo of some sort was being stacked outside the shiny, commercial airliner. They looked like rectangular boxes…aluminum boxes. Soldiers were loading them into the belly of the plane. As the marching men neared the jet, the smiles slowly disappeared.

One of them, an officer, saluted as he climbed the boarding ramp to the silver bird. A few of the troops made the sign of the cross. Death was always with you, a constant of war, even when going home. I learned with my first steps on Vietnamese soil that death would haunt me with a vengeance.

As I walked across the airfield with the other *volunteers*, I noticed *duece and a halfs* (2 and 1/2 ton trucks), waiting for us. The intense heat and humidity had already soaked my fatigues with a dirty sweat that was most pungent. I threw my dufflebag into the back of one of the trucks and climbed aboard, wondering, "What the hell have I gotten myself into?" Specialist 4th class, Michael W. Mason had arrived in-country. Those leaving went one of two ways possible…dead or alive.

The sights on the airfield were ironies and metaphors, screaming for attention. I gave little thought to the aluminum-cased war heroes. I was too into myself, eager for battle, and my own glorious adventures. The new *John Wayne* was in town and it wasn't big enough for both *Charlie* and me. I used to think there were a lot of pretenders like me. There weren't. I was 19. Some were 18. Teenagers still, yet, men going off to war.

I knew little, learned a lot, and lived to cheat death time and again. I grew up in a place of horror and lived to manhood by becoming a better killer than my enemy. I am ashamed to admit this, but I thrived on the killing and enjoyed it. It was never just duty, or a job; it was exhilarating fun. Death became my sidekick.

For eleven months it was fun. That was part of being a Baby Scout. I expected death every day and reveled in it. I woke every morning and strapped on a Colt 45. I never lived for tomorrow as I figured it would never come.

I lived for *search and destroy*, the *gunruns*, and the *firefights*. It was part of my daily life as a suicidal, teenaged gunslinger in the legendary Baby Scouts. We were all a little crazy, nuts, off the wall, and certifiable. You had to be to volunteer for the Scouts.

Eleven months after arriving in-country, I would cock my Colt 45 pistol and put it in my mouth. The life of a little Vietnamese girl ended under my gunsight and self-retribution seemed the only rational way back to humanity. I was wrong. I was wrong about a lot of things in Vietnam. My thrillride of a lifetime ended with the killing of that little girl. She is still with me, though. I talk to her all the time, at night, when I sleep. You see, she came home with me and never left. She'll always be with me. This, now, is how it all happened. Even after more than 30-years, it doesn't seem like all that long ago.

PROLOGUE

We left the way we arrived, with a walk across the blinding, sun reflecting tarmac of Tan Son Nhut Air Base. This time, however, I boarded a gleaming, silver, civilian jetliner instead of a C-141 converted cargo transport. The melancholy was interrupted by a cheerful greeting, "Welcome aboard." The pretty, blonde stewardess greeted us when we arrived at the top of the boarding ramp. I smiled at her, then looked back for a final glimpse of hell's frontier. On the horizon was a spiralling column of black smoke. It seemed a fitting epitaph and the irony did not escape me. The smoke was both human spawned and a godsend during my year in Vietnam. How the smoke originated is still a painful memory that eludes erasure.

As we soldiers entered the silver bird, another fifty were loaded into the dark belly of the aircraft. The aluminum coffins were stacked like so much cord wood. The men who went about the solemn task did so with a proficiency that smacked of experience. In Vietnam, *Graves Detail* personnel got all too much experience.

I took an aisle seat in the tail section. Understandably, I wanted a clear view of the stewardesses as they walked by. A thud and vibration ended my lustful daydreaming. The cargo hatch had slammed shut. The brave men, below, were secure in their dark sanctuary for the long journey home.

The boarding hatch closed seconds later. It was muscled home and sealed by the pretty, blonde stewardess. She wall tall, about five-nine, with a great figure, and looked to be pushing thirty. The woman wore her white blouse tightly tucked into her navy blue skirt. Her breasts weren't overly large but were nicely outlined by her tight-fitting garment. Her skirt rose to just above the knees and her shapely legs ended in matching blue pumps. She wore her hair long and with a slight wave that covered one eye whenever she cocked her head. Her eyes were blue and her nose was thin and upturned.

Her classic, American looks were topped off with full, sensuous lips lightly painted with red lipstick. In every way she was American...the first real American girl I had seen in a year. I didn't count the nurses or Red Cross *Donut Dollies*; they seemed too military, or uncivilian. The stewardess, however, was 100% civilian. I immediately formed a crush on her. She was a slice of American pie. She was the girl next door. She was…*Mom.*

The turbines suddenly increased their whine. We, almost as one, fell silent. Only the crane of our necks, toward the windows, betrayed our thoughts. Mom was giving the mandatory safety spiel but no one was listening. We were finally leaving the Republic of South Vietnam and were too intent on the happennings outside the plane.

The place where we lived, killed, or died, was slowly moving away and, hopefully, out of our lives forever. The pilot was talking to us over the intercom but we ignored him too. It was the moving landscape that held our attention. A year ago, to the day, I was aboard a military plane, rolling toward the terminal. Now, I was rolling away from it.

A sharp turn brought helicopter warbirds into view. The gunships were nestled in their protective bunkers of sandbags and steel. Beyond the sleeping war machines I saw a C-141 unloading its cargo of fresh *meat*. As this bittersweet vision slowly slipped past my window, I looked away. Strangely, I was thinking of my first steps on Vietnamese soil. A land that, over the course of a year, had damaged my soul and soaked up some of my blood.

The plane made an abrupt turn and the engines screamed. Reality slammed me back into my seat. The jet roared down the runway and rays of white light filtered in through the windows. Even in escape the tortuous Asian sun would cast shadows of a past I would never really leave behind. The rising pitch of the jets was an exclamation to the visions of a war that I was destined to never forget.

The front of the cabin rose upward and then there was the unmistakeable *Clunk* of the landing gear clearing the runway. That beautiful noise, and vibration, gave proof to my departure from the land known as *Hell on Earth.*

The silence. It was overwhelming. No one talked. All eyes were either closed in prayer or cast out upon the fleeting landscape. Faces were solemn. I stared at the back of the head of the soldier seated in front of me, yet, I did not see him. I was having visions of 51-caliber machine gun tracers and rocket propelled grenades being fired at the big, shiny, silver bird. Slowly, normalcy returned to my unreasoning brain. I was going home. I was also taking home with me a fear of flying. My hands had a death grip on the armrests. I had another brief lapse and envisioned a sniper taking aim at my shiny, silver bird. I didn't feel safe. Not yet.

I was leaving a land of unimaginable horror, yet I still didn't believe it. Then, all at once, a deafening, raucous cheer resounded throughout the cabin. It finally hit me. I was going home. I joined the chorus of cheers, shouting, and applause. Military hats went flying through the cabin and the tumultuous noise drowned out the turbines. A party was about to commence. However, in the cavernous belly of the plane, there was eternal silence. No party there. Only brave men sleeping a hero's slumber. They were going home, too.

When the thunderous roar subsided, I felt a sense of well-being. It was like shedding a years worth of sin, shame, fear, and guilt. For the first time in many months I was at ease with myself and with what I had done during my year in hell.

The countryside was rapidly falling behind. The silver bird was heading out over the South China Sea and the Republic of South Vietnam finally disappeared behind cleansing wisps of white clouds. Always the romantic, I thought them bandages for my tortured, fleeing soul. I had a lot of memories that needed bandaging.

As I turned from the window, a small, delicate hand, clutching a beer, was floating before my eyes. Mom was looking down at me, smiling, and showing perfect, white teeth.

"Beer, soldier?" I sheepishly smiled back at her.

"Sure. Thanks." I was tense and Mom noticed my death grip on the armrests. Her cheerful smile became a sympathetic one.

"It's ok," she said, looking at my name tag, "You're going home, Specialist Mason." I loosened my white-knuckled, death grip and looked into sparkling, blue eyes.

"I'm just a little nervous when I fly, Miss."

"Really?" she replied. Her eyes had noticed the silver wings on my chest. She was puzzled and was about to say something else but stopped herself. She had also seen the *Purple Heart* ribbon because her smile turned into a frown, and then a sad pout.

"Thanks for the beer, Miss. You've made this the best day I've had in a year." She stared at me for a few seconds, then the toothy smile was back, bigger than ever.

"You're welcome, Specialist Mason. I'll be here if you need anything." She turned with a flourish, blonde hair sweeping down over an eye, then she was gone. I watched her as she rolled the beer cart down the aisle. I watched her every move and discovered that my lust was gone. She, indeed, was Mom. She was taking care of her boys.

As the plane leveled off, a symphony of two hundred voices got quieter. In the background I heard a few men crying softly. A highly decorated infantryman hid his tear-stained face as Mom walked by. A few of us prayed. The rest settled in and got acquainted.

"Where you from?"

"New York."

"Oh yeah. I'm from Jersey."

"Do you believe Namath and those Jets?"

"I know. I lost a week's pay betting on the Colts."

"Yeah. That Namath. Who'd ever guess he could beat Unitas and the Colts?"

That's how the conversations went. There was little *shop talk* of the war. Mom was kept busy. She must have passed out five hundred beers and looked at hundreds of pictures of wives, babies, and girlfriends. After passing me a fresh beer, and noticing my more relaxed demeanor, she winked at me and then moved to those that needed her.

I got up and went to a vacant window seat. I sipped my suds and gazed out at the vast blanket of clouds. Resting my head on the cabin side, I thought about the Baby Scouts.

I thought about the black smoke on the horizon, and how those nasty, dark spirals had welcomed me to Vietnam exactly one year earlier. Of course, then, I had no idea what the ominous, black smoke was. I was a *FNG* and a *living ticket* for someone's journey home. I arrive, someone goes home.

Soon after arriving in country, I learned the significance, and irony, of the black smoke. Those filthy columns would even help guide me safely home after a mission over the infamous Iron Triangle.

I lived for a year in a wreckage of a country being held together only by the sheer numbers of American troops, advisors, and equipment. It was more luck than destiny that I found the Baby Scouts of the 3rd Squadron/4th Cavalry of the 25th Infantry Division. This 19 year old, Long Island suburbanite, would soon find his place in the war. I would find a home and a family to kill for.

Everything was coming back to me as the beer loosened my thoughts and the passing clouds soothed me to sleep. The party was still going strong but I was returning to my home…going back to the Baby Scouts and going back to war.

I felt something soft being placed behind my head. The empty beer can was pried from my red-knuckled fingers. Before darkness took me, I heard a soft, yet sad, melodic voice in my mind.

"Poor guy," said Mom, "I hope he sleeps all the way to Hawaii."

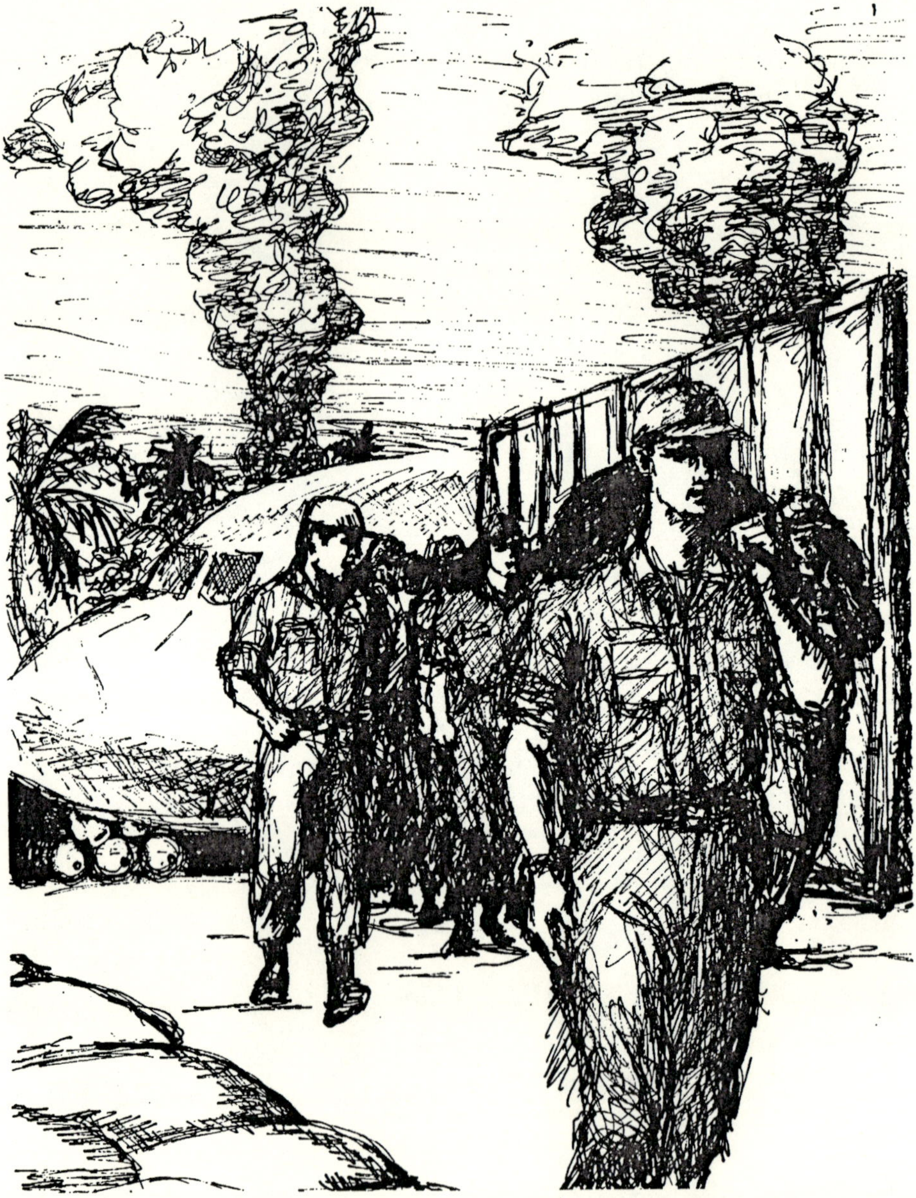

ONE

IN-COUNTRY

Flying backward into a backward country. It seemed appropriate. I was seated, among many, facing the tail section of the giant C-141 cargo jet. The Air Force thought it safer to have the troops facing the rear of the plane. I stared at the mountain of dufflebags behind the cargo netting. Except for the backs of heads, that's all there is to look at on a C-141. There are no windows and unless you sleep, or have a buddy to talk to, you just stared at a virtual mountain of green, canvas dufflebags.

My orders for Vietnam were cut for the 29th of January, 1968. Time in flight and the international dateline conspired to land me in the Republic of South Vietnam on the 30th. I would learn the significance of this very soon.

The hydraulic whine and thump of the landing gear startled me out of a listless sleep.

"Fasten your seatbelts," a coarse-voiced Sergeant bellowed. He was patrolling the aisle of the *stretched*, converted C-141. Now-and-then he would gently tap a sleeping soldier on the shoulder and say, "Buckle up, son. We're going in." Hundreds of metal buckles being fastened drowned out the engine noise. If only for a few seconds, the odd metallic noise was a welcomed break after fifteen hours of flight and screaming jets.

The enormous troop carrier dropped out of the clouds, over the South China Sea, and proceeded north over the Mekong Delta. The approach was straight and fast. I was thinking about a freckled-faced, red-haired, high school girlfriend when the plane touched down. A crude PA system crackled, "Gentlemen, welcome to the Republic of South Vietnam." The arrival was very suspenseful as we slowed and began the taxi toward the small, military terminal. We couldn't see anything and tensions were high. A corporal, seated next to me, whispered, "God, help me!"

Most on the plane were drafted into the army. However, I was different. I was regular Army, serial number 11813261. More interestingly, I was also a Vietnam volunteer. There weren't many *crazies* like me...the ones who volunteered for war. In my case, a *Dear John Letter* from that little, red-haired girl, and a cushy, boring assignment in Germany, led me to seek what few would want. The draftees had no

Michael W. Mason

choice. The letters *U-S* before their serial numbers meant United States. These *Uncle Sams* were government property and had no choice at all.

After basic training all soldiers are sent to A.I.T., or Advanced Individual Training. Many of us joked that the *I* stood for Infantry. It didn't seem funny, however, when the orders for Vietnam came in.

My M.O.S., or Military Occupational Specialty, was helicopter maintenance. The advantage of enlistment was being allowed to pick the training school you wanted. Draftees usually went to infantry school and then right off to Vietnam.

I was a helicopter crew chief and had spent the previous year working, and flying, on the OH-13. This small, observation helicopter is the *bubble* that has a metal, latticework frame attached to it. It's powered by a six cylinder, gas engine which propels the aircraft slower than some birds. In Vietnam there would be no bubbles for me. Something similar, yet far deadlier, was awaiting my special, untested talents. I would soon embark on the most thrilling roller coaster ride of my life. Dealing out death would become second nature and the adrenaline rush of aerial combat made marijuana seem like an impotent narcotic. Flying with the Baby Scouts would be better than beer, and even my mom's meatloaf, mashed potatoes, and gravy.

We were out of our seats before the plane rolled to a stop. As I stretched the kinks out of my sore body, the jet engines were throttled back, the sense of motion stopped, and the main hatch opened with a *Whoosh*! We moved toward the blinding, white light.

As I walked toward the luminescence, the soldiers in front of me disappeared like magic. When I stepped out onto the ramp my eyes lost all color and sight. I was then stopped in my tracks by a thick, brick wall of intense heat and humidity. Like dominoes, we all bumped into one another. My eyes slowly began to focus and the whites and greys were slowly replaced with colors. I had my first glimpse of Vietnam and the powerful, American war machine.

I walked down the ramp and witnessed the war effort in action. There were troops everywhere on the giant, Tan Son Nhut airfield. They were either marching off somewhere or busily working on the many aircraft that were parked in their protective revetments, or *bunkers.*

Helicopters were everywhere. Some of them were bristling with enough armament to level a small town. When I stepped off the ramp I felt both anxiety and elation…probably the only person happy to be in-country. If I was an Infantryman, I might have felt differently.

More than fifteen hours had passed since departing Fort Dix, New Jersey. There, it was thirty degrees with snow lightly falling. Here, I was welcomed by searing, hundred degree heat, blinding light, and a stifling, humid atmosphere that seemed difficult to walk in. I was already soaked with perspiration when I claimed my musty dufflebag.

The Sergeant, who had checked our seatbelts, took charge and lined us up into formation. A jeep pulled up and the Sarge saluted the driver, a Captain. After a short discussion, the jeep led us off the tarmac and toward a waiting convoy of *deuces*. The deuce-and-a-halfs are both the *Bekins* and the *Trailways* of the Army. Deuces moved everything and everyone.

The Captain positioned the jeep at the head of the convoy while the Sergeant directed the loading of the trucks. Sarge had walked over with us behind the jeep.

I respected that. As the loading continued, I took in the sights of the airbase.

Planes and choppers were everywhere and in constant motion. By far, most of the aircraft were helicopters. I didn't see any of my beloved OH-13s, but everywhere you looked…there were *Hueys*. The Huey is an all-purpose, utility chopper. It's the workhorse of the Army's aviation fleet. In Vietnam they were also the warhorses, packing enormous amounts of ordinance. Nearby, I saw an LOH-6A. This new, light observation helicopter was turbine powered and the replacement for the old, reliable bubble models. The *Loach* is shaped like an egg with a long, round, tapering tail section. I thought it looked funny. Soon, I would learn to love this baby of *hunter* ships.

The Sarge (I never knew his name), looked the convoy over, then twirled a finger over his head. All the diesels roared to life and then he climbed into the cab of the truck behind the jeep. I was in the third deuce back and watched the silent commands between Captain and Sergeant.

With a wave of the officer's hand, the convoy moved out. I didn't know where we were going. A sentry saluted the Captain as we rolled past a guard gate. Even on cement roads a deuce rides rough. My butt was numb by the time we left the smooth asphalt and were travelling along bumpy, dusty, dirt roads. Fortunately, the winds generated by the convoy kept us from eating too much dust.

Michael W. Mason

    I looked at the faces around me. They were young, like mine, but grim. Most were right out of A.I.T., and that meant infantry. I recognized the Corporal who sat next to me on the plane. We made eye contact and, with a dour expression, he slowly shook his head. His eyes were wide and I couldn't tell if his face bespoke anxiety or fear. I looked away before the Corporal noticed my indifference. My eyes wandered from face to sullen face. It seemed that I was the only one who was looking forward to duty in Vietnam. The others all had looks of despair.

    There wasn't much activity outside the airfield. All around were two-story, wood buildings. Some had air conditioners in the windows. Off on the horizon I saw columns of spiralling, black smoke. They rose hundreds of feet into a cloudless, blue sky and then mushroomed before dissipating in the wind. I asked the guy seated next to me what the smoke was but he just shook his head and said, "Beats me." I figured it was war related, a bomb or something. I also wondered why there was no sound from the explosions.

    It was late in the day when the convoy rolled into the Replacement Processing Center. The trucks came to a stop and so did the refreshing breeze. The trailing dust clouds caught up and settled over the trucks. Many of us held our breath or covered our mouths with shirt sleeves. The others just coughed.

    The broiling heat returned with a vengeance. It was a reminder that the cooler monsoon season was still months away. As much as I hated the dry season, I would despise the rainy season more.

    Until we became part of a paper trail we wouldn't officially be in-country. It's a classic *Catch-22* of sorts. I was here, but I really wasn't. I was alive, but not living in South Vietnam. At one time, or another, all soldiers enter the surreal world of *Captain Yosarian*. A rotor blade could cut me in half and my epitaph might read, "He disappeared while enroute to Southeast Asia and is presumed dead."

    My butt was thankful to get off the truck. Even a short ride on a deuce seems long. After a conference, the Captain and Sergeant led us to a large, rectangular, wood building. The two-story barracks looked similar to the buildings we passed on the ride over. Those buildings were administration offices. They were where the *brass* and the clerks worked.

    The sun was setting as we entered the barracks. It was military clean and had two long rows of metal bunkbeds. There were red-painted *butt cans* attached to support pillars. More than half of us lit up. I was reminded of my first *home away from home*, Fort Knox, Kentucky. It was where I took basic training.

I settled into a top bunk on the first floor. I could reach over and flick my ashes into a butt can without getting up. Smoking in bed is not allowed in the Army, but after basic training the Corporals, and most Sergeants, would usually give us some lattitude. I lay on my back and blew smoke rings. I daydreamed about Huey gunships.

"Hey! Where you from?" I looked over and saw a young, black private looking at me.

"Huntington Station, New York. How about you?"

"Columbus, Ohio." His name was Freddy and he was fresh out of armor school at Fort Knox, Kentucky. I told him that I took basic there and we formed a short-lived friendship.

Most of us talked about nothing of any great importance: home, girls, cars, and family. It was important to us, though. We showed each other pictures and shared smokes. Few of us knew where we were going. Freddy was one of the lucky few. He said, "I'm going to an armored cavalry unit near Saigon." Freddy was drafted, yet seemed eager to enter the war. He told me that he just wanted to get it over with and go home. I lied and told him the same thing. How do you tell someone that you volunteered to get shot at.

We went back to our own thoughts and I figured that Freddy was luckier than most of the guys in the barracks. They would be going to jungles and rice paddies as infantrymen. Freddy would get to ride in an *iron horse*. Of all the guys I came over with, I only remember Freddy and Sarge. The rest are nameless, faceless souls.

The mess hall was nearby and the Sarge led us there as a group, though mob was more like it. We marched out of cadence and smoked on the way. The Sarge was an oldtimer, a career man, a *Lifer*. He had a lot of stripes and hash marks on his sleeves.

He was a First Sergeant and would probably be assigned to a company as *Top Soldier*. This was his third tour of duy in Vietnam and he knew the ropes. When he talked, you listened. He was a big, tall, black man and sported a narrow, neatly trimmed mustache. He looked to be in his early to mid-forties. Sarge was courteous and commanded respect from us all. He was the last black man I would directly serve with in the war. Where I was going, Afro-Americans either didn't want to go, or didn't get the opportunity to go.

Michael W. Mason

More than half my bunkmates in basic training were black. They mostly came from the New York City area. Many of them seemed wise beyond their teenage years. A tall, gangly youth adopted me, sort of, and I called him *Big Daddy*. He called me *Son*.

Big Daddy helped keep me out of harms way during basic training and taught me some *street smarts*. He was all teeth when he smiled and was rarely seen without a grin on his face. Everyone liked him and sought his advice. He saved me many times from my own big mouth. Jokingly, after some of our talks, he would end our conversations with, "…my son."

Another of the big city boys was *Willie the Whopper*. Willie was a skinny kid, friendly, and usually kept to himself. He got his nickname because of his huge male *endowment*. He had the biggest penis in the company and had a penchant for playing with it. He also had a habit of masturbating in the middle of the night. Willie would lie on his back with his army blanket pitched over his erection. It looked like a pup tent. Some of the brothers would tease Willie about his nocturnal activity. He would just grin and answer, "With no bitches around, you do what you gotta do."

Everyone seemed to have a quirk of some sort. Some drank *After Shave*. Others would only use the latrine after *lights out*. My quirk, I guess, was *Clearasil*. The guys teased me about this and the Drill Sergeant called me, "Pretty Boy."

I remember most of the guys from basic. Sadly, I don't remember much about Sarge. No name, no face, just a few isolated incidents with the most memorable yet to come.

We all lit up after chow. The food was good. It's a tradition to gripe about army food, even when it's good. The army cooks took great pains to see that its troops were well-fed. I pulled my share of KP duty and can vouch for the quality.

In-country processing would start in the morning. The sun had set by the time Sarge had led us back to the barracks. There was a pretty, orange lume on the horizon and the beauty of it belied any semblance of a war zone.

After *shooting the shit* with a few of the guys, I made my bunk and took a long, hot shower. I figured it would be the last one for a long time. I combed my wet, dark brown hair. The grey was coming in fast and I wondered if I would be totally grey, like my uncle, before turning 25.

I put on my green boxer shorts and walked down the long aisle to my bunk. It was very quiet and the lights were already out. A few guys were smoking but most were already asleep. I climbed up onto my bunk and lit up. It seemed eerily quiet for a country at war. The only sound was the light snoring coming from Freddy. I blew a giant smoke ring, then tossed the butt into the can. I fluffed my pillow and thought about family, girlfriends, and my new home. When sleep finally came, I never had a chance to dream.

I startled awake, my body in midair, to the ear-splitting sounds of explosions, tearing metal, shattering glass, and screaming voices. I hit the floor, hard. I was tangled up in a knot of bedsheets, and then Freddy landed on me. My head was spinning but I was more bewildered than scared, or hurt.

A distant voice was yelling something about a rocket attack, and that our barracks had taken a direct hit to the roof. A Sergeant, but not Sarge, was shouting, "On the floor and pull your mattresses over you." I didn't argue.

The concussion from the exploding rocket was enormous. Thunder and lightning flashes could be heard and seen through the holes where windows used to be. One of the guys from upstairs slid under the bottom bunk next to me. I gave him half my mattress. His eyes were wide and he was shaking. It wasn't fear that I saw in his unseeing eyes, it was shock. The boy was in shock! I grabbed him around the waist and began to reassure him that everything would be fine. "It's ok, man," I said. "It's ok."

I patted his back and my hand ran across something jagged and wet. The soldier had a shard of shrapnel in him and my hand came away cut and wet with blood.

"*Damn*! You're hurt, man." As I was about to yell for a medic, the Sergeant yelled for everyone to get out of the barracks. I crawled out from under the bunk, dragging the wounded boy with me. He had me in a choke hold and wouldn't let go. Freddy saw this and came to my aid. He pried the soldier's fingers apart and then he and I put his arms over our shoulders and proceeded to drag him to the exit.

The Sergeant saw us and yelled for a medic. Ambulance-Jeeps and a deuce were already parked in front of the barracks. Two soldiers, wearing Red Cross arm bands, took the injured youth from us. They had to carry him as he had lost consciousness. I turned around to thank Freddy but he was gone. He had joined his infantry buddies and was busy telling them his first war story.

We were an unmilitary looking lot. Most of us were wearing nothing but shorts and dog tags. One guy wore only dog tags. He had snuck into the shower after lights out. When the rocket hit, he ran so fast he forgot his towel.

Off on the horizon were flashes of yellow light. The sound of thunder was distant and streams of red fire were coming from some of the moving lights in the black sky. The war had come to me. I was in it before my first day, in-country, was 24-hours old. It was at this moment that I discovered, to my own amazement, that I was happy to be here.

The Sergeant came over and asked me if I was alright. He had noticed the blood on my arms, chest, and shorts. I told him it was somebody elses. He laughed, looked at my shorts, and said, "*Damn*, son! For a minute there I thought you got shot in the *Johnson*." I looked down at my bloodstained boxers and then started laughing, too. When I looked back up, the man was walking away but still chuckling. I slowly stopped laughing and then wondered why the military called it a *Johnson*.

The Sergeant was conferring with the officers. After a few minutes he waved us over. The ranking brass, a Major, said we could reenter the barracks after the wounded were brought out. He never used the word, *dead*. We all knew there were dead guys in there. The Sergeant and the officers knew that we knew. They just didn't think that they needed to mention it.

The *walking wounded* came out first. Most suffered from concussions and minor shrapnel wounds. They were loaded on the jeeps. Then, the dead were brought out. They were carried on stretchers and covered with blankets. Dog tags dangled down the side of one of the stretchers. An arm was hanging out on another; there was no hand attached to it. A stream of blood left a trail to the waiting deuce. I counted four dead and at least a dozen wounded. "God!" I thought, "What a waste." I would pray that night to die in a fight and not in my sleep.

Shortly after the ambulance-jeeps and deuce left, we were allowed back in the building. There was splintered wood and broken glass everywhere. Bloodstained sheets and mattresses lay scattered about. The carnage was topped off with nasty, toxic water that had sprayed from the butt cans. We began cleaning without being told. No one talked. I was glad others were cleaning upstairs. I'd seen enough blood and death for one night. Little did I know that it was just the beginning of a long, bloody year...a year that would exact from me its toll in flesh, blood and, worst of all, horrific mental anguish.

It took hours to get the barracks close to normal. No matter how hard I tried, I couldn't get all the glass splinters out of my mattress and blanket. It really didn't matter as none of us would try to sleep.

I watched the distant lights through a hole in the wall that used to be a window. I was looking at my future and didn't have a clue. In just a few, short weeks I would be begging to join an elite outfit of teenaged killers. As I watched those lethal fireflies in the night sky, I wished to be there...raining down death from above. I would get my wish in about two weeks. Two weeks after the start of the *Tet Offensive*.

Tet was the big push by the North Vietnamese Army to disrupt the south and infiltrate the ancient, religious capitol, Hue. Even Saigon was attacked, as were major military bases across South Vietnam.

For the next fourteen days I would be going to indoctrination classes, jungle school, and pulling work details. In the military, details usually meant crap. In Vietnam it meant crap, literally. I would begin my education shortly after sunrise.

I moved away from the splintered hole and sat on my dufflebag. I lit up and looked around. Everyone was huddled about on the first floor. It was easy to spot the guys from the second floor. They were bunched together by the exit.

Freddy and a few of his new friends walked up to me. They wore only towels and carried shower bags.

"Let's go, Mike."

"Go where, Freddy?" I looked at him without understanding.

"The showers, man."

"I don't feel like a shower, Freddy."

"You got no choice," he said, laughing. "Look at yourself." I looked down and saw the dried blood. It was dark red, almost black. I suddenly felt nauseous.

The blood was everywhere. It caked my sparse chest hairs, covered my arms and the front of my shorts, and painted my right leg down to the toes.

"Ok, Freddy," I said, looking up at him, "Be there in a minute." Freddy nodded, then headed for the showers with his buddies. I was not far behind but made a detour into the latrine. I puked my guts into the first

Michael W. Mason

toilet I came to. Feeling better, I stripped my shorts and threw them into the trash can.

I walked into the hot steam clouds that billowed from the shower entrance. The dried blood became wet and began to drip down my body, leaving crimson trails that ended in a magenta pool on the shower floor. To my horror, my genitals were covered in blood. The others in the shower stared at me with much the same reaction. Then, Freddy began to laugh.

"Mike, man, that's the first time I ever saw a red Johnson. You gotta stop jerking-off all the time."

"Not funny, Freddy." I weakly smiled as I answered him. I looked down and saw the blood being washed away and down my legs. The water eventually became clear and I breathed more calmly. I took a bar of soap from my shower bag and began to lather up. My hand stung and I glanced at the jagged cut across the palm. I wondered, foolishly, if I was eligible for a Purple Heart.

I dressed in clean shorts and jungle fatigues. There was a soft, orange glow on the horizon as I walked to the mess hall. The Sarge would probably fill us in during chow. Someone did fill us in about the rocket and mortar attack. However, it wasn't Sarge who told us.

BABY SCOUT

Michael W. Mason

TWO

SANDBAGS AND FECES

"Four are dead and thirteen are wounded," said the Captain, as if giving the score of a ballgame. "The dead and seven of the wounded are going home," he added. The officer rattled off a few more sentences about war, bad luck, Tet, and Purple Hearts.

I finally learned what happened to the Sarge. He was one of the wounded. Many of us thought him killed when he didn't show up after the rocket attack. The Captain said the Sarge was asleep on the second floor when the rocket hit the roof. A Corporal, in the bunk above his, died instantly. The blast, and concussion, blew Sarge out of his bunk and sent him sprawling thirty feet down the aisle. He suffered busted ribs and massive shrapnel wounds down his backside. He also had concussion-induced nose and ear bleeds. The Captain added that he would recover but would probably never return to Vietnam.

I don't know if he retired after being sent home. I do know that I would have liked to have served with him. He was a man I respected and a man I would have been proud to drink a few beers with.

I didn't think much about Sarge after that. I would be too busy with my own life and the daily struggle to keep it. The rest of the morning was spent being processed into the Republic of South Vietnam. The paperwork was complete. I was officially…in-country!

I thought it funny that only now was I officially here. Many years later I would think about the rocket attack, and the dead and wounded. Were they ever really here, or were they caught up in a Catch-22. It was probably sorted out. The Army was good at finding solutions.

Processing was simply the presenting of our written orders to HQ (Headquarters). A clerk would process the paperwork and we would be assigned to duty in accordance with background, training, and needs of the army.

Almost all the guys from my barracks were gone. They left for exotic sounding base camps while I stayed behind. They were mostly infantry, armored, and artillery personnel. Freddy was gone, too, just hours after sunrise. The war effort needed him, and the others, immediately. They probably had training-enough to survive. My only war experience came

Michael W. Mason

from dropping paper bags of flour on tanks, from an OH-13, during war maneuvers in Baumholder, Germany.

After lunch, twenty of us were taken to the Jungle Warfare Training School at Bien Hoa. I was the only helicopter crew chief in the group. The rest were clerks, cooks, and mechanics. Along the way our two deuces acquired an armed escort.

Each of the two jeeps carried three soldiers and a floor mounted M60 machine gun. There was also an APC (Armored Personnel Carrier). This metal box on treads boasted a fifty caliber machine gun. The 50 is a prized weapon. It's very accurate and fires shells the size of large cigars. Imagine the power of *Dirty Harry's* 44-Magnum, the most powerful handgun in the world, then multiply that power by five. The 50 could bring down brick buildings all by itself. I had heard many stories about the fifty-caliber machine gun. After seeing one in action, for the first time, I believed them all.

Bien Hoa is northeast of Saigon and about 20-*klicks* (Kilometers), from Tan Son Nhut. There, I would begin my basic training in jungle warfare. The trucks dropped us off in front of a wood building. It had sandbags all around it and a corrugated, aluminum roof with sandbags on it, too. Only the doorways, at both ends, were devoid of the dirt-filled, canvas bags. A Sergeant and two Corporals were there to welcome us to jungle school.

We shouldered our dufflebags and were led to a big, green tent. It was encircled by a five foot wall of sandbags. We were told to pick a cot, leave our gear on it, and come back outside. Ten of us were loaded on a deuce and taken to our first work details.

The deuce and a half's huge, knobby tires kicked up a dust storm. I imagined that, from a distance, we might have looked like a stampede. I and two others were the last to be dropped off. A Buck Sergeant (three stripes), told us to strip our shirts and to join the sandbagging in-progress. Everywhere you looked there was sandbagging. After removing my shirt I was passed a shovel. I started filling a grey, canvas bag that another young man was holding open for me. The bags were either grey canvas, or green, woven plastic. When filled they were about the size of fertilizer bags, like the ones you bought at your hometown garden supply store. Other guys loaded the heavy bags onto a deuce. We took turns shoveling, holding, and loading.

There was nothing fun about sandbag detail. It was dirty, back-breaking work. We didn't bitch about it, though. We knew it was a necessary evil that resulted in saving lives.

For the next few days I sandbagged and pulled KP. I didn't mind *Kitchen Police* either as I thought that one day I might be a cook. I always enjoyed cooking and never minded the cleanup afterward. To me, it's just a necessary part of cooking.

At the end of each day I would shower, eat, and then relax in a makeshift *canteen*. This small, army bar was a small, wood building with a few tables and chairs. I was served a domestic beer by Vietnamese locals, hired by the Army to do menial tasks. The beer was just a notch above warm, and on the bottle the label read, "33." Even though it tasted bad, I would drink a lot of *33* during the months to follow. Bad beer was better than no beer.

Jungle training school began the next day. There were lectures about the country, the people, and the on-going *police action*. We all had a good laugh over that one, including the instructor. He mumbled something crude about politicians and then alluded to venereal disease. We laughed again, then settled down as the training film flickered on a white bed sheet that was nailed to the wall.

Military training films are professionaly produced and sometimes feature Hollywood stars. The films on VD were very graphic and showed what happens to soldiers who pick up girls and don't use protection. The explicit scenes of diseased male genitals were worse than the frostbite movies I saw in basic training. Those movies showed blackened, frostbitten toes being amputated with surgical pliers. If you have ever had, or seen, a cold sore, imagine a penis with much worse. The VD films probably helped save many soldiers from having to get penicillin shots during their tours in Vietnam. I learned to abstain or, at the least, carry a condom in my wallet.

One of the more popular horror stories to come out of Vietnam was *VD Island*. Rumor had it that it was an isolated island off the coast of Japan, and was where incurable VD cases were sent. The soldiers, inflicted with *Black Syph*, as it's called, lived the rest of their lives there. No one escaped. Those who tried were shot. Relatives of the *patients* were sent letters of regret, informing them that their sons, or husbands, were *MIA*, or Missing In Action. I never believed the VD story, but I never forgot it either. After hearing it, my wallet was never without two condoms. It was funny how

Michael W. Mason

some stories from Vietnam had a way of coming true. Then again, I never believed the *burning shit* story, either.

After evening chow we were issued full battle gear. I finally had a weapon in my hands and relished the sense of power. I looked forward to the training mission outside the barbed wire perimeter of the base camp.

After dark we were taken out past the perimeter wire. Barbed wire, razor wire, mines, and guards were part of every base camp's defenses. Earlier in the day I was taught about weapons, walking point, and booby traps. This night I was on a training patrol with a loaded M16 rifle, safety on. A Sergeant and a half-dozen infantrymen were with us, and they carried their weapons with safeties off.

During the training mission we learned to watch out for punji pits, trip wires, and *baited souvenirs*. I learned to be wary of anything and everything. I looked down most of the time and safely stepped over some *planted* booby traps. It became apparent that my eyes and ears were every bit as important as my rifle.

I made it through clean. A few of the guys were chewed out by the instructors for setting off fake traps. One guy must have really pissed-off the Sergeant because the other infantrymen were joking about the poor asshole getting *shit burning detail* in the morning. This was when I finally figured out what those black columns of smoke were. I always thought *shit detail* was just another name for sandbagging or KP. I never dreamed of taking it literally.

Shit burning detail is just that. The burning, by fire, of shit. I was one of the lucky few not to get assigned to this work detail while in jungle school. I learned from others how it worked. Two or three guys were assigned to the dreadful task. They would go to the officer's and enlisted men's latrines and drag out the metal barrels of waste. There was one under each of the holes that ran the length of a long wooden plank. Toilet seats were rare as it was more efficient to just cut holes in the wood.

Diesel fuel was poured into the cans and ignited. The waste erupted into flames and billowing clouds of black, acrid smoke would rise into the sky. The amazing thing was how the smoke would form these spiralling, ebony columns that rose straight up, sometimes to a thousand feet or more.

Mercifully, the nasty detail usually went quickly as the cleansing fire scoured the steel cans in short order. The worst part of the job was dragging the sloshing, stinking cans out from under the latrine. Your face was right over the can and getting dry heaves was the price-exacted for being unlucky enough to get on one of those dreaded work details.

Indoctrination was over. After two weeks in-country I found myself on a Huey gunship, flying north to a base camp named *Cu Chi* (Koo-Chee). I was finally joining the war.

I was assigned to D Troop, an aviation outfit, of the 3rd Squadron/4th Cavalry in the 25th Infantry Division. Cu Chi is one of the largest base camps in South Vietnam and is located about 30 klicks northwest of Saigon.

I was the only passenger on the Huey. It was one of the older but powerful C-models. It was rigged out as a *Hog*. It got its nickname from the bulbous, 40mm nose cannon, and the fact that it carried so much armament, it routinely scraped its nose in the dirt on takeoff. These war birds were also called *Frogs* or *Mini-Hogs* in some aviation outfits.

Besides the nose cannon, a pilot and co-pilot, the Mini-Hog also carries 24, 2.75 inch rockets in side mounted pods, and two modern day gatling guns. These *miniguns* can be tuned to fire upwards to 16,000 rounds a minute, 2,000 for helicopters. There are also two door gunners, each manning an M60 machine gun. One of the gunners is usually the crew chief. Some pilots won't fly unless the chief flies with the ship. They think it guarantees that the maintenance will be done right. A true Hog is fitted with a nose cannon and two rocket pods carrying a total of 48 rockets. If miniguns were added, the overburdened chopper would never be able to get off the ground.

The Hog is the battleship of the Army's helicopter fleet. It is the heavy hitter, the unseen killer from up high. Soon, I would become a hunter. Together, hunter and killer would form the deadliest partnership in the history of the Vietnam war.

The flight to Cu Chi gave me my first real look at the country that I was there to defend. Looking past the starboard gunner, I saw a myriad landscape of jungle, rice paddies, open fields, and mountains.

There were rivers and streams, and quaint villages dotted the green countryside. Green! Everywhere I looked, there was green. The land was rich with lush vegetation, but amidst all this natural beauty were the scars of war. Moon-like craters seemed to be everywhere. The brown potholes were pronounced in their sharp contrast to the greenery. I tried to spot people on the ground but found it nearly impossible as the gunship was flying at 3,000 feet.

Michael W. Mason

There was a lot of vehicle traffic on the road below that the flying battleship seemed to be following. I saw tanks, APCs, deuces, and jeeps. The column of steel was heading south, toward Saigon. It kicked up a voluminous dust storm as it thundered along the infamous *Highway One*. Above the convoy, but far below the Hog, were what looked like insects, buzzing back and forth. That's what those little bubbles looked like to me. They weren't OH-13s, though. I recognized them as OH-23s, or *Ravens*. They were undoubtedly the ugliest helicopters in the Army's fleet.

The Raven has a long, round, tapering tail section and looks not unlike a dragonfly. I was startled from my sightseeing when one of the door gunners tapped me on the shoulder, pointed, and yelled, "Cu Chi!"

I looked past the pilots and saw a huge oval of brown dirt. It was like a massive wound in the middle of living, green flesh. As the Hog made its approach, and banked to the right, I saw barbed wire, tanks, helicopters, and sandbag-fortified buildings. I grimaced when I saw black columns of smoke rising from different areas of the giant base camp.

The Huey leveled off and began losing altitude. As the distinctive *whomp* of the chopper's rotor blades got louder, I knew we were on final approach. The pilot pulled pitch and the Hog flared into a slow hover down a long, dirt and grass airfield.

On both sides of the airfield were helicopters with white *Centaurs* painted on them. The mythical, half-man/half-horse, figure held a spear as if ready to launch it at an enemy. My heart sank when I spotted Ravens sitting in bunkers with their rotors sticking up above the five-foot walls of steel and sandbags. I had hoped I was going to an outfit that only flew gunships.

The Hog slowly hovered into one of the empty bunkers and landed in a whirlwind of dust. The crew chief was out the door before the skids touched down. The co-pilot turned around and gave me a thumbs up. I gave him one back and then jumped out and onto the base camp called Cu Chi.

The crew chief pointed me in the direction of a large, corrugated aluminum, maintenance hangar. I grabbed my dufflebag and strode down the flight line of D Troop of the 3/4 Cavalry. I stayed to the side as the airfield was alive with the motions of war. Helicopters were taking off, landing, or being worked on in their protective bunkers. Miniguns were being loaded, M60s cleaned, and pilots and crew chiefs were performing pre-flight inspections.

In one bunker, a rotor blade was being replaced on a gunship. It had a few holes in it and what appeared to be a long crack. The tail section was being looked over by a Lieutenant, and a crewman was patching holes with some kind of aluminum tape. Both men were laughing as they went about their business. "All in a day's work," I thought to myself.

A mechanic at the hangar directed me to *Operations*. A wood-planked walkway led me to the screen door of the little, headquarters building. The mechanic had called it a *hootch*. Unsure of protocol, I knocked before entering. I was hoping for an assignment that included flying and guns. What I didn't know was how easy it would be to get my wish. I could simply volunteer and end up getting the fight of my life.

After the door slammed behind me, I heard the familiar, distinctive sound of Hueys taking off. I was hoping for a gunship, maybe even the mighty Hog. My destiny was already written, however. On the flight to Cu Chi I had witnessed my future. It was to be those little insects that buzzed the tree tops, daring the enemy to shoot at them.

Very soon, I would strap on a gun and lower my life expectancy by about fifty years. All this was ahead of me. I was about to embark on the thrillride of a lifetime by joining an elite outfit known as…Baby Scouts.

Michael W. Mason

THREE

BABY SCOUTS

"Specialist Fourth Class, Michael W. Mason reporting as ordered, sir."

"At ease," said the OD (Officer of the Day). The Chief Warrant Officer gave me one of those lazy, officer salutes in return. The young W1 wasn't much older than me. He never gave his name but his stitched-on name tag said, "Dunne." In the Army, Warrant Officers always seem to be pilots. I never met a Warrant who didn't have wings on his uniform.

I passed the OD my orders and he immediately noticed that I was a volunteer. He cracked a smile, shook his head, and continued to read. A minute later he looked up and asked, "Why are you here?"

I answered, "Boredom and a desire to fight, sir."

He laughed. "Cut the crap, Mason. Why are you here?"

I told Mr. Dunne about the little Army airfield in Baumholder, Germany and how a *Dear John Letter* sent me over the edge. The Top Sergeant there offered me OCS (Officer Candidate School), if I would stay in Germany and reenlist. I turned him down, saying that I needed the change for my sanity and self respect. The Sergeant retorted, "Mason, what you'll find in 'Nam is bullets." At the time I thought he was joking.

I had just turned 19 and never thought about my mortality. The possibility of dying had never occured to me. My outfit in Germany was sent to Vietnam a year after I left. I would have ended up in-country anyway.

The W1 got up from behind his desk and said, "Ok, Mason. I buy that story." He added that the XO (Executive Officer), would evalute my records, troop needs, and then decide my fate. "In the meantime," Dunne added, "you can sack with the Baby Scouts. Mr. Dunne tossed my file on the clerk's desk as I followed him out the door.

"What the *hell* are Baby Scouts?" I thought to myself as we walked along the creaky walkway of wood pallets. The Warrant pointed toward the barracks and called them hootches. As we got closer to the buildings he showed me the mess tent, officer's country, and a large, round pipe sticking three feet out of the ground. It had a wire-mesh screen over the opening and was about twenty feet from the main road. "That's the pisser," he said, "and over there are the latrine and shower hootches." I was relieved to see that the toilets, like the showers, were enclosed in a small hootch. I've always been a modest person and the idea of urinating into a pipe, by the side of the road, was bad enough. Even though the pipe had a four foot high aluminum shield curved halfway around it, everyone knows what you're doing as they walk or drive by.

Once, a jeep carrying four *Donut Dollies* drove by as I was relieving myself. They glanced my way and waved. Red-faced, and with my free hand, I waved back. The thought of those ladies knowing what I was doing embarrassed the hell out of me.

Mr. Dunne said the 25th Infantry Division called itself, *Tropic Lightning*. He added, "D Troop is the aviation arm of the 3/4 Cav. We provide aerial support to the ground forces." He went on to describe how the fleet of choppers was used to insert infantry, extract infantry and the wounded (dustoffs), and to fly search and destroy missions. I liked the sound of *search and destroy* and thought that being a door gunner might be cool. The nickel tour ended abruptly when we stopped in front of a hootch. Shirtless boys were busy filling sandbags and placing them around the rectangular, wooden building. One of them said, "Hi, Mr. Dunne."

Fifteen feet to the right of the hootch was another young soldier. He, too, was shirtless and was stirring a huge, black cauldron. It rested upon a crude, rock-encircled fire and hot, soapy water sloshed out of the top as a wood paddle lifted out a pair of green boxer shorts. The cauldron was the Baby Scout's washing machine.

Damp clothes were spread out along the wall of sandbags that surrounded the hootch. That was the dryer. A few of the guys looked at me as I stood on the threshold of the large, wood hut. Above the doorway was a rusted and pitted, metal sign. It had a cartoon OH-23 painted on it. The caricature had two hands that held firing-M60s, and a bubble wearing a blue baby's bonnet over a smiling baby face. Written above the painting were the words, "Baby Scouts."

I followed the Warrant Officer through the door. It was on a spring and slammed behind us. The hootch was dark and musty.

"Hey, guys. We got a FNG here. Any empty bunks?"

"Hi, sir," said a spec-5 who was sitting on a nearby, empty bunk. He stood and pointed. "There's an empty one down on the right."

Bunks, and a few cots, lined both sides of the hootch. Half a dozen guys were either sleeping or cleaning weapons, like the Spec-5. He walked over and offered me a dark, meaty hand. I shook it while he told me his name was Danny Narvone. He was old, almost thirty I guessed. His hair was jet black and his skin was very tanned and leathery. A gleaming, white smile clashed with his Navajo Indian darkness.

Narvone was the Flight Line Chief. He decided who crewed on what ship and when.

"You can have that cot over there, Mike." His voice was surprisingly soft and pleasant, and his demeanor showed him to be a man I was going to like. Mr. Dunne said Narvone and the other Scouts would orient me. "Good luck," he added, then walked out the door. The brilliance of the day flooded through the swinging door and then darkness returned with a resounding slam.

I felt alone…a solitary stranger in the company of soldiers called Baby Scouts. Narvone placed a hand on my shoulder. "You'll catch on soon enough. In a few days you'll have your duty assignment. Until then, welcome to the Baby Scouts, Mike."

I walked down the aisle to the empty cot. I threw my dufflebag on it and began unpacking. Narvone came over a few minutes later. He said to take the rest of the day to get situated.

"Mike, after unpacking, walk the grounds, including the flight line, and see what we're all about."

I looked at him and asked, "Do you think I'll get assigned to the Scouts?"

"No, I don't think so. This is a volunteer outfit. You might get hangar duty, though. We always need good chopper mechanics." I was puzzled and wondered why you had to volunteer to become a Baby Scout.

I had pretty much figured out that the Baby Scouts flew, and crewed, the little OH-23s. However, I didn't understand why you had to volunteer to get in. Before I could ask, Narvone said he had to go to the flight line to prepare for dusk patrol. He said to finish unpacking and to get acquainted with the Scouts. He walked to his bunk, picked up an M16 rifle, a bandolier of ammo clips, and a flight helmet. "See ya later," he said as he kicked the door open and disappeared into the brightness that enveloped him.

I had a cot, army blanket, pillow, and a wood foot locker. My living space was a 10 by 7 piece of dirty, concrete floor. I resumed my unpacking and a few of the Scouts came over and asked where I was from. They, like Mr. Dunne, were amazed that I gave up Germany for 'Nam. Three of the four guys were crew chiefs. The other, *Hutch*, was infantry and assigned to the Baby Scouts as a gunner/observer. He was about five-eight and very thin. His ears were too big for his small head and he was covered with freckles. Hutch was a straw-haired Kansas boy and every inch the farmer's son. He also had one of those grinning, smart mouth personalities. Hutch had a wisecrack for everything and always got away with it. I liked him. He and the other Scouts seemed like regular guys. They made me feel…like I was home.

The Scouts went back to whatever they were doing and I finished unpacking. At last! No longer did I have a forty pound dufflebag to carry around. I folded it and happily kicked it under the cot. My clothes and toilet articles went into the foot locker. I was amazed that my little bottle of *Aqua Velva* had survived the trip. Shaving rarely, I hardly ever used the stuff, but a few guys in basic had dozens of bottles. They were the alcoholics who drank the stuff to keep the DTs (shakes), under control.

Sitting on my cot, I gazed about the hootch. Everyone had their own little space. There were sixteen bunks, or cots, eight on each side. My little cubby was spartan compared to most of the others. Empty beer cans littered the floor and glass ashtrays were lying by most bunks.

Some of the living areas were decorated with pictures of family and girlfriends. Others had *Playboy* centerfolds nailed to the wall. A few even had chains of grenade rings hanging from the rafters. This wasn't the Army I was accustomed to, but it seemed so right.

The hootch suddenly got bright as five soldiers entered. They were the Scouts on sandbag and laundry detail. They were all filthy. They also had another thing in common. They each wore shiny, silver wings on their jungle hats.

They saw me sitting on the cot and one of them said, "Hi. How are ya?" They all stripped, wrapped towels about their waists, then headed off for the showers. They each carried a shower bag as they went out the back door. I tagged along, at a distance, to see where the shower hootch was. They turned right and followed the boardwalk toward the road. Two of them veered left and headed toward the latrine. The other three went right, following the walkway to a square, wood hootch with huge, plastic water tanks on the roof. Gravity fed the water into pipes that ended in shower heads. The tanks soaked up a lot of sunshine, so the showers were usually lukewarm.

BABY SCOUT

The shower hootch was a luxury we all appreciated and never took for granted. Warm or cold, the showers reigned supreme on my short list of home comforts.

Feeling the need, I headed for the pisser pipe. Standing there, under the hot sun, relief came slowly as I watched an armored unit rumbling down the dirt road. I tried to hurry as the trailing dust clouds closed in. The ground was vibrating from all the treaded tonnage, and the pisser pipe was beginning to sway. I started to back up, before finishing, and was buttoning up as I broke into a flat-out run.

I got clear of the dust clouds but heard, "Shit!" echo from the latrine. As the dirty fog fell over both latrine and shower, I began my tour of D Troop of the 3rd Squadron/4th Cavalry. D Troop occupied a rectangular 1/4-mile area of dirt, sparse grass and weeds. Two thirds of this was the flight line where the Gunships, Slicks, and Scouts were bunkered. The little Ravens were kept further down the line, away from the more powerful Hueys and their ferocious rotor wash. Near the Scout ships sat a grey, metal cargo container. It served as a maintenance and ammo locker. Hanging on the outside was a small blackboard with *SHORT* chalked across the top. Underneath was printed, "Kirkwood, 29 days." In about nine months I would envy these *shortimers* and would count the days until I could write my name in chalk.

The maintenance hangar separated the flight line from the living area. The first hootch behind the hangar was OPS, or Operations. It was sometimes called HQ, or Headquarters. A hundred yards further back were three rows of living quarters, mess tent, and bar. The bar wasn't much, but it served cold beer and was a social gathering spot. If you drank enough of the 3.2 beer, you might even get a buzz. Most of us in the bar were teenagers but, by military standards, we were grown men entitled to adult priviliges. Back home, I'd be using a fake ID or having someone buy beer for me.

The hootches quartered the troops by caste and MOS. The first row housed the Gunship and Slick crews. *Slicks* were Hueys that were bereft of armament, except for two door gunners. They transported the infantry or the casualties of war. Further up the row were the officer's hootches. The second row housed the Baby Scouts, more officers, and the mess tent. The third row billited the the infantry platoons. We didn't socialize with them much at all.

Also in that row was the *Kit Carson* hootch. It quartered the South Vietnamese infantrymen who were assigned to D Troop. When the Slicks took them into battle, it was usually covert and very bloody. Some of them brandished enemy body parts on their clothes, and sometimes from their ears and around their necks. A Kit Carson Scout would wear an earring…literally.

Rumor had it they kept severed heads and genitals in their hootch. I was never eager to prove this story true. It meant having to enter their living quarters to witness something everyone knew was true. I learned quickly that, in Vietnam, the strange and bizarre went hand in hand with the truth.

Even in war there is a social order. When invited to an officer's hootch it was usually to go over a flight plan or to get chewed out. Salutes were rare in the living area and virtually non-existent on the flight line. Lieutenant Hank Kerns was the exception. He was *Academy* all the way and expected to be saluted everywhere and by everyone his junior…even the Warrant Officers. The other Baby Scout pilots would just ignore him. That really made him mad and then he would take it out on one of the crewmen. He locked my heels, once, on the flight line, for not saluting. Another Lieutenant came over and reminded Kerns of the *no salute policy* for the flight line. The rebuffed officer strode away, angrily kicking dirt and imaginary butts. It took months before the Lieutenant stopped soliciting salutes on the flight line, but only after being told that enemy snipers target the person returning the salute. Although a smart, good pilot, Lieutenant Hank Kerns was a pain in my butt for a long time.

I walked around for hours, familiarizing myself with the layout of D Troop. The heat was intense and my uniform was soaked. My stomach was also growling. I returned to the dark, musty coolness of the Baby Scout hootch. A Staff Sergeant was waiting for me.

As I was about to collapse on my cot, Sergeant Oliver Jenkins walked over and said, "Narvone told me about you." Jenkins was a career man, a *lifer*. He also was a living caricature of *Ichabod Crane*, the reluctant hero of the Disney cartoon movie, *The Legend of Sleepy Hollow*. Jenkins was in his forties, looked fifty, and was very gaunt. Being very thin, he also had a pronounced *Adams Apple* that captured your eyes whenever he talked.

While Danny Narvone was in charge of flight line operations, Jenkins was in charge of the Scouts when they weren't flying or working on the flight line. He told me that I would stay with the Baby Scouts temporarily and would pull sandbag duty in the morning.

"You'll probably get hangar duty," he said and then added, "It's time for chow."

The red sun was low on the horizon as I followed some of the Scouts to the mess tent. I wasn't one of them so I kept a discreet distance. The mess area was outside, under a large tent. There were wooden tables and benches and the scouts seemed to have their own private section. It was self-serve, much like a buffet. There was never a menu but the food was usually fair, sometimes good. Most importantly, it was hot. Meat and potatoes were the usual faire. There were vegetables and sometimes even cake, pie, or pudding. My favorite meals were the ones when real, cold milk was served. Also, there was the *Kool-Aid*. For breakfast, lunch, and dinner, there was the big pot of Kool-Aid. It, and the milk, sometimes made me think of home.

After serving myself, I took a seat at the end of one of the scout tables. I ate and listened to talk of girls, cars, music, movies, and killing *Charlie*. Charlie is the nickname for the Viet Cong, the guerilla fighters, and the enemy the Baby Scouts encountered the most. It was rare when we battled the NVA (North Vietnamese Army). It was usually our ground forces that engaged the NVA regulars.

Two of the Scouts got up and one of them said, "Later."

"Shoot 'em up," was the group reply. Hutch saw my puzzled look and told me that they were going on dusk patrol. He said the Scouts flew dawn and dusk patrol every day. They were reconnaissance missions to make sure Charlie, or the NVA, weren't creeping about the base perimeter or anywhere nearby.

Usually, two OH-23s flew dawn and dusk patrols. One ship flew high cover, the other at tree top level or lower. The low ship was supposed to ferret out the elusive and well-hidden enemy. The real search and destroy missions took place throughout the day. He concluded, "That's usually when all hell breaks loose." I soaked all this up and Hutch went back to his chow. I started thinking to myself, "I've got to join the Baby Scouts."

On the walk back to the hootch I heard the two scout ships before I saw them. The little Ravens had just taken off for dusk patrol. Two machine gunners were standing on the skids of each ship. I watched them until they banked left and disappeared from sight. "What balls," I thought, "This is for me."

Michael W. Mason

I resumed my course for the hootch when Lieutenant Kerns came out from his quarters right in front of me. I saluted with, "Good evening, sir." He returned the salute, smiled, then responded, "Evening, soldier." That was my first encounter with the man who would be General. I think that I put him in a good mood for chow.

It was dark in the Baby Scout hootch and eerie shadows were dancing on the walls, cast by the lanterns and flickering candles. I lay on my cot and took in the sights.

There was a poker game going on in one corner. In another, a Scout was cleaning an M79 grenade launcher. The other guys were either reading, writing letters home, or just listening to the Armed Forces Radio Network on a cheap radio. Top forty rock and roll prevailed but there was never any of the new rock. There was no Jefferson Airplane, Grateful Dead, or Bob Dylan. At the time, I never knew there was a rock music revolution going on back home.

Sergeant Jenkins and Narvone were writing letters, probably to their wives. The night was usually a peaceful time in the hootch. Sometimes there was horseplay, but mostly the Scouts used the night as a time for quiet solitude. It was also the only time when the war seemed far away.

A few hours later, four Scouts walked into the hootch. They were the two from chow and the two who missed chow due to an earlier mission. One of them looked very familiar. He took the bunk closest to the door. He was a stocky Spec-5 with a waxed, handlebar mustache. It was my classmate from aviation school, Chuck Bryer.

"Buck, is that you?" I yelled.

He turned, locking eyes with me. "Mason, *damn*!" He tossed his rifle and flight helmet on his bunk and walked over. I stood and we shook hands. Buck is one of those guys whose face reddens when excited. We reminisced awhile.

"You know, Mike, everyone was jealous of your Germany assignment. I can't believe you volunteered for 'Nam." Buck had only three months left before he'd be short. I asked him the question I was saving for the right moment.

"Buck, can you get me into the Baby Scouts?"

"What? You're nuts. You gave up a dream assignment to come here, and now you want to join the Scouts? You're crazy."

"Yeah," I said, "that's about it." We argued pros and cons for five minutes. He had no answer for me when I said, "You volunteered for the Scouts. Am I any crazier than you or the others?"

He sighed and answered, "Ok, I'll talk to LT about you."

"Who's LT?"

"He's our platoon leader, Lieutenant Larry Tinder."

"Thanks, Buck."

Our conversation went back to the usual stuff, like cars, girls, and home. Buck broke off the reunion and got ready for a shower. When he passed my cot on the way out, he said, with a laugh, "Mason, you're still nuts."

I had sandbag detail in the morning so I decided that taking a shower was pointless. The other guys seemed more friendly after watching Buck and I talk about old times. I settled into my cot and wrote a letter home to mom. I didn't mention the Baby Scouts.

My mom, Mary Pauline Mason, was the prettiest *three striper* to ever put on an Army uniform. She served in the WACs (Women's Army Corps), during World War Two. She was petite but you didn't want to rile her. As a Buck Sergeant in the WACs, she had the authority to back up her commands. *Polly* was from a military family and married into a military family. My mom was also very smart. She would never understand why her only son would want to sign up with a suicide squad of teenage warriors.

My letter told her that I was working on aircraft and that I missed her, dad, and my two sisters. I ended the letter with my customary XXXOOO.

It was still early when I stripped to my shorts and hit the sack. Tomorrow would be a long, dirty day of sandbagging. I fell asleep while thinking what it must be like to fly, standing on the skids of a helicopter.

Michael W. Mason

FOUR

VIRGIN FLIGHT

Morning came in darkness with Sergeant Jenkins rousting me from a deep sleep. It was six a.m. and morning formation was in half an hour. I used the latrine and brushed my teeth. I remembered to forego the shower. I didn't see the need to shower before getting dirty.

Formation was held on the large, dirt field behind the maintenance hangar. Part of this area was taken up by two aluminum poles, set in round buckets of concrete, with a volleyball net stretched between them.

I lined up with the Baby Scouts. The gunship crews lined up together as did the pilots and the infantry platoon. The Kit Carson Squad rarely attended the formations.

As we were forming up, two Scout pilots and four crewmen walked past and toward the flight line. The dawn patrol crews never had to attend the morning gathering. The rest of us came to attention and saluted as the American flag was raised.

A few speeches about the Tet offensive were given by the XO and the Commanding Officer. The CO was Major Richard Arbogast. He was a short, stocky man in his late thirties and very military. I thought he was probably just like Lieutenant Kerns when younger.

The major dismissed the formation and turned us over to the platoon leaders. While most headed off to the mess hall, Jenkins pulled me and two others, aside. He told us that sandbag detail would be at the troop bunker. He said to report for duty after chow at 0800 hours.

I headed for the mess hall and heard the dawn patrol overhead. I looked up and saw four *skidriders* entering the orange lume of the rising sun. It was an eerie sight but it made my heart skip a beat. I froze and watched the two ships bank to the left and fly into the rising fireball that was lighting up the horizon. The little ships disappeared into the sun and the morning light began to cast shadows. I hurried off to chow as Cu Chi began to come alive.

Except for the occasional rocket and mortar attacks, I usually slept well. Cu Chi was heavily guarded with sentries, barbed wire, and land mines. Nothing, however, can stop those random missiles falling from the sky. This is why we sandbagged everything of importance, including the pisser pipe.

For the next two days I helped sandbag the newly-built underground bunker and the Baby Scout hootch. The troop bunker was usable but needed a few extra layers of sandbags. Since I was bunking with the Baby Scouts, it seemed only right that I helped sandbag there, too.

Near the end of day two, Buck came up to me and said that Lt. Tinder would be dropping by to talk with me. Buck said, "That's all I know," then headed off to the showers. I crossed my fingers and went back to work. An hour later, Sergeant Jenkins told us to knock off for the day.

A shower, clean uniform, and a full belly were taken for granted in D Troop of the 3/4 Cav. However, being a FNG, I appreciated it all. In the field, *grunts* didn't fare as well. For days, even weeks at a time, infantrymen would subsist on cold rations, salt tablets, and canteens laced with quinine. Mosquitoes and sweat-soaked jungle fatigues were the norm for those poor souls, and a dry pair of socks was a rare luxury.

After evening chow, I went back to the hootch and nervously waited for Lt. Tinder. By the time he arrived, I was a stressed-out wreck. He walked through the door to a loud chorus of, "LT!" He waved to the Scouts and smiled. I stood and he noticed my unfamiliar face immediately. He walked over and held out a hand as I was preparing to come to attention.

"At ease," he said as he shook my hand. Right away I liked this young officer. He was not much older than me.

Lieutenant Lawrence Tinder was a small man, almost half a head shorter than my five foot, ten inches. He was, maybe, 140-pounds, if that, and could probably whip any guy in the hootch. He had that wirey build that reminded me of a boy in high school whom everyone knew not to mess with. He had a good crop of brown hair, too long by Army standards, brown eyes, and a face that was young and always, it seemed, smiling.

LT commanded respect with his self-confidence and mutual respect for others. He told me to sit, then joined me on the cot. Sergeant Jenkins came over but remained standing.

He wanted to know why the Lieutenant was talking to the FNG.

"Buck tells me you want to join the Scouts, Mike. Is this true?"

"Yes, sir."

"Have you really thought this over? It will be like nothing you've ever done or can imagine in your wildest dreams. You'll be flying in a piece of *bait* and will get shot at by an enemy you'll probably never see." I stared LT in the eyes and answered.

"Yes, sir. It's what I want. I volunteered for Vietnam and I want this. I want to join the Baby Scouts." Tinder, expressionless, looked me in the eyes, then continued.

"We have a slot open for a crew chief. It's yours if you really want in, but you have to tell me again that you want to join the Baby Scouts. This is a volunteer outfit, you know. All the guys are volunteers. Buck and Danny think highly of you and I think highly of their opinions. Say the words, and you're in."

"I want to volunteer for the Baby Scouts, sir."

LT smiled, then stood and yelled, "Baby Scouts, assemble." Suddenly, I was encircled by all the Scouts. The Lieutenant said, "Gentlemen, welcome our newest Baby Scout." A tumultuous roar went up and I was pounded on the back and shoulders.

LT was looking down at me, smiling, and I realized that I forgot to stand. I shot up quickly and slurred, "Sank thew, thir." LT laughed at my consternation.

"Mike," he said, "listen to Jenkins, Narvone, and Buck. They and the other scouts will break you in."

"Thank you, sir." I shook the Lieutenant's hand and then he turned and walked toward the door. Buck walked in as Lt. Tinder walked out. LT kept walking but in passing said to Buck, "He's in!"

Buck came over and joined with the others in welcoming me to the fraternity. Narvone came in a few minutes later and said he'd heard the news. The Flight Line Chief stayed long after everyone else went about their business.

He filled me in on Baby Scout duties. The first thing I needed, he said, was a weapon. Narvone said he'd take me to the supply hootch in the morning to requisition an M16. At the same time I would be issued flight gear.

"We'll break you in right, Mike, on dusk patrol." Spec-5, Danny Narvone was one of the few who called me by by first name. LT was the other. *Mason* just happens to be one of those names that people use in lieu of my first. Mason this and Mason that. I never really cared. It has always been like that.

"Mike," Narvone said, "tomorrow is training day for you. You'll be going on a real mission and will fly high ship with Mr. Dunne and Hutch.

Michael W. Mason

Do what they tell you. No discussion. Understand?" I nodded agreement and Narvone smiled.

"Good. See you in the morning, and welcome aboard." He walked away and over to Hutch to brief him on his new, *cherry* partner. After Narvone went back to his bunk, Hutch looked at me and gave a thumbs up. I grinned and returned the gesture.

Before hitting the sack, I thanked Buck for helping me get in the Scouts. He said, "You're welcome, Mason, but you're still nuts." I laughed and told him that I was no more nuts than any of the Scouts. He suddenly got serious and said, "You really don't know what you're in for, do you?"

"Flying, shooting, stuff like that, right?"

"Geez, Mike. This isn't a shooting gallery. Here, the targets shoot back."

"What?"

"The Baby Scouts just don't go out and capture Charlie, you idiot. We hunt Charlie and we kill him, or he kills us. Most of the time, he gets off the first shot."

"*Damn*, Chuck!" I was beginning to feel a little less exuberant about joining the Baby Scouts.

"That's right, Mason. Hardly a week goes by without one of us getting shot up. We either come back with a ship full of holes, or a body full of holes, or both. Charlie sometimes has a better rifle than we do, and he stays hidden most of the time. When we do flush him out, it's usually in a firefight."

"Alright, Chuck, I get it. You've got me a little scared, too."

"Good. You should be. I'm scared all the time. We all are. We just don't show it. It's good to be afraid, I think. It helps keep us from going ballistic and doing something stupid."

"All I want is to fit in and do my job. I'll handle it."

"I hope so. The Baby Scouts isn't for everyone. Have you ever heard of the First Air Cavalry?"

"Yeah. Everyone has. So what?"

"We do what they do, only in our own backyard. They're the elite in hunter-killer search and destroy missions and they lose a lot of men. It's not a game and it's definitely not fun. Wait until you get shot at for the first time. You'll see."

"Ok. I get the point. I'll try and keep a level head."

"Good. Now, I guess we better hit the sack. I've got dawn patrol and you've got a full day of training. Oh! By the way, Mason, you're still nuts."

"You too, Chuck." I laughed and got ready for bed. As I lay in my cot, I thought about what Chuck had said. It was good advice, but I missed the point entirely. All I knew was that I was a Baby Scout. I was going to fly, cradle a machine gun in my arms, and shoot Charlie. Getting shot never occured to me. I was as immortal as any 19-year-old could be. I fell asleep quickly and dreamed of skidriding over a green, jungle canopy. I awoke the next morning feeling refreshed and was eager with anticipation. Whatever Buck told me was forgotten. Months later I would wish I had taken him seriously.

After morning formation, and chow, Narvone took me to the supply hootch. I signed for an M16, two bandoliers of ammo clips, two boxes of shells, flight helmet, and gloves. All the while, my eyes couldn't stop staring at a dull, dark brown, piece of hardware. It was an army model Colt 45 semi-automatic pistol. It was beautiful and I imagined it strapped to my waist and riding low on my leg, resting in a leather holster.

I asked about the Colt and the Quartermaster said I would have to turn in the rifle for it. Narvone looked at me and said, "Don't be silly. The pistol is useless. It's about as accurate for about as far as you can throw it." I nodded and knew he was right. The Colt was the last thing I needed. I only knew, though, that I had to have it.

We returned to the hootch and dropped off everything but the M-16, clips, and ammo. Out on the flight line the Scouts were either working on the Ravens or cleaning weapons. Buck Sergeant Tom Donald was cleaning an M60 machine gun. It was broken down into many pieces, most of them being brushed clean in a bucket of solvent. Another M60 was leaning against the maintenance locker, waiting its turn in the toxic bath.

Tom Donald was an infantryman assigned to the Scouts. He's the son of a St. Louis supermarket owner and would some day run the family business. He was drafted and volunteered for the Baby Scouts shortly after arriving in-country. He has a shock of light-brown hair, a thin mustache, and an infectious laugh. He always seemed to be laughing about something and telling stories or funny jokes. Tom found humor in almost every situation. He also loves to perform to an audience. Half the time he would talk to you in his other *persona*, George Burns. Tom loved the old, cigar smoking comedian, right down to his mannerisms. When it came time for a mission, though, Tom was the Baby Scout you wanted covering your ass.

Tom, like the others, volunteered for Baby Scout duty. Many of the troop's door gunners were infantry volunteers. Most grunts, though, didn't want any part of the Scouts, muchless helicopter duty. As far as they were concerned, we were just flying targets in the Vietnam shooting arcade. Tom didn't fear getting shot out of the sky. He thrived on the hunt and was one of the best gunners in the outfit.

Narvone told the guys to teach me the ropes. He wanted me somewhat prepared for dusk patrol. Baby Scout school had begun and the fellas treated their student like he knew nothing at all. I was painfully aware that it wasn't far from the truth.

My training began when Narvone left for the maintenance hangar. The first lesson was field-stripping and cleaning my M16. I was taught to do this blindfolded. Tom explained that I might have to clean the weapon in the dark sometime. I asked why and he answered, "You never know when you might get shot down. You could be on the ground for minutes, even days." I looked at him with a serious look on my face, though on the inside I was smiling. I couldn't fathom the notion of getting shot down.

Next, I was told to load the ammo clips with the metal-jacketed bullets. I did, then placed the clips back in the cloth bandoliers. I slammed one clip into the breach of my freshly cleaned rifle. I checked to make sure the safety was on. I was told to keep the rifle loaded at all times, but to never *home* a round until out past the perimeter wire.

The next subject was my favorite...the M60. This would be my primary weapon and Tom was the best teacher I could have. He and Chuck were known as the best gunners in the Scouts.

After a brief lecture on the weapon, he had me watch him assemble the one he had just cleaned. An accomplished pro, he made it look easy. Then, he took it apart under my watchful eyes and, then again, reassembled it. He put it aside and grabbed the one that was leaning against the locker. He passed it to me with the seriousness of life and death, saying, "Your turn."

I took it apart, slowly, and put the parts in the solvent. I brushed them clean and then began to solve the puzzle. A perfectionist, Tom made me go through the process three times, even though I got it right the first time. He then showed me the tricks to quickly solve some inflight problems that would most certainly occur, such as breech jams and overheated barrels.

BABY SCOUT

Ammo belts for the machine guns were hanging over the locker doors. Tom showed me how to look for *short-rounds* in the belts. Short rounds were bullets that were not aligned with the others. They were the main cause of jams. I learned to correct the problem by using my fingers to push the misaligned round through its connecting link so it lined up flush with the others. A perfectly aligned ammo belt meant fewer jams. Driven by my desire to do well, I would make it a habit to check the belts before every flight.

The locker also housed an assortment of grenades. There were smoke grenades in different colors such as red, white, green, or yellow. Further back were the explosive grenades: fragmentation, thermite, and WP. The latter we called *Willie Peter*. It is a white phosphorous grenade that looks like the *pineapple* grenade that you saw in the old war movies. It was a light blue-green color and exploded in a shower of sparks, smoke, and burning, hot phosphorous.

Your enemy might elude a frag, but Willie Peter rained fire and acid. Nothing could stop it, save cutting off its oxygen supply.

Thermite grenades aren't explosive but, in their own way, are just as lethal. They burn white hot, and even under water. If you want to burn a hole in something, anything at all, you use thermite. In the months ahead, I would use thermite once. It was one of the many things in Vietnam that I would regret doing.

I would toss many of these horrible bombs during my year in country…many of them after a cowering or fleeing enemy. I threw them into hootches, down spider holes (tunnels), and into canoe-like boats called sampans. Willie Peter was my grenade of choice. It exploded like fireworks, set fire to everything it touched, and was *damn* fun to watch.

I looked up and into the sun. Out of its glare came the returning dawn patrol. The two Ravens flared to a hover over the airfield. The Scouts quickly moved the freshly cleaned weapons into the ammo locker. The main rotors of the little ships were kicking up a dust storm. Slowly, they moved toward the bunkers. The six-cylinder, aircraft engines sounded like noisy Volkswagons with bad mufflers as I watched the pilots work the controls. The gunners were standing on the skids, cradling their M60s. The choppers slowly entered the bunkers, the pilots deftly manipulating the two control sticks and foot pedals.

The skids touched down gently and the gunners unhooked their *Monkey Straps* and hopped off. The left gunner attended to the pilot's skid-mounted

Michael W. Mason

machine gun. The right door gunner walked to the locker and leaned his weapon against it. The pilots cut the engines and began filling out their log books. All the while I just stood there, mesmerized, and engulfed by the swirls of dust that slowly began to fall, much of it on me. It never occured to me to seek shelter with the others in the locker.

The pilots got out while the rotors were slowly freewheeling to a stop. The crew chiefs would sign off on the log books after a visual inspection for bullet holes. The pilots grabbed their personal weapons and walked down the flight line toward Operations. The crew left their flight gear and personal weapons in the ships as they would be going up again, later.

The gunners began to tear down the machine guns, including the skid gun. The crew chiefs began their visual inspections. Finding no bullet holes, they began cleaning the air and fuel filters, checking the main and tail rotor hubs for grease and loose fittings, and finished their post-flight duties by washing and polishing the bubbles.

The birds checked out ok and the crewmen walked over to the locker, sat down, and lit up. Benny Hutchinson was the gunner I'd be paired with for dusk patrol.

"Narvone wants you to fly right seat," he said. "That's the crew chief's position." Hutch would fly left seat, the gunner/observer position, with his M-60 and smoke grenades. He would also help the pilot with map reading and keeping tabs on the aircraft's position in relation to the base camp.

We spent the rest of the morning going over the skid gun. Hutch showed me how to load and arm it. I loaded the ammo box with 500 rounds while he watched. He seemed impressed when I found, and fixed, two short rounds. "Let's go eat," he said. I walked down the flight line with a bounce to my step, and feeling like a Baby Scout.

On the way to the mess tent, I asked Hutch about all the activity on the flight line. Since my arrival in the Troop, choppers were in and out all day long and into the night. I was curious about it. He explained that the Tet offensive was keeping everyone busy, especially the Gunship crews and the Baby Scouts. Hutch said that the Cav's armored units were in the thick of it, and that the Scouts were doing a lot of reconnaissance.

"We were ordered to Tan Son Nhut Airbase a week ago," he said, "to support our armored guys. They kicked butt and we kicked butt while flying search and destroy missions with the Gunships. We also flew convoy cover to keep Highway One open."

BABY SCOUT

It suddenly dawned on me that those *insects* I saw, on my flight to Cu Chi, were the Baby Scouts. Hutch said, "I popped two Charlies on the convoy patrol and Tom Donald got four on a S&D mission." Listening to this made me wish that it was already time for dusk patrol. Like a racehorse, I was chomping at the bit. I couldn't wait to get into the air and blast Charlie.

When we reached the hangar, Narvone joined us for the walk to chow. He said the 25th Infantry Division bailed out Bien Hoa, Tan Son Nhut, and, to some extent, Saigon.

"If it wasn't for us," he said, "those places would have been pounded but good." I listened attentively as we continued to walk. I thought to myself, "Hunting will be good."

The mess hall was crowded but there were always seats for the Baby Scouts. Outsiders rarely took seats at the table that was known as Scout territory. Even the Kit Carson soldiers respected our space.

The food was good. The cooks served up sliced beef, powdered mashed potatoes, biscuits, and gravy. Hutch said the meat was probably Water Buffalo. I looked at Narvone and he laughed. "Don't worry, Mike," he said, "You only have to worry about the food on hot dog day." I looked at Hutch and he was grinning and nodding. He and Narvone busted out laughing from the look on my face. I smiled and continued to eat. I figured they were kidding me and, besides, the meat or whatever it was, tasted good.

After chow, Narvone said to take the rest of the day off. The hootch was empty except for the three of us. Most of the Scouts were off defending an embattled Saigon. Narvone began to write a letter. Hutch slept while I daydreamed about my upcoming mission. When I finally fell asleep, I had a strange dream about *hot dog day*.

Later, I was wakened by Narvone who also woke Hutch. He said to grab some chow, then to report to the flight line. I ate light, concerned about impressing the other Scouts. I didn't want to puke on my first mission. After chow, Hutch and I went back to the hootch. We had to pick up our flight gear.

LT, Buck, and Tom, were already prepping their ship when Hutch and I got to the flight line. We put on our flight helmets and placed our rifles and bandoliers in our ship. We then went about the task of pre-flighting our little bird of prey. I untied the main rotor and began checking the filters and fluid levels. Mr. Dunne walked up and put his carbine in the ship. While he performed his own pre-flight check, I got the M60 from the ammo locker.

Hutch was arming the skid gun when Dunne yelled, "Let's go!" They both climbed in while I grabbed the onboard fire extinguisher and stood in front of the bubble. The pilot yelled, "Clear!" He fired her up. The engine started with its characteristic *Bang* and a thick cloud of black smoke from the exhaust.

The rotors gained speed rapidly. The blades revved faster and the engine relaxed into a smooth idle. Anxious to go, I stowed the extinguisher, put on my flack jacket, and climbed in. It was time for me to join the war, already in progress.

Hutch had his M60 resting on his lap, muzzle pointing outward. I buckled in with my monkey strap and then, carefully, stepped out onto the skid. My weapon was heavy, yet it felt very comfortable cradled in my arms. I opened the breech plate and loaded the ammo belt. Confident the belt was properly loaded, I closed the plate and it clicked smoothly shut. I refrained from cocking the bolt. I remembered the rules about not having *hot rounds* inside the base perimeter. Mr. Dunne was setting the instruments and unlocking the two control sticks. The cyclic was the *steering wheel* and the collective stick gave pitch to the blades. It also had a rotary hand throttle, much like that on a motorcycle.

In front of both gunner seats was a length of wire that stretched from instrument panel to door frame. On the wire in front of Hutch were different colored smoke grenades. In front of me were two smokes, a white and a red, two frags, and two Willie Peters. I thought, "God help Charlie."

"Clear!" yelled Mr. Dunne as he brought the RPM up. Hutch and I looked back and behind the ship and then gave the pilot two thumbs up. He pulled up on the collective stick and the Raven began to rise. Dunne controlled the ship's forward and lateral motion with slight movements of the cyclic stick and foot pedals. Carefully, he pulled back on the cyclic and the chopper began to back out of the bunker. The foot pedals controlled the tail rotor which kept us from spinning in circles. LT was already hovering over the flight line when we cleared the bunker. Mr. Dunne lined up behind him.

I was in *John Wayne* heaven when the radio sqawked, "Cu Chi tower, Centaur one-six, dusk patrol, for takeoff from the corral."

"Roger, Centaur one-six. Cleared west. Exit left base at the gate."

"Roger that, Cu Chi. Centaur dusk patrol is on the go."

As LT finished his request for takeoff, we were moving down the airfield in a nose-down attitude. I was watching the maintenance hangar getting closer as Mr. Dunne followed LT and gained speed rapidly. A sudden pull on the cyclic stick sent us up and over the hangar. We cleared it by only a few feet. Mr. Dunne, smiling, was looking at me. In the days to follow, all flights took off to the left of the hangar. I never asked, but figured my first takeoff was an initiation into the Baby Scouts.

We gained altitude and I noticed how out of place the base camp seemed. It was like a scar on the green skin of the world. Cu Chi base camp was a large, brown oval surrounded by miles of barbed wire. We banked left over the main gate and were soon past the perimeter wire.

Underneath, the Vietnamese village of Cu Chi went by in a blur. It was *lock and load* time. I cocked the M60 and was ready for battle. Hutch also cocked his machine gun and the pilot flipped the *Hot* switch for the skid gun. Our little scout ship now had some big teeth.

LT led us to the firing range. It was a large, open field that the Baby Scouts used to test fire their weapons. I watched as LT nosed his chopper over and began a simulated gunrun on an old, wooden ox cart. He fired his skid gun and then his gunners joined in. We stayed behind, and above, so not to get pelted with spent cartridges. The ox cart was splintered as the bullets found their target. LT pulled pitch and banked left at the same time. Buck kept firing as the OH-23 pulled out of its attack dive. He was covering their retreating backside.

Now, it was our turn. Mr. Dunne nosed the Raven over and we dived on the ox cart. He fired a short burst from the skid gun. Taking a red, grease pencil, he marked a small *X* on the bubble. Firing again, the rounds danced around and on the cart. This time, he marked another X on the bubble and circled it. Now, my pilot had a crude but accurate gunsight.

Hutch fired off a burst and his weapon jammed. While he was cursing, and digging out the bent shell from the ejection port, I opened up with my M60. This was my first time using the weapon and I was amazed at how little recoil there was. The tracers helped my aim as I zeroed in on a flock of white egrets.

Tracers were the rounds (every fifth), that were coated with red phosphorous. My gun literally spat fire and lead. I loved the sight of the red, glowing bullets streaming to earth. In the days to come, I would learn to lead my victims with the tracer rounds and let them run right into the deadly hail of copper-jacketed lead. In time, I would also learn how to follow my prey, and to use the flying dirt, or water, as guides to their fleeing backsides.

The tracers also helped in conserving Willie Peter grenades. A short burst from an M60 would turn a bamboo hootch into a raging bonfire.

"Mason," said Dunne over the intercom, "leave the birds alone and try to hit the cart." I answered the pilot with a stitching of the field, right up to the ox cart. It exploded into pieces and a small chunk of splintered wood began to burn.

"Good. Good. That's enough." I nodded to Mr. Dunne, and even Hutch seemed impressed. We left the training field with all weapons in working order.

LT came up on the radio saying, "Going low."

"Going high," answered Mr. Dunne.

LT went to tree top level as we climbed to 500 feet. The low ship is the *Hunter*. The high ship is his cover. When a gunship flew high cover, it was called the *Killer*. I watched as LT zigged and zagged over the sparse vegetation. At times, he was fifty feet off the deck, skimming the top of lush, tropical palm trees. Other times, he was only five feet above the watery surface of rice paddies. This went on for an hour. I never let my eyes wander. I felt responsible for the safety of LT and his crew. In the weeks ahead, I would learn most of what I needed to know in order to do my job right and to increase my chances for surviving a year in-country.

The Baby Scouts flew from first light to last light, seven days a week. Night missions were rare. You couldn't see anything in the dark, anyway. The missions usually went like this…

The low ship reconns the rice paddies, jungle, bushes, open fields, villages, rivers, and anywhere else the enemy might hide. The high ship flies cover, always keeping the low ship in sight. Ideally, the prey was spotted by the hunter and quickly blown away with machine gun fire.

Sometimes, a smoke grenade was tossed to mark the location of the hidden enemy. The high ship, listening in on the radio, would then transmit the map coordinates back to Operations. Then, it would make a gunrun on the smoke. Both ships would engage the enemy with miniguns and M60s. If all went as planned, Charlie would be blown to hell.

If a Gunship was flying high cover, the Scout, after spotting the enemy, would move aside and let the killer make the gunrun. The assault helicopter would fire 2.75 inch rockets, 40mm grenades, and thousands of rounds from its miniguns.

Sometimes, the elusive enemy would disappear into the thick foliage of the jungle or would crawl down a spider hole. That's when the brave *tunnel rats* of the infantry were called in. If a large number of enemy soldiers were discovered, artillery might be called in by the pilot. He would relay the map coordinates to the fire base, and then the heavy bombardment would commence.

The way missions usually went caused me to nickname my job, *bait patrol*. The low ship, or decoy, would tease the enemy into firing at it. Then, with the hiding place revealed, we could engage the *hunted* in a firefight.

At times, I felt like I was strapped to a moving target with whooshing rotor blades that noisely announced, "Here I am. Please shoot me!" How could Charlie resist such an appetizer. Fortunately, Chuck was a lousy shot…most of the time.

Dusk patrol was routine. The VC were hunkered down for the night. Darkness was closing in and LT radioed us to return to base. He stayed low, us high, on the flight back to base camp. My virgin flight was coming to an end. However, the adrenaline in my body was still fueling my racing heart.

I wanted to stay in the air forever and hunt my prey. The machine gun, grenades, and the rush of wind against my body, combined to make me drunk with power. Suddenly, I was a nineteen-year-old going in harms way and loving it. I had the John Wayne fever.

In our own way, we Scouts were suicidal. For instance, I, like the others, drew enemy fire for a living. Sure…it was a volunteer assignment and this was war, but one flight hooked us all. We were as addicted to the adventure as some are to alcohol or tobacco. I became addicted as soon as I fired the machine gun. Flying, riding the skids, killing Charlie, they all were bonuses for being a Baby Scout. Even a day without a kill was a *high*. A mission, any mission, was better than drugs.

If you don't count alcohol, I never took any drugs during my tour in country…not even pot. I didn't need to. Flying with the Baby Scouts and engaging the enemy at close range were my glorious *acid trips* of the war.

My legs were turning numb from supporting me, the M60, and its heavy ammo belt. Since we were going back, I decided to sit on the cockpit seat. I sat with my left cheek on the seat and my right leg hanging out the door. My foot was pushed back by the rushing wind and by moving it laterally, or vertically, it acted much like an airfoil. My *flying foot* would become my trademark and some discussion of debate among pilots and gunners. It would also end up causing me much pain.

"Cu Chi tower, Centaur one-six."

"Cu Chi tower."

"Centaur one-six, dusk patrol, requesting right base, POL."

"Roger, one-six. Clear to land, POL."

LT and Dunne landed at the Petroleum and Ordinance Depot. Buck and I gassed up our ships. While refueling, I saw our Hog taking on rockets and grenades. Both crew chief and gunner took part in the reloading of the weapons. I noticed that the rocket pods were almost empty and thought, "The Gunship must have had an interesting mission." The Hog was never wasted on routine sorties.

"Cu Chi tower, Centaur one-six."

"Cu Chi tower."

"Centaur one-six, dusk patrol. Two for the corral from POL."

"Roger, one-six. Cleared for takeoff. Watch for the outgoing Gunships and land at pilot's discretion."

"Roger, Cu Chi. Dusk patrol on the go."

I was still on a high as we crossed over the perimeter wire. Hutch and I cleared our weapons. The pilot flipped his hot switch to off. We came straight in and over the *Muleskinner* liftship outfit. The Muleskinners were a CH-47 company. These huge, tandem rotor, cargo helicopters were used to transport infantry and supplies. They also would go out and *sling* back downed aircraft. Rumor was…they also had a *Spooky*.

The United States Air Force had the original Spooky, though they called it *Puff the Magic Dragon*. At night, with its many miniguns, and gatling cannon firing, it looked like a fire-breathing dragon. In fact, when Spooky first appeared in the night skies of South Vietnam, many natives, including Charlie, thought that's exactly what is was.

This military DC-3 (AC-47), could decimate an entire village in mere seconds. The guns fired so fast you couldn't hear a pause between the firing bullets or cannon shells. The weapons sounded like *whirring* chainsaws that were running at full throttle. When Spooky was called into the frey, you knew that things were hot and heavy.

The Muleskinner outfit was behind us as we made our approach. Darkness was imminent and the pilots wanted to put the baby warbirds to bed. I didn't want my first adventure to end, however getting shot down at night usually meant certain death.

BABY SCOUT

Our ships flared as they slowed to a hover over the Centaur airfield. The pilots guided the choppers to the bunkers nearest the ammo locker. Narvone and Donald scooted inside for protection from the oncoming dust storm.

As the skids settled into the dirt, throttles were cut and the mission came to an end. Danny and Tom peeked out the locker and looked at me, the new guy. I grinned big and gave them a thumbs up. They laughed and returned the gesture. I realized immediately that I must have looked like a school boy after his first day in class.

Hutch was out and attending the skid gun. I unhooked my Monkey Strap, climbed out, and carried my M60 to the locker. Narvone walked over.

"How'd it go?"

"Great," I said, still high with excitement, "but I need more practice with the M60."

LT walked over and talked to Dunne. With Narvone's help, I began the visual inspection of the ship. The Baby Scout leader and Mr. Dunne were still conversing as I began to clean the filters. I was feeling nervous and a little self-conscious.

After lashing down the main rotor and signing the log book, I grabbed my rifle, bandoliers, and helmet. Hutch said he wanted to stay and give his machine gun a good going over. He also offered to clean mine. I protested but he said, "Beat it, Scout!" He had a smirk on his face. I smiled and turned away with great joy. I was, for the first time, accepted as a fellow Baby Scout.

I headed down the flight line with the others. LT told me, along the way, that I did good.

"Thanks, LT." He looked at me funny, then smiled and shook his head. I guess he was surprised that a FNG would be so familiar with him. Buck, the Lieutenant's crew chief, laughed. He was amused, but also a little relieved that I didn't screw up and let him down. As the others walked, I began to strut. I was thinking, "Watch out, Charlie. There's a new Scout in town and he's coming after you." I didn't realize it but I was already showing signs of John Wayne Fever. There is no cure for this mental affliction, save horrific rendering of body and soul. In Vietnam, it literally means pain and suffering.

The sun had set and the sky was red over the horizon. As we walked, or strutted, down the flight line, I watched the Gunships warming up in

Michael W. Mason

their bunkers. They were going out on a night mission. The mighty Hog was one of them. The flying battleship led the way out and over the base perimeter. I thought, "It must be important if the Hog is going."

The pilots veered off and walked to OPS. The others headed for the hootch. I said I'd be along, shortly. I stood facing the red-colored horizon and watched the Centaur Gunships disappear into a crimson twilight. I sat down on the boardwalk and felt special.

My initiation was over and I had passed the test. A new, young candidate had gained admittance to a select club of suicidal, teenage warriors. As I watched the stars flicker on, my only thoughts were, "I'm a Baby Scout. I belong."

BABY SCOUT

Michael W. Mason

FIVE

KOOL-AID AND BUNKER RATS

The days are always interesting and exciting in Vietnam. In-between the dawn and dusk patrols are the search and destroy missions, or S & D. There is also the occasional convoy cover, and the more frequent *ash and trash* or *milk runs*. D troop's milk runs are usually flights to Tan Son Nhut, or Saigon, for booze, beer, and cigarettes. Other sorties like these included the picking up of replacements, ferrying the brass around, or taking soldiers to Saigon or Vung Tau for R & R. *Rest and Relaxation* is something that everyone looks forward to.

After six months in country you can take two weeks off from the war. You are allowed to vacation almost anywhere in the world and at Uncle Sam's expense. Married soldiers mostly go to Hawaii to see their wives and kids. Single guys usually visit the more exotic places, such as Kuala Lumpur and Bangkok.

I heard many stories from soldiers who returned from these *Shangrilas*. Many came back with custom made suits, Seiko watches, Japanese cameras and stereos, and unbelievable accounts of erotic adventures with beautiful, passionate women. The prices were dirt cheap, including for the women.

Some came back from R & R with a venereal disease. This earned the careless soldiers a trip to the base clinic and a penicillin shot in the butt. The best, and safest, vacations were had by the guys who hooked up with just one girl. In Bankok, for instance, the girls existed to serve the vacationing, war-weary soldiers. They were all young, beautiful, and usually owned or rented their own homes. They owed everything they had to the eager, but lonely boys in uniform.

The way it worked was…you'd move in with the girl of your choice. You might meet her in a bar, night club, or on the street. Besides money up-front, you paid for food, drinks, tourist trips with your girl, whatever. In return, you had a loyal, endearing companion for the duration of your R & R.

She literally became your girlfriend. She cooked for you, waited on you, bathed you or with you, and treated your body and senses to the most

Michael W. Mason

erotic, sexual pleasures imaginable. The girls all spoke English and made for good company on excursions to interesting places.

Some of the girls were older than the teenaged warriors they soothed. I think many of us lost our innocence to these *working girls* of the Orient. After hearing all the stories, I sometimes wished I had.

These exotic women became wallet and album photos for many of the returning soldiers. I suspect many a grieving family, or widow, wondered about those pictures when going through the personal effects of their fallen heroes.

If you couldn't get out of country, for whatever reason, there was always Saigon or Vung Tau. Saigon had the lure of city life: night clubs, museums, grand hotels, and the occasional rocket and mortar attacks.

Vung Tau was south of the big city and situated on the shore of the South China Sea in the Mekong Delta region. It was a village with an airbase that shared its name. The little community was a smelly place of open sewers, open garbage pits, cheap bars, and even cheaper whores. You didn't find quality girls in Vung Tau, only VD if you weren't careful about where you shopped.

The only nice thing about Vung Tau was the beach. Some called it *China Beach.* There was another China Beach further north. In fact, many beaches along the Vietnam coastline had the same name. Only one, however, was relatively safe for R & R. That was the one in Vung Tau.

Vung Tau is where many soldiers, and civilians, pay cheap prices for cheap tricks and get the *Clap*, or a minor venereal infection, for their discount shopping. I once visited a *whore factory* near China Beach. I was so sickened by what I saw, that I ran out and puked in the middle of the street. This less than memorable moment came during my last month in-country.

When not working at war, I worked on the choppers. If my maintenance was caught up, I filled sandbags. When there were no more waste cans to set ablaze, I pulled guard duty. There was little idle time in D Troop of the 3/4 Cav. The funny thing was, how I hated the *down time*. Strangely enough, I discovered that I was happiest when cradling a *locked and loaded* M60 machine gun.

There was always something to do. Sometimes, I would run errands in the headquarters jeep. I picked up mail, delivered reports, and chauffeured the brass. Other times, I would goof off with the little vehicle. The jeep was fun!

BABY SCOUT

  I was joy-riding in the jeep one day as the sun was setting. The *Wolfhounds* compound was at the far edge of the camp and, for some reason, I got a strange urge to visit this legendary and somewhat mystical place. The Wolfhounds are the elite of the infantry and legendary for bravery. The outfit is also notorious for its ferocity in battle. It was dark when I found the compound. In front, just off the road, was a sign that read, "Beware! You Are Entering Wolfhound Territory." That sign, along with the many, scurious shadows in the darkness made me timid. It was scary, in a halloween sense, so I stayed in the jeep, motor running. I felt like an unwelcomed guest, a trespasser, and decided to move on.

  Further up the road was *MARS*. The Military Affiliate Radio System is the AT&T of Cu Chi. I stopped by there frequently to make phone calls home and to see my good friend, Barney Peller.

  Barney is a communications expert whom I first met in Germany. He ended up in 'Nam because his radio expertise was sorely needed. Barney was a friend from saner times and a *bunker rat* by occupation.

  Barney's heavily fortified *commo center* is the mouth and ears of Cu Chi. This was where I made my infrequent calls home. Barney always had a phone available for me. In return, I got him a flight on dusk patrol. I was glad we came through that flight without incident. Having Barney onboard compromised our safety, somewhat, but he could read a map better than any pilot and was an expert with the M16 rifle.

  Barney Peller was the nicest lifer I ever met. He was married to a very large (huge), German woman and sired four children. Barney was also somewhat of a medical and sexual marvel. Years earlier, he suffered *Elephantitis* of the testes. One of his testicles swelled to the size of an orange, then slowly shrunk to the size of a pea. Barney once told me, "Mike, I was left with one nut and a nine inch penis that can last for hours." He said that his wife loves him even more than ever, and that her girlfriends are all envious of her. Barney and Helga will probably live happily ever after. I also think Willie the Whopper would have envied Barney. I just admired him for being a good man and friend.

  After the visit, I drove back to D Troop. It was late, dark, and few lamps were burning in the camp. I drove with the headlights off. That is standard procedure when driving at night. I parked next to OPS, grabbed the jeep's log book, and went inside to report to the CQ (Charge of Quarters).

Michael W. Mason

At night, the officer of the day is called the Charge of Quarters, or CQ. He asked me why I was late. My brain reeled for an answer and seconds later I said, "I'm not late, sir. My duties took me this long to complete." The young W1 dwelled on my explanation for a few seconds and said, "All right, Mason. Fill out the log and you can go." The tall, skinny Warrant Officer was fresh out of flight school in the states. I left OPS not knowing that W1 Jimmy Latham and I had a future together that would redefine the meaning of *wet behind the ears*.

Whenever I had free time, I'd usually just hang out in the hootch. I'd write letters home, chat with the guys, or just catch up on some sorely needed sleep. Chow was a good time, too. The food was hot and usually pretty good, considering where I was. For some reason, I was always in the minority on this opinion.

Chow time was also good for people watching. I always get a kick out of people, even if they're just scratching an ear or grooving to rock on the radio. Everyone seems to have a funny quirk. Tom Donald had his George Burns facial expressions, Hutch always had a smirk on his face, Narvone had a stone face that brought him good luck at poker, and Buck couldn't go five minutes without twirling his handlebar mustache between his fingers. Mine, I guess, was strutting. I still strutted whenever I walked the flight line. Hutch told me once, "Mike, it's like a switch. As soon as you pass the Hangar, or leave the ammo locker, you strut like you own the airfield." I laughed when he told me that. Secretly, I knew he was right. I did feel powerful before and after Baby Scout missions. It would be many months before my strutting would cease, and it wouldn't end voluntarily.

If there was a constant of the war at chow, it was the *Kool-Aid*. We always had this bellywash at chow…morning, noon, and night. It might be cherry. It might be grape, but it was always Kool-Aid, every day. I had some almost every day and thrived on it. I think many of us did. It was like a part of home was always with us. We, after all, were part of the original Kool-Aid generation. We grew up on it, even sold it as kids for pennies a glass. Thanks to Kool-Aid, mom was with me every day.

Being who I was, I watched the crews all the time. Leaning back against the tent pole, I took in the sights and sounds while sipping my sugary, grape delight. The Gunship crew is a tight bunch, much like the Baby Scouts. The Hog crew always seemed frazzled. They were wired, always on edge. I don't know if anyone else noticed this, but the pilots looked much the same.

BABY SCOUT

One night while on guard duty, I dove for cover during a rocket attack. I was on the flight line and tumbled into a Gunship bunker. I ate dirt, and a little something extra while cowering next to the sleeping Hog. I had landed in someone's little pot garden.

Marijuana was being cultivated on the flight line. It was mixed in with the tall scrub grass that grew all around the bunker, so it was very hard to spot. Weed was used in the Cav and, though I never witnessed anyone smoking it, I smelled it often, usually when walking by the infantry or Gunship hootches. I was glad there were no *potheads* in the Baby Scouts. In time, though, that would change.

After chow, there was always the same walk back to the hootch. On the way I always passed the underground bunker. It was finished and I had a personal investment in it of many hours and sweat.

It was March and very hot. One evening, I was sleeping when an explosion woke me from a deep, sweat-soaked sleep. Fully awake, I got my pants on as two more rockets landed close by. I heard the sound of tearing metal coming from the direction of the maintenance hangar. I hoped no one was pulling night maintenance duty. Another rocket landed and the concrete floor vibrated under my feet. I put on my flack jacket, grabbed my M16 and bandoliers of ammo clips and boots, and ran for the underground bunker. I saw a mortar round explode on the airfield and I hoped Hutch, who was on guard duty, was ok.

The inside of the bunker was hot, musty, and dark except for a few flashlights and a lantern. About fifty of us were crowded together. I sat on the dirt floor and put on my boots. A few cots were present but they belonged to a pilot and a gunner.

The pilot was one of the Baby Scout officers. The gunner was a gunship crewman. Both were getting short; only a few months left before going home. They both were very afraid of dying in a rocket attack.

The two men still performed their duties, but at night this hole in the ground became their home. None of us thought any less of these men. Most of us thought them to be pretty smart. Living in the bunker, at night, increased the odds that they wouldn't go home in a flag-draped, aluminum coffin.

I flew with the bunker-slip rat pilot a few times. He was a bit nervous, and touchy, but a good pilot. If I ever became a bunker-rat, I hoped to do my job as well.

Michael W. Mason

A few nights later there was another rocket attack. This one sounded further off so we didn't run for the bunker. We Scouts didn't always do the smart thing. For some reason, when the explosions sounded far away, our bravado got bigger and our brains, smaller. It was just the Baby Scout way.

This rocket attack took on a different twist. A rumor began to circulate that the VC had breached the outer wire of the perimeter. Someone was running through the Troop, telling everyone to standby and stand armed. None of us Scouts would put on the steel pot. We had our false sense of pride and would rather die wearing our beloved jungle hats, than play by the sensible rules of war.

Danny Narvone went back in the hootch. A minute later he came out wearing his steel pot. He was one of the few Scouts who realized there was little difference between vanity and foolishness. Sergeant Jenkins and Hutch were the others. Personally, I didn't think any less, or any more, of these hard hat soldiers. I only knew that, if killed, I would die looking good in my jungle hat with silver wings. Most of the infantry-bred door gunners knew better. We crew chiefs, however, didn't know any better. We just believed, for some inane reason, that it was important to die looking good.

Sergeant Jenkins came by wearing full battle gear. In the darkness he looked like a black and white caricature of a World War Two soldier. He told us to standby and then he left for OPS. Fifteen minutes later he returned and told Hutch and me to report to Operations. He added, "Full gear and steel pots." Jenkins told everyone else to stand down, but to keep weapons close by.

When we reported to OPS, the Commanding Officer told us that we were *volunteered* for perimeter duty. My first thought was, "*Damn!*" Hutch remained his usual calm self. He was trained infantry and no stranger to perimeter duty.

We were transported by jeep to a CP (Command Post), near the main gate. The jeep dropped us off near a tank that was blocking the main entrance to the base, its cannon turret pointed outward. Also on the tank was a manned 50 caliber machine gun. A Captain and Sergeant explained the situation to us.

During the rocket attack, movement was spotted outside the perimeter wire at two different locations. The Tet offensive had reinforced the *better safe than sorry* axiom and a command decision was made to beef up the perimeter defenses.

Hutch and I were the contributions made by D Troop of the 3/4 Cav. Our orders were to patrol five hundred yards, up and down the road, on the inside of the perimeter. We were told to *lock and load* but to keep our safeties on. Any movement inside the outer wire was to be fired on. In case of an all-out assault, Gunships would drop flares and then commence gunruns on the encroaching enemy. The flares, like miniature suns on tiny parachutes, would also help us perimeter guards to see what we were shooting at.

Before sending us on our way the sergeant Said, "If we need her, Spooky is on standby." Against all the American defenses, I didn't see how the enemy could stand a chance. I asked hutch for his opinion and he said, "No chance at all. Cu Chi is just too big and too powerful and like the Sergeant said, we've got Spooky."

The Captain and Sergeant left us to our duty. We patrolled the road and I felt like a slow moving target in a sniper's crosshairs. I needed to be in the air, moving low and fast. I always felt safe doing that. That's when I feel invulnerable and in control of everything in front of my gun barrel. Here, I was cherry, again, and somewhat dependent on Hutch and his experience. We walked our patrol with rifles pointed toward the wire. I was a little jumpy but managed to keep my nerves in check. Even in darkness there are shadows. I would be seeing phantoms throughout the long night.

For two hours we ambled up and down the dirt road. My craning neck hurt and my eyes were strained from looking at shadows. A jeep, with lights out, came toward us. Hutch clicked off his safety. I did what he did. A familiar figure got out of the vehicle. I heard another click. I put my safety back on, too. The Sergeant said to hop in, that we were needed to reinforce a machine gun post further up the road. He dropped us off about three hundred yards on the other side of the main gate. The Sergeant said, "I'll be back for you at first light."

The jeep rumbled out of sight and we took cover behind a clump of dirt and broken sandbags. We were about a hundred feet from the machine gun bunker. If there was an assault on the perimeter, we were to give flanking fire.

Hutch turned his back to the mound of old, torn sandbags and sat down. I joined him and we lit up. Hutch could sometimes be a smart-ass and a pain in the butt, but he was always cool. I even approved of him writing my little sister, who was a junior in high school. She and Hutch corresponded until he rotated back to the states. I didn't have a girlfriend anymore. Except to my mom and uncle, I didn't write home much at all.

"*Whoomph*!" Hutch and I were startled by the noise and we clicked off our safeties. We rolled over on our stomachs and crawled to the top of the dirt mound. We aimed our rifles toward the wire.

"What was that?"

"Claymore," said Hutch.

Claymores are anti-personnel mines. They're rectangular, concave, and about the size of a one inch thick, 12 by 5 inch book. The plastic casing is filled with high explosive and hundreds of steel pellets. Three little legs, like a camera tripod, folded out from the bottom. The claymore rested on the ground, on the little legs, concave side facing outward. The Claymore is the anti-personnel explosive of choice in the Army. It's light, portable, easy to set up, and deadly. It can be detonated by trip wire or electric current, sending lethal, steel balls at high velocity on a wide killing swath.

Thankfully, the rest of the night went by without incident. We guessed that an animal set off the Claymore, or maybe a nervous bunker guard with an itchy, trigger finger. At first light the Sergeant picked us up and said the alert was cancelled. He said the Tet offensive had made everyone tense and a bit more careful. He thanked us as he dropped us off in front of the maintenance hangar.

We reported to OPS where the OD logged us in from TDY (Temporary Duty). Tired, I stowed my gear and hit the showers. The water was lukewarm and, as I lathered up, I heard two Ravens fly overhead. You can set your watch by dawn patrol.

Back in the hootch, Hutch was out cold on his bunk. He was still in full battle dress and boots. His M16 was resting by his side. On the floor was his steel pot. Inside were three frags. "*Damn*!" I thought. "I didn't know he had those."

I, too, was tired but liked going to the mess hall. It was a recreational time for me. I enjoyed the people-watching more than the food, and the Kool-Aid always made me think of home and of my little, wood stand in front of my house. Some days I charged a nickel instead of the usual two cents a glass. When I earned a quarter it was a good day. That was a lot of money to a kid back in 1957.

I was nine years old, living just outside of Portland, Oregon. The small community of Hillsdale was as American as it gets…milk and cookies, soup and sandwiches, fish on Friday, and parents not unlike Ward and June Cleaver.

My other tv role models were Robert Young, Fess Parker, and James Arness. Our family tv was black and white and our family car was a pink and white Dodge Coronet with huge tail fins and a dash-mounted, push-button, automatic transmission. In 1957, all cars had lots of chrome and big tail fins.

Hillsdale was a wonderful place to live and grow up. Daughters played house with *Barbies* and rode girls bicycles. Sons played *cowboys and indians* and *war*. Toy guns were all the rage, then. Mine were so realistic that the federal government cracked down on the toy makers.

My guns were the realistic *Mattel Shooting Shell* models. They were made of metal and used spring loaded cartridges. They fired grey, plastic bullets. I used to stand in front of the tv and outdraw *Paladin* every Friday night. I usually lost on Saturday night to Marshall Matt Dillon.

I also had a shooting shell rifle and a shooting shell belt buckle. A small, shiny, silver derringer would swing out from the buckle and shoot a plastic bullet. I was very sad, and angry, when these toys were banned by the government.

After my guns were taken away, I took up sword fighting with a homemade, wooden sword, and an aluminum garbage pail cover for a shield. After a few cuts, eye injuries, and cracked heads, those too were confiscated by my concerned, over-zealous parents.

All the kids in the neighborhood suffered the same fate. We were distraught and without our tools of war. Being nine years old, I and the other kids came up with new games of war. The best was the weekend *dirt clod* battle. If our parents ever saw what we did, all of us would have been paddled and grounded for months.

The dirt clod war pitted one army of kids against another. There were about eight on each side. We would gather on opposing ridges of a deep ravine in the nearby woods. Each army spent about fifteen minutes digging up rock-size dirt clods. We also dug trenches and bunkers to hide behind. Only fifty feet separated each army of pre-pubescent warriors. Out of the chasm, that separated the combatants, grew a giant oak tree. From a strong, thick branch hung a knotted, hemp rope. The dirt clods, trenches, bunkers, and the rope, were all our weapons and defenses. An impartial referee, usually a girl, would yell, "War!" The battle was on.

Dirt clods rained down on both sides. Some of us had garbage pail covers or pieces of plywood for protection against the incoming missiles. The bravest among us would run for the dangling rope and swing across to the other side. While holding on with one hand, the suicidal insurgent would throw one dirt clod at the enemy. He was a hard target to hit and rarely got hurt. I tried it once and got hit in the back. It stung but only a minor bruise resulted. The battle ended when all the dirt clods were used up. Neither army ever won a concisive victory. That wasn't the point of the war. We just had fun doing it.

The attrition rate was high. There were cuts, bruises, black eyes, and fat lips. Concerned mothers started keeping their kids home. Few and fewer showed up for the battles. Then, on a rainy day, the war ended. Someone threw a muddy clod, wrapped around a rock, and hit the boy on the rope in the head. He lost his grip and fell thirty feet into the ravine. He survived but suffered a broken leg. After that, parents interveened and called for an end to hostilities. The great dirt clod war of 1957 was over.

My dad was of the *Greatest Generation*, a veteran of World War Two. He brought back an M1 carbine. He went hunting with a neighbor and shot a Doe by mistake. He never went hunting again. There was a gentleman's code back then. Females were to be protected and taken care of. Even if it was a deer, my dad was crushed by the incident. I was brought up the same way…respect women and fight fair. I kept those values, even through the Vietnam War.

The mess tent was still busy feeding the troops. I got some powdered eggs, a meat something, toast, and some Kool-Aid. I sat at the Baby Scout table and began my surveillance. My ears caught interesting gossip coming from the officer's table. They were talking about the new Cobras and Loaches that were coming to D Troop.

The AH-1G, or Cobra, is the Army's newest, high-tech, assault helicopter. It made the Huey Gunships obsolete. Even the mighty Hog would one day be supplanted by the Cobra. For now, though, the Hog is just too powerful a weapon to be put into mothballs.

The Cobra is long, sleek, and only three feet wide. It seats the pilot aft and the weapons officer (gunner), forward. This incredibly fast war machine carries rocket launchers, minigun, and, sometimes, an automatic grenade launcher. Some Cobras were rigged with two minguns. It was rumored to have an attack speed of over 185 knots, or about 200 miles per hour. Some pilots would brag that they did 220 knots on a gunrun.

The biggest rumor about the Cobra is that if the pilot doesn't pull out of an attack dive before 1500 feet, the chopper would plow into the ground. Before leaving Vietnam, I would be the victim of a comedic Cobra pilot and this not so funny rumor.

When I heard one of the officers say *egg*, I knew he meant, *Loach*. That's the nickname of the LOH-6A. The official Army nickname is Cayuse, but no one ever calls it that.

The Loach is a jet turbine powered, light observation helicopter. I had seen a few of these ships before, mostly up north in the Tay Ninh Province. They belonged to the legendary 1st Air Cavalry. There are many tall tales about the 1st Air Cav and I believe them all. It was the Air Cav that pioneered chopper warfare in Vietnam and bred the first generation of suicidal, teenaged gunslingers.

The Air Cav racked up the highest body count in Vietnam. It also lost the most men and ships. Once, a *pink team* went screaming by my OH-23 like it was standing still. A pink team is a Loach and Cobra flying as a hunter-killer. The new Cobras and Loaches revolutionized helicopter warfare. They also helped launch the Baby Scouts into the elite of legendary fighting forces.

In D Troop of the 3/4 Cav, the Baby Scouts were the white team. The gunships were the red team, and the slicks, which carried the infantry, were the blue team. I don't ever remember being called *pink* when paired with a Cobra or other Gunship. It may have been out of respect for the 1st Air Cavalry. Their casualty rate is high and when we went hunting and killing, we were following in the footsteps of the pioneer of search and destroy, aerial warfare. One thing is for sure. None of us would ever admit to wanting to join the 1st Air Cav. The life expectancy with the Baby Scouts is low enough as it is.

Something was definitely blowing in the wind. Something was changing in the 3/4 Cav and I was to be part of it. This change would result in making me a more effective killer. It was going to be the wilding time of my life and the reason I almost lost it.

Michael W. Mason

SIX

BUSTED CHERRY

The weeks went by and the killing continued. A lot of *them* died and only a few of *us* died, or were wounded. We racked up the body counts and kept the enemy busy, running and hiding from our murderous intent.

The 3/4 Cav's armored and infantry units also did the 25th Infantry Division proud. While I flew the clear, blue skies, the ground pounders scoured the rice paddies and jungles. I always considered it an honor to give aerial support to the grunts. Soon, I was going to love them.

They came in the middle of the day. I was busy doing maintenance when I noticed everyone staring into the sun. I heard the unmistakeable *Womp, Womp, Womp* of Hueys and hurried with the gas filter before the coming storm undid my work. I hopped to my feet and checked the rotor tie-down. Seconds later, two killers emerged from the blinding, white glare of the radiant sun.

They were brand new Huey AH-1G Gunships, or Cobras. I had never been so close to one of these assault helicopters before. My little Raven, as well as the old Huey gunships, seemed like *Tin Lizzies* in comparison.

As the futuristic warbirds slowly hovered toward the hangar, everyone on the flight line stopped what they were doing and fell in behind the slow moving ships. It was a *Pied Piper* spectacle that would happen one more time. That would be when the hunters flew out of the blinding, Asian sun.

Trucks on the road stopped to watch and guys from the armored units crossed the road to get a closer look at the lethal war machines. Pilots and crews from the adjacent 25th Air Battalion crossed their flight line to get to ours. It was apparent that I wasn't the only one who hadn't seen a *Killer Cobra* up close before. I joined in the procession of witnesses to the future. A week later I was on my way to Loach school.

The week-long schooling was at Bien Hoa. There, I excelled and was at the top of my class. The days were spent learning about the airframe, jet turbine, and the ship's flight characteristics. I also learned minigun operation and maintenance. Some pilots attended the school. They were the maintenance officers who needed to know as much as the crew chiefs.

The Loach is a small, egg-shaped helicopter. To me, it's funny looking. To Charlie, it's a demon. The little ship has teeth and can riddle the enemy

Michael W. Mason

with its minigun in an attack dive of over 140 knots. Besides the minigun, the crew chief sits in the right, rear jumpseat with an M60 machine gun and a box of grenades.

The pilot flies right seat and the observer is in the left. The observer usually has an M16 but sometimes he takes along an M79 grenade launcher. The Loach, fully armed, is a mini-fighter/bomber. Together, the Loach and Cobra could take on anything and win.

The LOH-6A really does look like an egg. If you removed the main rotor, tail section, skids, and painted it white, it would look just like a giant egg, complete with big and little ends for the *Lilliputians* to fight over. I grew to love the egg. It made me a better Scout, a more efficient hunter, a deadler killer, and lengthened my life expectancy by a few, precious seconds.

I don't know where they went but shortly after Loach school started, the OH-23s disappeared. I graduated at the top of my class and returned to Cu Chi. In the Baby Scout bunkers sat four, new Loaches. Mine was #395. I took real good care of her and figured that she would take good care of me. I worked hard to make her the best hunter in the fleet. As the assigned crew chief, I kept the log book. In the months to come, I would only have to *Red-X* her four times. The first, unfortunately, was less than a week away.

Mr. Dunne became the assigned pilot for #395. He's a big man, and he barely fit in the cockpit. He was the OD when I first reported for duty in D Troop of the 3/4 Cav. Chief Warrant Officer Dunne always seems to be in a good mood. Like me, he also loves a good scrap.

We made a great team and my growing reputation with the M60 made him a more confident pilot. W1 Dunne would go on to distinguish himself in the war. Besides the Air Medal, with many clusters, he would earn the DFC (Distinguished Flying Cross), for bravery. He never asked for medals or sought them out. He, like me, just loved a good fight. My nickname for him is *Gun-Gun* Dunne. Gun-Gun got a kick out of that.

It was early May when the Baby Scouts were ordered to support an armored unit just outside of Saigon. The city's *suburbs* suffered heavy pounding from the months of Tet.

Bomb craters, burned out hootches, and crumbled buildings were everywhere. The mission called for a gun team, so my Loach had a Gunship for a partner...the Hog.

The ground units were going from building to building, searching for the elusive enemy. This was to be a simple *mop-up* operation for the armored and infantry units. AK-47 fire and RPG (rocket propelled grenade), attacks changed that in a hurry. That's when the Baby Scouts were called in.

The Hog stayed at 500 feet, keeping #395 in sight at all times. Mr. Dunne zipped the Loach just above, and through, the maze of exploded buildings. Like all hunter pilots, he flew keeping the AO (Area of Operations), off the right side, and under the gunsight of his backseat gunner. It also helped having two sets of eyes searching for Charlie. We reconned ahead of the advancing, slow moving, ground forces.

"Got one! Got one!" I yelled, as I opened up with the M60. A VC in *black pajamas,* and carrying an AK-47, was running toward a small, bamboo hut. I stitched him up the back with a trailing burst of machine gun fire. The impacting rounds slammed his *rag doll* body through the hootch doorway, but not before I saw his head explode in a crimson shower of blood and fragments.

His refuge became his tomb. Dunne saw the body go through the door but not the kill. He said, "I'm going to make another pass. Lob a Willie through the door." Dunne pulled collective, pulled back on the cyclic, and gave the ship some right pedal. We spun on our axis as he then evened the pedals and forced the cyclic stick forward. He did the maneuver in one quick motion. The old Raven could never do that. This new, turbine chopper could stop, turn, and spin on a dime.

The pilot brought the Loach in at tree top level. I pulled the pin on the Willie Peter and dropped it about fifty feet in front of the smoldering doorway. The tracers from my machine gun had started a small fire. It was like watching in slow motion as the grenade fell to its target. It tumbled end over end like a small football.

As we flew over the roof, I watched the white phosphorous grenade go through the doorway. Seconds later the hootch exploded into flame, smoke, and cascading sparks. The fireworks rose fifty feet into the air. The hut became a burning funeral pyre for the dead Cong inside. Later, the advancing grunts would look through the smoldering ashes for bodies, weapons, and spider holes.

Mr. Dunne didn't see the actual kill so I only got a *probable* body count. I was really mad that Gun-Gun wouldn't confirm my kill. I wasn't angry at him, just the bad luck. I don't remember Mr. Dunne and myself ever getting mad at each other.

We engaged in several more firefights and set a number of buildings on fire. The awesome power of the Hog was needed only once. Half a

Michael W. Mason

dozen VC had holed up in a two story, brick building. The advancing ground units were half a mile away.

We made one pass at the building with minigun and M60 blazing. The observer dropped a couple of frags. The well-protected enemy fired back with, at least, half-a-dozen automatic rifles. After the one pass, the observer tossed a red smoke grenade and the pilot called in the Hog.

The Gunship pilot radioed us to move away and for the ground forces to hold their position. This was the first time I ever saw the Hog in action. It moved off about a mile and climbed to three thousand feet. We climbed to five hundred feet and sought the safety of distance, about half a mile..

The Hog suddenly banked and came around in a nose down attitude. The pilot came up on the radio and said, "Centaur two-six commencing gunrun." I was about to witness what would be the terrified enemy's last few seconds among the living.

The Hog came straight in at the building. It loosed rocket after rocket and long bursts of automatic grenade fire. Both door gunners were rocking and rolling with their M60s. Just before pulling out of the attack dive, the Hog opened up with its twin miniguns. There was so much smoke you couldn't see where the thousands of rounds were impacting. When the ship pulled out of its dive and banked left, only the left door gunner opened up with cover fire. It took minutes for the smoke and dust to clear and allow a visual inspection of the destruction.

The rockets had blown away the roof and most of the front wall. The grenades exploded inside and brought the second floor down on top of the first. The miniguns peppered the rubble with two thousand rounds of ammo. If anything survived, it wouldn't be human.

Mr. Dunne radioed the Hog and said we were going in for a closer look. The Gunship stood by at 500 feet while we flew in slow circles around the pile of debris. It was clear that nothing could have survived the onslaught of the Army's battleship. The concussions alone, from the exploding ordinance, would have killed anyone inside the building. Dunne radioed the Hog, and ground forces, that the enemy was destroyed. No survivors.

It was getting dark so the search of the crumbled building would have to wait until morning. We signed off station and climbed to join our cover ship. The commander of the ground forces radioed back, "Roger, and thanks." As #395 climbed and slowly banked to a heading of north by northwest, toward Cu Chi, tracers lit up the darkening sky. I returned fire, aiming at the muzzle flashes.

Then the bottom fell out and the pilot yelled, "*Shit*!" The Loach shuddered and dropped like a rock before Mr. Dunne pulled collective with forward cyclic. We nosed over and the screaming, red-lined jet turbine propelled #395, and crew, toward the ground. I kept firing at the invisible enemy while thinking about my certain death. The earth of a Vietnam battlefield rose to meet the falling casket with #395 painted on its side.

The wounded hunter ship plummeted toward the ground and probably set a speed record as the airspeed indicator redlined. We were headed right for the armored unit's night encampment. "*Damn*!" I thought, "We're going to take some of our own boys with us."

Suddenly, my back was slammed against the rear bulkhead. The Loach shuddered and the rotor blades popped loudly in protest as the little warbird flared and banked to the right. Only the heavy *G*-forces kept me from falling out.

"It's all right. We're under control," said Dunne over the intercom. He switched to radio and explained our situation to the Hog and the ground commander.

"Enemy fire took out our battery and instruments. I've got to set her down."

"*Damn*!" I thought to myself. "At least we're landing among friends."

"Roger," radioed back the Hog. "Any casualties?"

"Negative that," answered Dunne, "but it looks like the ship will need a few band aids." The ground commander came up on the radio and gave us permission to land within the perimeter of the armored unit's encampment. Mr. Dunne keyed the intercom as he laughed out loud, saying, "As if he could stop me."

We landed gently but sent grunts running for cover from the swirling dust clouds. The Hog radioed that it had enough fuel to stay on station for ten minutes. Mr. Dunne had landed near a tank and sent its crew scrambling to avoid the rotor wash. He throttled back and I got out to inspect the damage.

There were several bullet holes in the front underbelly of the ship. One had smashed though the battery box and severed some wires at the main junction. There were also two exit holes in the plexiglass above the pilot's seat. Mr. Dunne had escaped death by inches. Also, I realized, if he had been shot we all would have perished.

Michael W. Mason

    I checked for other bullet holes in the doghouse, the cowling that protected the main shaft linkage and also housed the main air filter. There were none as was the case with the rotor blades, engine doors, and tail section. A five minute inspection of the ship found nothing else wrong. Dunne looked at the holes above his seat and shook his head. He smiled at me and said, "I always wanted air conditioning." I forced a smile but didn't laugh.

    We had radio power during the ordeal only because of residual power from the slowly dying battery. Now, it was completely dead. Mr. Dunne said he didn't think we could make it back to Cu Chi. I didn't argue. I told him the battery was a goner and that only a new one would get #395 back into the air. Also, especially since it was night, flying back with even a slightly damaged battery would be perilous. Going down in the blackness of night was certain death, even with the Hog present.

    While I continued to inspect the ship, the observer cleared the minigun. His name was Earl and he was on loan from the infantry. He came along to see if he wanted to join the Scouts. He didn't. I never saw him again after that night, except occasionally at the mess hall.

    I told Mr. Dunne that I could repair the damage but without a new battery we weren't going anywhere. He agreed as he cut power to the ship's turbine. The Loach wouldn't start again without a new battery. A Major and Sergeant appeared. Dunne climbed out of the Loach and walked over to meet them. He didn't salute. He knew better.

    After a few minutes of discussion with the two soldiers, he turned, waved, and said, "I'll be back in a few." He left with the two armored cavalrymen. With little else to do, I went back to assessing the damage. It was minor stuff. I could repair it in about half an hour. All I needed was a new battery. Reluctantly, I took out the ship's log and entered a red X. It seemed a silly thing to do, considering the fix we were in. I just thought it was the right thing to do.

    While Earl and I tended to the wounded loach, the armored unit went about setting up its defenses. Much like the wagon trains of the old west, the metal machines formed a circle with turret cannons pointed outward. The smaller APCs filled the gaps between the tanks.

    Soldiers began placing claymore mines outside the perimeter of steel. Sentries guarded the men setting the mines. I watched all this while leaning against the Loach, having a smoke. The respite was short-lived as the Hog *Whomped* in unannounced. Its powerful rotor wash sent soldiers scurrying for cover, including me. I ran around to the other side of my little ship.

Mr. Dunne materialized out of the dust storm. He walked over and told me that he and Earl were going back to Cu Chi. The Major had let Dunne radio the Hog, which, in turn, radioed OPS. A decision was made to leave the crew chief, me, with the Loach until morning. Dunne said he'd be back with a new battery. I asked him to also bring back a roll of electrical tape. I had a small tool kit onboard that had everything else I needed to repair the ship.

The observer was already walking toward the Hog when Mr. Dunne said, "I'll be back with the dawn patrol." He grabbed his flight helmet, M16, and then ran toward the waiting gunship yelling, "Take care." Even in the midst of so much armor, firepower, and men, I felt alone. I watched the powerful Gunship depart, leaving me with a broken ship and a racing heart.

Claymores were placed where the Hog had been. I watched the mighty battleship until its lights faded into the night. The only lights visible now were the glowing embers of cigarettes. I sat down on the left skid and lit up. "Hey, fly guy." I looked over at the nearby tank and saw a group of soldiers waving at me. One of them yelled, "Here. Come on over." I got up, grabbed my rifle, and walked toward the uncertainty of strange men and machine.

As I approached, a black Buck Sergeant asked, "What happened, man?"

"Took a few rounds. One knocked out the battery."

"Have a seat," said one of the others as he gave the tank a pat. I climbed up on the dirt-encrusted treads and sat on what might be called a fender. There were four of them. A black Sergeant, a white Corporal, and two black PFCs. The corporal asked how long I'd been in-country. I answered, "About four months. I arrived the day Tet started."

"*Hell*! Mike, is that you, man?" I looked at the Sergeant and recognition came quickly.

"Freddy. *Damn!*" We stuck out our hands at the same time and shook.

"Hey, guys," said Freddy, "this is the guy I told you about…the dude with the red pecker who went through the rocket attack with me. You should have seen him, blood all over the place and on his Johnson."

"Freddy," I said, laughing, "is that all you remember, my dick?" The others joined in the laughing and Freddy, thankfully, held back his answer to my straight line. He *shooshed* us all and I began to look nervously around the camp.

"It's all right, Mike. I doubt if the gooks can see us."

"Freddy," I said, "it looks like you got what you wanted and a promotion, too. Just don't put me on shit burning detail, ok?"

We all laughed and passed the time telling stories and sharing smokes. One of the black guys asked me what it was like to be a flying target. I said it was exciting and a pure head-rush everytime you got in a firefight.

They all seemed to relate to the fighting, but not the flying. In their minds, I was just a target to be shot out of the sky. Freddy said I was just lucky that Charlie was such a lousy shot. I countered with arguments about big, metal bullseyes for RPGs and booby traps. They came back with, "Yeah, but you have a long ways to fall. We don't." They had me there and I conceeded with, "You win."

We also talked about home, cars, and girls. We shared more smokes and our dreams for the future. I started getting tired and told my friends that I had to get some sleep. The Corporal gave me a box of C-Rations and it suddenly occured to me that I was very hungry. I thanked him for the food and looked over at Freddy.

"Don't fall out of the sky anymore. Ok, fly boy?"

"Ok, Freddy. Be cool."

"Always, my man."

I hopped off the tank and walked slowly to the Loach. Behind me, I heard Freddy say, "Shut your mouth, man," after one of the other guys had said, "He aint never going home." I smiled inwardly thinking, "Well, that's what everyone says about the Baby Scouts." I threw my rifle in the back and climbed into the observer's seat. I opened the box of canned food. I took out the little P38 (can opener), and slowly cut the lids off the small, round cans. There was spaghetti, a fruit cocktail, and vanilla cookies.

The P38 is a little, matchbook-size can opener that fits on your key ring. It also tightens or loosens screws, cuts rope, splices wire, cleans your fingernails, and picks your teeth. I never left the hootch or went flying without one on my key-ring.

The C-Rations also had a miniature pack of *Marlboro* cigarettes. After wolfing down my cold food, I lit one. The inhale calmed me. I didn't feel quite so alone anymore.

BABY SCOUT

I was asleep when the attack came. The first thing I saw was that the far side of the perimeter was aglow from an exploded APC. I grabbed my rifle and dived out of the Loach. I crawled under the ship and pointed the rifle barrel toward the perimeter. Fifty caliber machine guns could be heard over the firing of M60s and M16s. In the background, I also heard the distinctive *Whoomphs* of M79 grenade launchers.

Although the firefight was on the far side of the camp, I felt vulnerable under the flimsy sheet metal of the Loach. I crawled out, slung my rifle, and grabbed four grenades, stuffing them into my pockets. Next, I tore off a few hundred rounds of ammo and grabbed the M60. Under all this weight it was a slow trot to the neighboring tank. I slid underneath and took a prone position on my stomach. After loading the M60, I placed the rifle and grenades next to me. Freddy and his crew were probably at the perimeter with their weapons. I felt alone, again, and a little scared. On the ground I was out of my element and knew it.

It was over in a few minutes but seemed like an eternity. The enemy attack turned out to be just a couple of very foolish Viet Cong. One of them had fired an RPG into the camp and destroyed an empty APC. The rocket powered grenade is an armored unit's worst nightmare. It easily blasts through the metal skin of APCs, then explodes inside, killing everyone onboard. One was fired at me once. It happened on a rare, night mission over the Iron Triangle. It's a scary sight, seeing a rocket grenade coming up at you, especially at night. Fortunately, they weren't fired at helicopters very often.

The two VC who attacked us were holed up in a brick building about 400 feet from the camp. While they sniped at the perimeter, fifty calibers were disintegrating the building around them. A tank commander ended the farce with a single blast from his turret cannon. The building vaporized into fragments of brick, wood, and body parts. The rest of the morning was quiet but everyone stayed alert on the perimeter. Out of place, I stayed under the tank and nervously waited for sunrise.

The dawn patrol arrived out of an orange sun. One Scout stayed high while the other flared to a gentle landing just inside the camp. Mr. Dunne was in the observer's seat. I crawled out from under the tank and gathered up my weapons, ammo, and grenades. It was a heavy burden and I walked slowly to the wounded Loach. I placed my tools of war in the ship, then walked over to greet my pilot. He pointed to the back of the ship, and next to the crew chief's feet I saw the new battery, some tools, and a roll of electrical tape. I scooped it all up and went back to my ship. By the time I got to the Loach, Mr. Dunne was at my side and the dawn patrol ship was taking off.

"Well, how'd it go, Mike?"

"Fine, sir."

"Come on, you were scared to death," he said, laughing, and added, "Weren't you?"

"I smiled sheepishly, then thought, "How'd he find out about the firefight?"

I went to work replacing the battery. While I made repairs, the pilot gave the Loach a visual inspection. He even checked and cleaned the engine filter for me. I quickly finished hooking up the battery and then started the tedious job of splicing the many severed wires.

While I was trying to sort out all the different colored wires, Mr. Dunne climbed into the cockpit and began a preflight check. He had seen me working on the main wiring harness so I knew he wouldn't throw any power switches. I ignored him and went about my repairs.

As I was bandaging my surgery with electrical tape, I asked Mr. Dunne to reset the circuit breakers. As he did this, I suddenly heard the sound of diesel engines coming to life. I looked up and saw the armored unit poised for departure.

"Just great," I thought, "We're going to be left here, alone, without any protection." I hurried my efforts and just as the armored cavalry began to roll, I yelled, "Fire her up!" Mr. Dunne started throwing switches while I scooped up the old battery, tools, and other loose stuff and threw them in the back. I heard, "Clear!" and then the familiar sound when a pilot pushes the ignitor button.

The ignitor began its rapid, distinctive clicking while I held my breath and crossed my fingers. The turbine *whooshed* to life and I breathed again, though very rapidly. As the rotor came up to speed, Dunne grabbed me by the arm and said, "In front." First, I secured the M60, grenades, and other loose stuff. As I climbed into the observer's seat, I noticed a nearby tank. There were four guys on it, waving. It was Freddy and his tank crew. My friends had waited to see us off safely. Even a squad of VC would hesitate before taking on a battle tank.

I plugged in my helmet and waved back at them. Mr. Dunne saluted. Freddy returned the salute with a flourish just as collective was pulled. Dunne added some forward cyclic and we made a running takeoff. Clearing the battle zone quickly, we looked back. Smiling, I saw Freddy's tank kicking up a storm as it rumbled after the departed cavalry of iron horsemen.

Dunne pulled back on the cyclic and we quickly climbed to 2,000 feet. He knew I was lousy with maps but at this altitude it didn't matter. Heading north by northwest, we would eventually run into our giant base camp. I settled into my seat and began to enjoy the leisurely flight to Cu Chi. I was feeling calm and listened to the wind rushing by. My thoughts went back to the previous day and the events leading up to the present.

I had my baptism of fire and survived. LOH-6A, #395, was wounded but brought us down safely, albeit with a little help from the pilot.

My first, big adventure was over and it was the greatest time of my life. Even the time on the ground, though scary, was exciting. It was cowboys and gooks, and the cowboys won. The Loaches were all they were cracked up to be. I didn't miss the old Ravens at all. We seemed to take more chances with the Loach. It made us more confident and gave us a feeling of great power and invulnerability.

I was flying home with what we called a *busted cherry*. It's a crude description but accurate. No longer was I flying a ship with its sheet metal intact. The bullet holes were almost like badges of courage, or honor. I now felt like I belonged to some club or honorary organization. Also, after spending the night with the ground forces, I even had points towards a CIB (Combat Infantry Badge).

Mr. Dunne tuned in the Armed Forces Radio Network. The music was soothing and I found my foot tapping along to the beat. Dunne began to conduct the band with lateral movements of the cyclic stick. We flew north by northwest and sang as our little ship rock and rolled to the beat of the Rolling Stone's *Satisfaction*.

Michael W. Mason

SEVEN

GREASE GUNS AND GUNSLINGERS

The ensuing days were filled with new adventures. I was disappointed because they were mostly for the other Scout teams. They were racking up the body counts while I was blowing up empty hootches and sinking sampans. Sometimes it was aggressive search and destroy tactics that got us into a firefight. Other times it was just plain, dumb luck when we drew enemy fire. Bad luck was not getting your ship shot full of holes. It was getting your body shot full of holes.

I was in the Baby Scout hootch when one of the guys crashed through the door.

"LT's been shot!" We all reacted vocally at the same time. The profanity we yelled was one word, and it wasn't *Crap*.

I never saw LT again. He got the *million dollar wound* and was sent home. There were rumors that he died but Buck said that was ridiculous. I only flew a couple of missions with the Baby Scout leader. Buck was his regular crew chief. It took days for us to get over the loss of our leader. The smallish, young Lieutenant gave us direction and a resolve to be the premier outfit in the 25th Infantry Division.

Buck moped around for a week until the new scout leader walked into the hootch and yelled, "Baby Scouts, assemble!" His name was Nathaniel Reese. He was a Lieutenant, respected by the troops, and would fill LT's boots quite well.

Lieutenant Reese is a regular guy and has a laid back attitude. Buck took to him immediately and became his old, cheerful self again. I flew with Reese often and we would share some harrowing moments. As Baby Scout leader, his call sign is one-six. One designates him as a Scout. The six means he is in command. Other Scout pilots are one-two, one-three, and so on. The Gunship leader is two-six and the Slick's boss is three-six.

D Troop's commanding officer is *Six*. Whenever I hear Centaur Six on the radio, I know the old man is flying.

Lieutenant Henry (Hank) Kerns is cut from the same green cloth as the old man. He can fly and shoot 'em-up as well as anyone, yet he always has this propriety about himself. He's the only officer who likes to salute on the flight line. When he finally learned that it was hazardous to his health, he settled for salutes around the hootches. I flew with Kerns a lot. We worked well together in the air but not on the ground. The man who would be General always made me tense.

I was on the flight line when Hutch ran up and said, "Narvone's been shot."

"*Damn*! Not again," I said out loud.

"The clerk told me," said Hutch, "as I was walking out to the flight line. The gun team is on the way in."

We ran to the hangar and waited with other anxious Scouts. The CO and the XO were both there. Kerns saluted. No one else did.

A jeep with two medics, and a stretcher, pulled up in front of the hangar. A minute later the gun team, moving fast, flared to a hover over the airfield. The gunship moved to its bunker but the Loach kept coming. It made a running landing on its skids, and must have slid over thirty feet. The ship came to a stop just ten feet from the hangar, but not before a little right pedal spun the Loach ninety degrees, left side facing the hangar. Lt. Reese was the only pilot who could do that.

The medics grabbed the stretcher and ran up to the Loach. Danny Narvone was in the observer's seat. I saw Buck get out of the back. He looked shaken. Enemy fire had stitched the left side of the ship, and Danny's left leg. His boots rested in half an inch of blood and he looked pale, weak, and groggy. Blood had splattered Lt. Reese and much of the cockpit.

There was a hole in Danny Narvone's leg the size of a fifty-cent piece. The blood was gushing out in spurts, matching his heartbeat. A medic applied a compress to the gaping wound and then tied it to the shattered leg. He and his partner lifted Narvone out of the ship and placed him on the stretcher. The jeep then took away one of my role models and I never saw him again.

This is Vietnam and the replacements never stop coming. The dead, wounded, and the shortimers made for a never-ending cycle of fresh meat. Most of the new guys were 18 or 19, like me. Buck was promoted to Spec-5 and succeeded Narvone as Flight Line Chief. I started flying with Lt. Kerns regularly and Buck assigned himself to Lt. Reese most of the time.

The Baby Scouts began flying missions as far north as Tay Ninh. The AO included war zones C, D, and a relatively unknown jungle area known as the Iron Triangle. For months, I flew every day and many nights.

BABY SCOUT

Though unknown by most, the Baby Scouts earned as much distinction as the other Scout outfits. We also lost a lot of good friends along the way. Earning distinction in the Vietnam War always exacted a price. The cost...too many lives.

The Black Horse Squadron is an anomaly to me. Their Loaches are literally tied together with wire and duct tape. The crews have death in their eyes.

After one joint mission, a Black Horse Scout ship went off on its own. Its killer escort left the AO for refueling. The Baby Scouts, 1st Air Cav, and other Black Horse crews were on the Tay Ninh flight line when the prodigal hunter returned. It was yawing and bucking, obviously out of control. It landed hard, bounced, and narrowly missed a Gunship that was warming up on the airfield. The bullet-riddled Loach sat on the scrubby field, smoke pouring out of the engine compartment. No one got out of the ship. I was one of many shocked and confused spectators.

Finally, a Black Horse crew chief got out of his Loach and ran up to the smoking, rocking ship. He froze in his tracks just before reaching the devastated chopper. Then, he slowly walked up to it, reached inside, and neutralized the control sticks. He twisted the throttle grip to idle and then shut down the turbine. I wondered why he didn't wait for the jet turbine to cool down. I watched as the crew chief turned around and then slumped to the ground. He sat on the right skid and his head slowly fell into his waiting hands. "My God," I thought. "He's crying."

Other Black Horse crewmen walked over. Then the Baby Scouts and the 1st Air Cavalrymen joined them. I, and the others, just stood there and stared. No one spoke. The vision before us needed no words.

There seemed to be more holes than sheet metal. Everywhere I looked there were bullet holes and ragged tears in the thin, aluminum flesh of the horribly wounded bird. The rotor blades were also riddled and the bubble was virtually non-existant. Most of the canopy's plexiglass was scattered all over the inside of the shattered warbird.

Three figures sat frozen and almost looked alive in their mortal slumber. The pilot's hands were still griping the controls. His face was pocked with blood and, yet, he looked peaceful. His chin rested on his chest and his eyes were closed. There were bullet wounds to his legs and stomach. He landed the ship just seconds before he bled to death. The observer had no face. His M16 was dangling outside the door, its sling wrapped around the crewman's wrist. His right leg was severed at the knee joint, and held in place only by his tight-fitting pants.

There was blood and pieces of flesh splattered all over the instrument panel and the inside of the cockpit. Thick streams of blood trickled out the door frames and puddled on the ground. I stood there, transfixed by the horror in front of me. It didn't frighten me, though. It just made me angry and hungry for revenge.

In the back of the ship sat the still body of the crew chief, M60 resting between his legs, the muzzle resting on the floor. The ammo box was empty, as was the grenade box. The chief had one major wound. The top of his head was gone, just above his eyes. His flight helmet was missing and had probably been blown out of the ship. It was apparent he had the fight of his life before succumbing to the bullet that had his name on it.

We slowly moved away from this ghost ship. Two stretcher jeeps pulled up about the time we got back to our own ships. I strapped in and loaded the M60. I slammed the breech plate shut and cocked it. The grenade box was filled with frags and Willie Peter. I was ready for whatever was going to happen. I had a feeling this was not going to be a good day for Charlie.

Lt. Reese got on the radio. "Black Horse one-six, this is Centaur one-six."

"Black Horse. Go Centaur."

"The mission's yours. Take us out."

"Roger, Centaur one-six. Lock and load. Black Horse on the go."

"Roger, Black Horse. The Baby Scouts are on the go" The other hunter-killer ships radioed their allegiance.

"Air Cav. Roger that."

"Hornets. On the go."

"Black Horse one-six, Centaur two-six. Your ass is covered."

"Alright!" I said aloud, "We got the Hog."

The Black Horse ships led us out and only radioed the control tower after clearing the airfield. Tay Ninh tower wasn't amused but none of us much cared. It was payback time and payback was going to be bloody justice of the vengeful kind.

Black Horse led us to the last known position of the ghost ship. It was deep inside the AO known as the Iron Triangle. I was flying with Mr. Dunne and was very trigger-happy.

BABY SCOUT

The observer didn't bother with map reading. If we got shot down over the thick, jungle canopy, no one would be able to land to rescue us anyway.

"Black Horse one-six to all Scouts. Let's go find Charlie!"

"Roger that," went the chorus that sqawked from all the radios. The Cobras went high and the Hog even higher. It was comforting knowing that the Gunships were there.

We buzzed the jungle canopy like angry bees. Like never before, we dared the enemy to shoot at us. The Cobras formed a *Daisy Chain* at a thousand feet. They circled, expecting all hell to break loose. They were right.

A Black Horse Scout ship opened up with all its guns and a red smoke grenade. "Here we go," I thought, as we and the other Loaches converged on the red smoke. We poured thousands of rounds into the well-hidden enemy camp. Fire and smoke from Willie Peter grenades filled the air. The enemy engaged us with AK-47 fire and a few errant RPGs. It was a slaughter as we swarmed the camp and overpowered the surprised foe.

"*Damn*!" said Mr. Dunne. "They've got uniforms."

"It's the NVA!" I yelled. "It's the North Vietnamese Army."

It turned out to be a full company of NVA and a few Charlies in black pajamas. Mr. Dunne got three of them with the minigun and I blew away two with the M60. Lieutenant Reese and Buck accounted for six. It was easy pickings, but only because we surprised them. The NVA is well-trained, unlike the Viet Cong.

The slaughter lasted five minutes but seemed like an hour. Black Horse one-six came up on the radio and said, "All Scouts clear the area. Gunships, bring it on." The circling Cobras unleashed the deadly daisy chain. One by one the Gunships attacked and fired their arsenals of rockets, grenades, and miniguns. Each Cobra would attack, then join up with the other gunships that were circling, awaiting their turn.

The daisy chain rained down a seemingly endless supply of ordinance on the hapless victims. When one Cobra pulled out from its attack dive, another was right behind. I watched in amazement and wondered how something so destructive could be named after so delicate a flower.

"Black Horse one-six, Centaur two-six is joining the party."

"Roger, Centaur two-six. All Cobras, break off. The Hog is coming in."

Michael W. Mason

    The Cobra Gunships broke off the daisy chain and went in search of their respective Scout ships. Mr. Dunne was circling the AO at 500 feet, about half a mile away. After the last Cobra had made its gunrun, I settled back for the big show.

    The old Huey is much slower than a Cobra, but that disadvantage has an upside. The Hog has more time to deliver its massive amount of firepower to the target.

    The Hog came in from two miles out. It fired rocket after rocket. The Centaur Hog was fitted with two pods, each holding 24, 2.75 inch rockets. A third of them had warheads filled with fleshettes. These were tiny, steel darts that rained down on the enemy after the warhead exploded overhead.

    The Hog fired its 40mm automatic grenade launcher. Not to be left out, both door gunners let loose with their machine guns. Even a *Spooky* crewman would have been impressed by the awesome sight. One Cobra could have made two gunruns in the time it took the old Huey to make one. Therein lies the advantage of the modern, high-tech Cobra, and the beauty of the old, obsolete battleship.

    "This is Black Horse one-six. Let's go home."

    "Roger," squawked all the radios in the aerial fleet.

    We left behind us a smoldering hole in the Iron Triangle. Mostly, though, we left behind our hatred, anger, and vengeance. We were satiated from the retribution and were bereft of any lingering emotions.

    The battle, or slaughter, had taken only twenty minutes and, except for a few bullet holes in a few ships, we came away unscathed. The infantry would find dozens of bodies that we accounted for. There were too many corpses for the few NVA survivors to take with them as they disappeared into the safety of the jungle.

    I never flew with Black Horse again. Now and then their ships would cross my path and I would marvel, and shake my head, at their sustained battle damage. It was if the patched bullet holes and shrapnel damage were badges of honor.

    I finally understood why those Scouts had death in their eyes. While we Baby Scouts went looking for a fight, the Black Horse crews went looking to die. We always thought we had a chance, though slim, of going home. They thought they never would.

    During the next few months, D Troop would lose a Cobra, two Loaches, and all of its Slicks in combat. My best and worst times lay just ahead. They included the two lost Loaches. Unfortunately, I would be on them at the time.

During those months my attitude and personality would change. I went from eager to please combat crewman to gunslinging hot-shot. I formed an opinion that nothing could hurt me. I became immortal in my own mind. I became the *Duke* of aerial gunfighters, and invincible.

I had the *John Wayne Fever* and it turned me into a suicidal, thrill seeker. If the 1st Air Cav or even Black Horse requested my services, I would have reported for duty without hesitation.

I know a *snake driver* who feels somewhat like I do. This Cobra pilot has the heart of a Scout pilot and secretly desires to fly with the 1st Air Cav. He's also the first pilot to paint the ominous shark's teeth on his ship. He always wears his big cavalry stetson and his nickname is *Cousin Brucie*. The lanky officer sports a wicked handlebar mustache and he swaggers when he walks. Cousin Brucie is one of the older guys, about 25. He's also one of the best, most aggressive snake drivers in the troop.

My transformation from crew chief to gunslinger began with a routine milk run to Vung Tau, the R & R village on the South China Sea. This ash and trash mission, as we sometimes called milk runs, is a one day journey. It would lead me down a new and different path, and I would get caught up in the evil and inhumanity that only the Vietnam war could manifest.

In the days ahead, I found myself relishing the kill. It was something I looked forward to. My first kill was the VC that I machine-gunned as he dove through a hootch door. I never really gave his death much thought. I was doing a job. Nothing more. Soon, killing would become a chore I would look forward to. The job would become fun. Killing would become fun. It's all about the gunslinging world I was about to enter.

Lieutenant Kerns had to chauffeur some Colonel to the Vung Tau airbase. As crew chief, I got to go along. The hour flight was at 3,000 feet and very boring. I never even loaded the M60. The *Brass* flew left seat and got some stick time. Most of the time we flew without the left cyclic stick. It got in the way during missions. Senior brass, though, love to play pilot. It was always a good idea, and smart diplomacy, to keep the brass happy.

At altitude you can see what a beautiful country Vietnam really is. South of Saigon is the Delta region. It's a thick carpet of lush greenery with rivers and streams snaking their way to the South China Sea.

Michael W. Mason

When flying close to the ground, I thought Vietnam the ugliest, most barren place on earth. From up high, though, its natural beauty rivaled that of any American national park.

Vung Tau isn't the blister on the landscape that Cu Chi is, but it still has to have its perimeter wire, guards, and other security measures. As we neared the R & R village, Lt. Kerns took back the controls and requested permission to land.

There isn't any dirt, or dust, to kick up as the airfield is paved. Lieutenant Kerns landed near some strange looking airplanes. They were twin-engine, Army OV-1s, or *Mohawks*. The exotic looking, turbo-charged, propeller aircraft are used for electronic surveillance. It's rumored the Mohawk can find the enemy at night, even through the thick canopy of the jungle.

The Mohawk's capabilities remind me of stories I've heard about so-called *sniffer* choppers. Supposedly, the Army and the CIA are experimenting with electronic equipment that, literally, sniffs out the enemy using infra-red, heat-seeking technology.

I first heard of the Huey sniffers from Tom Donald. He told me that Army Intelligence and the CIA were testing stuff all the time and that Vietnam made for the ideal testing ground. "Besides," he told me, "who's going to care what happens to one insignificant village or its people. Casualties of war, Mike. Casualties of war."

Once, while on a mission, my pilot received a rude radio transmission telling us to clear the area. The pilot asked why but was rebuffed with, "Get out, now!" To this day I would swear to hearing an M79 grenade launcher firing at machine gun speed.

Later, in the hootch, I was told that new weapons were being tested in the AO that we were ordered to leave. The automatic grenade launcher that I heard was just that…a 40mm, automatic machine cannon, or grenade launcher. Called *Thumper*, this powerful weapon failed to impress chopper pilots, but eventually found a home with some armored, ground units.

I heard a lot of stories while in-country. I never discounted any of them. To this day, the one about *VD Island* still brings shivers to my fragile, wounded pysche. At 19, doing what I do for Uncle Sam, and seeing what I saw on a daily basis, I am inclined to believe every story I am told..

Lieutenant Kerns said I had four hours to do whatever I wanted. He and the Colonel went to the operations hootch. I walked the opposite way, out the gate, and into the village of Vung Tau. The further I walked into the village, the more it stunk. The smell was like garbage dumpsters ripening under a hot sun. Young boys constantly badgered me, tugging on my sleeves and asking, "Hey, mister, want girl? You want boom-boom? You come. Get girl. five dong."

I never expected anything like this. I said no at least a dozen times as I toured this R & R resort community on the South China Sea. A few of the young *pimps* also said, "My sister very pretty. Boom-Boom good. You have my sister. 10 dong." A few times I saw soldiers going off, and down alleys, with these pubescent hustlers.

I felt naked without my rifle. I wasn't allowed to carry it off the airfield. While looking at crafts at a streetside bazaar, something caught my eye and my imagination. It was something that would change me into a wholly different person.

Right in front of me, hanging from a wood peg on a vendor's cart, was something I didn't need but had to have. It was a shiny, black leather gunbelt and holster, not unlike the one *Paladin* wore. It was beautiful with cartridge loops around the belt. It had a silver buckle and even a gunfighter's leg strap.

I knew I would buy it before even trying it on. The old vendor asked for twenty Amercan dollars. I haggled him down to twelve. The leather rig was probably made from Water Buffalo, but leather is leather. Even if it was made of vinyl, I still would have bought it.

The old man put it in a paper bag for me and I swaggered back toward the airbase. I had to run the gauntlet of young pimps, but I ignored them and their promises of sibling flesh. Unlike many soldiers in Vung Tau, I didn't partake in the offerings of female companionship. It really didn't matter. I had found what I didn't know I was looking for.

I had only a short wait for the Colonel and Lieutenant Kerns. The paper bag, concealing my new persona, was hidden in the grenade box. I grabbed the fire extinguisher and stood-by as Kerns ignited the turbine.

We were soon airborn and flying north to Cu Chi. We leveled off at 3,000 feet and the Colonel resumed his stick time. Kerns was instructing him on Baby Scout tactics while I daydreamed about the kind of pistol to fill the holster with.

The first chance I got, I went to the supply hootch and traded in my M16 for a sidearm. After much thought, I got an old Colt 45 automatic

Michael W. Mason

with three ammo clips and a box of shells. The Colt was blued steel and cold to the touch. It filled my hand nicely and filled the holster perfectly.

Once back in the hootch, I cleaned the weapon, filled the cartridge loops with 45 caliber shells, and strapped her on. I wore the rig low on my left leg. My transformation was complete. In my mind I was a gunfighter, a gunslinger in a repressed land that needed my special services. The daydreams of Matt Dillon, Paladin, and Wyatt Earp were over. I was one of them, now. There was no longer any need to dream about childhood fantasies. I was now living it in my own, strange reality.

I loaded the two spare ammo clips and put them in the black, vinyl pouches I had bought for the belt. With jungle hat cocked to one side, I walked the walk. I took some flack from some of the Scouts for giving up the M16, but didn't care. I told them that I still had the M60 in case anything happened. Hutch teased me the most. He said, "Well, you can always throw it at the gooks, but a rock would be more accurate."

He and the others were right. It was foolish to trade in an automatic rifle for a semi-automatic pistol, but damn if I was going to give up my boyhood dream of being a cowboy. Besides, I always liked Paladin better than *The Rifleman*. I would keep my new identity close at all times, riding low, strapped to my leg.

There were other gunslingers around. Those few carried either the Colt, or the 38 caliber revolver. One pilot carried a *Grease Gun*. This slow firing, 45 caliber, automatic weapon looks like a mechanic's grease gun. It has a round, steel body and a short barrel. It you saw one lying around the motor pool, you might mistake it for one.

It's also very accurate at close range, and so steady that you can write your name with it on the side of a building. I got to fire a grease gun once. It was fun and as easy to do as writing my name in the snow.

While I played gunfighter, the other Scouts played soldier. One of the best is Tom Donald. Tom is infantry and someone you want on your side. When not on duty, Tom entertained us with stories, jokes, and impersonations. He did a mean Groucho, Manfred Mann (drummer), George Burns, and showed us how to dance the *Turtle*.

Tom is also the master at lighting *Blue Flamers* through his shorts. He would lie on his back, legs in the air, and light farts with his Zippo lighter. Tom enjoys performing in front of an audience. Lighting farts is his show stopper. He caught fire once, and only because his over-filled lighter leaked during ignition.

The blue flame was easily a foot long and it lit up the hootch. It also lit up Tom's shorts. We applauded and cheered, then laughed as Tom scooted around the floor trying to extinguish his burning boxers. The show stopper lasted only a few seconds, but it was the stuff that legends are made of. Tom's only injuries were a few singed hairs, a red butt, and a wounded pride. Nothing he did in the future would top that night's entertainment. In the drama category, however, his best was yet to come.

June, July, and August were the months of Tay Ninh, Dau Tieng, and Go Dau Ha. Both NVA and Charlie were there. So were the Baby Scouts. The fighting was intense on the ground, and not much easier for us. We flew 16 hours a day trying to find the elusive and well-hidden enemy.

Our foe liked to hide, especially under the thick, jungle foliage. A lot of defoliation chemicals, like Agent Orange, were used to clear the growth but the enemy just moved on to plusher, greener surroundings. During this time I was also witness to a B-52 strike. It was the first and only *Arc Light* mission I ever saw.

We were scouting near the Iron Triangle when a radio message warned us to clear the area. We knew what was coming and the pilot moved us three miles out from the designated target. I searched the sky for a glimpse of the huge Air Force bombers but they were too high up. I thought, though, that I saw vapor streaks across the blue background that was a clear day.

Time passed slowly and the minutes seemed like hours. The pilot kept the right side of the Loach facing the impending devastation that was to come. Lieutenant Reese and I had the best seats in War Zone C. Hutch, flying left seat, had to look past the pilot to see what was about to happen.

Suddenly, billowing clouds of dark, dirty smoke erupted before our eyes. The sounds from the massive explosions came seconds later. So did the concussion waves that slammed into our little warbird. Even from five miles out we could feel the might and the power of a B-52 bombing raid. The Loach handled the air storm with little problem and Lt. Reese began a slow circle around the area of destruction. It was catastrophic, at least for the enemy. An entire square mile of earth and wood was vaporized. We slowly moved in for a closer look.

It took twenty minutes for the smoke and dust clouds to clear away. We began to reconn what was left of the target. We discovered not much at all. What once was green, plush flora, was now dirt and massive, deep craters. Tree stumps were on fire and little else remained. A few human body parts were scattered over the square mile of total devastation. There was an arm here, a head there, but nowhere did we find an entire body. The blasts tore everything to shreds and splinters. There were more animal parts present than human. Deer, monkey, and what might have been the remains of a tiger were half-buried in the huge mounds of soft dirt. On the fringe of the target we found the remains of entire bodies, but only those of animals. There were deer, monkeys and a few snakes.

Never had I seen such destruction. Even the mighty Hog couldn't do what one B-52 air strike could. I thought that this must be the closest thing there is to a nuclear blast. It instilled fear in me and respect for more powerful gods than the Baby Scouts.

We headed home. The Arc Light left us with nothing to search and nothing to find. I never saw the bombers or their bombs. The convincing evidence that the Air force was there was the desolate, moonscape-like nothingness it left behind.

The war was going well for us. The NVA and VC were suffering heavy losses in all the war zones. North of the DMZ (Demilitarized Zone), strategic targets were being pounded by fighter jets and bombers. The Armed Forces Radio Network and the *Stars and Stripes* newspaper kept me informed on the war. It was one victory after another, and the people back home were proud of their boys.

The newspapers from home printed a different story. The war, they said, was one of attrition and journalists reported on peace rallys that protested the conflict in Southeast Asia. Many politicians, and even celebrities, were condemning the bombing and newspaper editorials called for a stop to the escalation of the war. It was all very depressing and I stopped reading the papers from home. It wasn't that I didn't want to know the truth...I just didn't want the truth to be what was being written or said. My feelings didn't make any sense so, to forget, I buried myself in maintenance and mayhem. With every bolt I tightened, or every Willie Peter I dropped, my mind kept telling me, "You're here for a purpose. Screw the politicians and screw the journalists."

President Lyndon B. Johnson, as Commander in Chief, would soon halt the bombing of North Vietnam. He would also not seek another term as President of the United States. The attitude of the 3/4 Cav was one of defiance. Most of us in the troop believed in what we were doing and the *bleeding hearts* could go screw themselves. We would continue to do our duty even though the American people, and the government, seemed to be turning against their sons.

1968, the year of Tet, was the year we kicked butt and made thousands of women widows and thousands of children fatherless or orphans. It was also the beginning of the end of the Republic of South Vietnam. There was to be no more escalation after this bloodiest of years.

In America, escalation was a dirty word and had already toppled a President. I didn't know much about politics but knew that a war run by democracy was a losing effort. I bitched about the politics of war and kept throwing my frags and Willie Peter. I still loved my work.

These were busy months and there was little time for cleaning, laundry, and other such domestic chores. To help us out, the brass brought in mamasans from Cu Chi Village. They became our *hootch girls* and cleaned our hootches, washed our clothes, and even polished our jungle boots.

Some hootches got old mamasans...women in their thirties and forties. The Baby Scouts got Mei (Me). She was sixteen, smart, and cute as a button. She was shy and, at first, aloof and wary of us young, boisterous Scouts. She spoke little English but understood a lot. Mei became a bright spot in my dark, lonely world of gunfighting.

Her shyness went away after a week. She discovered that we were just boys who, when not off fighting the war, showed off for her attention and amusement. She was the first *gook*, or *slant*, that I met up close and personal. She taught me a little about her country and ways and I taught her a little about mine. I once showed her a map of the United States and she pointed to a city in Southeast Florida.

"Miami," I said, and she went nuts and started hitting me on the shoulder.

"Miami! No say, Miami. Miami bad!"

"Ow! Stop it, Mei."

"My, you no say, Miami." Mei couldn't pronounce my name or most words that had a *K* or a hard *C*. She called me, *My* and I figured that was close enough.

"Miami bad word. You never say to Mei."

"Mei, that's only the name of a city in America."

"It bad city." I choked back a chuckle as I didn't want to get hit again.

"No, Mei. It's just a name, like Saigon, or Cu Chi."

"Mei understand. It bad, Vietnam. It good, America."

Michael W. Mason

"Well, yeah, something like that." I rubbed my shoulder. The little girl had sharp knuckles and I learned never to get her mad at me. Her punches really hurt.

The little hootch girl caught on quickly. She told me that Miami is one of the dirtiest words in the Vietnamese language. I never quite understood its full meaning, but figured it was the Amercan equivalent of saying, "Go fornicate yourself!"

After being around Mei for a few weeks, I stopped using words like gook and slant. She helped me see the Vietnamese people as more than just backward inhabitants of a third-rate country. She gave her people an identity. Mei helped me see that they were like most people in the world. They only wanted what was best for their families and their country. In that respect, I learned the vast majority of South Vietnamese were not much different from me. Mei probably taught me more than I was able to teach her. We became good friends and she always laughed at my prudity. It took a long time before I was able to walk around in front of her in my boxer shorts or a towel.

Being so young and cute, I called her *Babysan*. One day, she and the other mamasans were doing laundry in the shower. I was sandbagging outside the hootch when I saw one of the Gunship crewmen, wrapped in a towel, walking toward the shower. A few minutes later all the mamasans, including Mei, ran out of both shower hootch doorways. I figured the crewman must have chased them out.

A few of the older mamasans hung around one of the doorways. Slowly, more of the ladies returned to join the older women. Even the young ones, including Mei, came back. The mamasans began to giggle and chatter amongst themselves. Mei looked the most embarrassed, but kept glancing in the shower.

"Out, *dammit*! Get out!" The crew chief yelled and most of the mamasans scattered. Only two old ones stood their ground. The crewman left the shower hootch, laughing. I was confused as I thought he was mad. The women went back to their laundry chores and, even from fifty feet away, I could see that Mei was still giggling and red-faced. I laughed and went back to my sandbagging. It was a funny incident that I soon forgot.

A few weeks later I was taking a shower when this same crew chief walked in. We said, "Hi," and went about our business. The Baby Scouts didn't fraternize much outside the hootch. The Gunship crews stuck to themselves as well.

A few mamasans gathered by the doorway. They were holding laundry baskets. I was embarrassed and wondered why they had to show up now. I was about to yell when the other guy bellowed, "Out! Get out!" I was startled and turned to face him. I realized immediately why the mamasans were at the shower.

The Gunship crew chief had a penis a donkey might envy. He hung halfway to his knees and the mamasans couldn't keep their eyes off it. I turned around real quick and hoped the chief didn't see my downward glance. I had accidently broken one of the two rules of shower etiquette. You don't drop the soap and you don't look down.

If a lot of guys are in the shower, dropping the soap is cause for a lot of jokes, teasing, and laughter. Looking, however, is forbidden. In the men's shower, or locker room, you look each other in the eyes.

All the hootch girls returned and the crew chief just sighed and went about his washing. I figured if he didn't mind the prying eyes, I would finish my shower as well. It was one of the weirdest moments in my life and I was very self-conscious about it. My upbringing was very proper and I wouldn't even let my mother see me in my shorts. "Grin and bare it," was how I was feeling at this particular moment...until I saw Mei peeking around the corner.

"Oh, man!" I whispered out loud. I grabbed my towel and wrapped it around me. I looked over at her again but she was looking right past me, and at something even Willie the Whopper would envy. I grabbed my shower bag and left through the opposite doorway.

Five minutes later, Mei came in the hootch. I was combing my hair when she walked up to me and said, "My, you funny." I grinned, sheepishly, and asked what she meant.

"You funny in shower when face turn red."

"Well, Mei. You..." The little Babysan cut me off in mid-sentence.

"You not worry. I see little brother all time. No clothes. You no worry." I didn't know whether to laugh or be insulted. I wanted to tell her the water was cold, but thought better of it. I stood there, in my towel, and was speechless. The Babysan looked at me and started laughing.

"My, I never see man like him no more."

"Mei," I said, "there's not many men like him anywhere."

"That for sure," she said, grinning like a Cheshire cat. "He big like buffalo." I laughed and then she laughed with me.

87

Her laughter turned to giggling and she added, "You look good in shower, too, My." She then ran off, still giggling, and I saw my face turning red in the mirror. I was dumbfounded. This little, sixteen year old girl had just given me back my manhood and pride. She was not only smart, but handled me as only a mature woman would know how.

Feeling good again, with pride intact, I went back to the mirror that hung from a nail in the wall. My handlebar mustache was growing in just fine, I noticed, as I twirled the ends to sharp points.

The battle for the Tay Ninh Province was heating up and the Baby Scouts began flying night missions. At night you can see the enemy's tracer rounds coming up at you. An even more frightening sight is watching an RPG coming toward you. It looks like a giant, slow-moving fireball. Bullets we might survive. A hit from a rocket powered grenade meant few remains to send home in a flag-draped, aluminum coffin.

During the months of July, August, and September, *Operation Toan Thang* was in full swing. The campaign was headed by ground and air troops of the 25th Infantry Division. The mission was to stop the enemy from attacking the supply convoys that rumbled along Highway 1 between Tay Ninh and Cu Chi, and to keep Tay Ninh airbase from being attacked, possibly over-run by the NVA and Viet Cong.

These were the months of night missions. The mighty gunships and the infantry slicks were kept busy in their support of the ground forces. The Baby Scouts flew at night, too.

It was scary, but exciting. There wasn't anything we could do, except act as *muzzle-flash spotters*. We just circled the AO at a thousand feet and kept our eyes open. When we spotted those tell-tale flashes, the pilot radioed the coordinates to the Gunships. We were also acting as *Mini-Slicks* during night missions. In an emergency, we might be called to *dustoff* some wounded. The worst case scenario would be the Loach's crew chief, me, staying on the ground, at night, while the Loach flew the wounded to Tay Ninh hospital. Fortunately, for me, that never happened. It was bad enough just having to fly in the black void of a Vietnam night.

During the battle for Tay Ninh, two RPGs were fired at #395. One missed by fifty feet, and the other by only a few. My heart pounded so hard I could feel my upper ribs vibrating. Seeing a rocket propelled fireball coming at you, at night, is something you never forget.

My Loach is a potent, aerial, gunnery platform. With its minigun, M60, and grenades, it could pulverize an enemy position. On the other hand a Cobra Gunship, or the Hog, would vaporize it.

The rescue of Tay Ninh seemed a never-ending story. It involved most of the 25th Infantry Division and most of its many brigades, regiments, and squadrons. I flew in a joint effort with other helicopter outfits. The Baby Scouts received its fair share of bullet holes, too. We also got our fair share of the killing.

Tomorrow would be July 31, 1968…my birthday. I was hoping to celebrate it with a high body count. The VC would crash my party, though, trying to keep me from celebrating another year. It was going to be a birthday to die for.

Michael W. Mason

EIGHT

BLOWN OUT OF THE SKY

Turning twenty is a big deal to a teenager, or at least I thought so. Growing up, I looked forward to birthdays. Turning 13 was special, as was 18 which made me legal for most things in the adult world. Turning 20 is like finishing a seven year marathon filled with all the obstacles of a burdening adolescence: puberty, acne, drugs, and the scariest of all, girls. I looked forward to the finish line…21.

Presently, I was waking up in the hootch. I'm 20 and don't feel any different. I made formation, ate chow, then returned to the hootch. I reached under my cot and pulled out a *care package* from my Uncle Rusty. I received it a few days earlier but saved it for today. I used my P38 to cut the heavy twine and tape. Inside, I found a letter. It said that all was well with my uncle and aunt. Digging deeper, I found some of my favorite foods. There were cans of soup, candy, and a box of *Milk Bone* dog bisquits.

Years ago, as a little kid, I tried a dog bisquit and liked it. Everyone in my family thought it strange but since I also ate frozen hot dogs right out of the freezer, they indulged me. I like dog bisquits because they appeal to my taste. I thought them like hard cookies, or pretzels, and they went down well with milk or beer. I also have the nicest, whitest teeth in the family.

I grabbed a few bisquits to munch on during the walk out to the flight line. I didn't have dawn patrol but my M60 needed cleaning before the next mission. I replaced the barrel as it was worn and pitted from the thousands of rounds that had been fired through it. Everything was ready when Lieutenant Reese showed up. A Spec-4 was with him. He was new to the Scouts and this was the first time I spoke to him.

"Hi. I'm Mike. How ya doing?"
"Hi. I'm Bill Peters. Call me Willie. Everyone does." I laughed.
"You're kidding. Willie Peters?"
"Yeah," he said, "I get this all the time."
Still laughing, I said, "Ok, Willie. Let's go."
Willie's somewhat chubby but looks fit. He has red hair, a round face, and big cheeks covered with freckles. He also seems to smile a lot, but

Michael W. Mason

that's normal for FNGs. He climbed in the observer's seat. I had already armed the minigun. As Willie buckled in, I asked if there was anything he needed to know. He said, "Yeah, where are we going?"

"The Iron Triangle." I answered.

"What's that?"

"A bad place, Willie. A very bad place." He just looked at me, squeezed the stock of his M16, and nodded. His FNG smile was gone.

I grabbed the fire extinguisher and stood in front of the ship. I was crewing a different Loach today. Mine, #395, was assigned to dawn and dusk patrols. After the turbine roared to life, I stowed the extinguisher and climbed into the back of #384. We backed out of the bunker and joined a Cobra that was hovering over the airfield. Most of the time the Scout ships were paired together. When we teamed with Gunships, especially the Cobra, we became a true hunter-killer team.

Lieutenant Reese radioed the control tower and got clearance to depart the corral. The Cobra followed us up and out over the perimeter. It carried twin rocket pods, 40mm grenade launcher, and a minigun. Its freshly painted shark's teeth make it look like the killer predator it is.

The snake driver took his ship to a thousand feet. Lt. Reese leveled off at five hundred. My M60 was loaded and cocked. We were on our way to the AO. The brass wanted us to check out an area west of Tay Ninh. We were to identify NVA trails leading into Cambodia. After that, our orders were to refuel and then search the fringe of the Iron Triangle. My machine gun was ready and my grenade box was freshly stocked with frags and Willie Peter. My flying foot was comfortably floating in the breeze. I had a feeling that it was going to be a good day of hunting.

Lieutenant Reese talked to Willie over the intercom. He was giving him basic training in visual reconn and map reading. We reached the AO and Reese radioed the Cobra.

"Centaur one-six is going low."

"Roger, one-six. Got you covered."

We depended on the high ship to keep us covered at all times. While the Gunship watched over us, we went in search of prey. Most of the time the prey spotted us first. I never liked that part of being the hunter. Charlie was good at hide and seek and my M60 rarely got in the first shot.

The AO is huge. It's five square miles of open fields and rice paddies for us to search. We zigzagged back and forth checking dikes, hedgerows, and hammocks for clues. Everything was routine but, as always, exhilarating.

BABY SCOUT

The landscape moved by quickly in a blur. My eyes, though, were thoroughly trained in low level reconnaissance. If something moved, I noticed it. If there was a color that was out of place, I noticed that, too. Much of the time, though, I just enjoyed the thrill of the hunt. There was not a ride anywhere that could compare to low level, aerial hunting. Not Coney Island, not even Disneyland. I was attuned to every vibration of the little ship. I knew the sounds of the rotors on every bank and turn and I could feel the steady hum of the turbine through the sole of my left boot. My right foot was alway out the door and flying as if it was on a mission of its own. It was both counterweight and stabilizer. I learned to use it to steady myself when firing the machine gun. I turn my foot to the right, and the bullets go right. I turn it left, the bullets go left. I got so good at it that I didn't need to use my eyes to line up a target. My foot became my gunsight.

In a large, grassy field was a lone hammock. It was a big clump of dirt covered in tall, thick grass. My pilot decided to do a quick fly-by to check it out. At about twenty feet off the deck, he made his run. The Loach was doing about forty knots and the grassy knoll passed quickly by on the right. Potential targets are always kept to starboard.

The hammock was a hundred feet away as we flew by. Suddenly, this routine mission went into the toilet. AK-47 assault rifles opened up on us from the grassy, island hideaway. Instinctively, I returned fire before locating the target. As my tracer fire hunted for the tell-tale puffs of smoke, the Loach shuddered violently and threw me back into the bulkhead. My machine gun fire went up and narrowly missed the rotor blades. The last thing I saw was Lt. Reese fighting the controls. The last thing I heard was him yelling, "We're going in!"

The mortally wounded Loach was coming apart in midair. Above me, the rotor hub linkage was shot to pieces and, behind me, the turbine had blown up internally from the invading bullets. We never had a chance. The ship was falling apart around me, but hit the ground before breaking into pieces.

The ship slammed into the soft earth at forty knots. It hit first on the front curvature of the skids. The pilot had no control whatsoever. Only my Monkey Strap kept me from being ejected from the ship. The Loach bounced, then rolled for what seemed like an eternity. The world was a blur and I was being jostled as if in a large clothes dryer. My body was pelted, and bruised, by ricocheting grenades. The ammo belts slapped me and became wrapped around my neck and torso. I was feeling no pain, just amazement at what dying in battle was like. I kept tumbling in that clothes dryer and expected a fiery death at any moment.

Slowly, the tumbling ended but the broken aircraft continued its slide on the muddy field. The Loach slid on its left side and I had faint glimpses of a clear, blue sky out of the right doorway of the ship. The Loach then slammed into a dike, flipped over it, and kept sliding down the grassy, muddy field. Everything happened within seconds, but it felt like an eternity. The Loach slowed quickly and when it ceased its death slide, it was leaning to the left at a forty five degree angle. The mangled, but still intact, left skid kept the shattered warbird from completely rolling over.

My head was spinning and I was on my back, tangled in ammo belts. The grenades were gone and I couldn't find my M60. Its severed bungy cord was swinging free in the door frame. My senses slowly returned and my first rational thought was, "I'm alive."

I quickly determined that my continuing survival depended on getting clear of the smoldering ship. Quickly, I began to untangle myself from the constricting ammo belts. I heard moaning coming from the observer's seat. Willie sounded like he was hurt bad. Lieutenant Reese was cursing, so I knew he was probably ok. The distinctive sound of AK-47 fire filled the air. Bullets ripped into the dead bird but were deflected by the turbine and its transmission.

The Loach had slid far past the hammock and ended up with its tail section facing the men who had shot it down. Our very lives were saved by those happenstance events.

"Mason, you ok?"

"Yes, sir. How about you?"

"Knocked out for a minute, but ok. Willie's hurt bad, maybe wounded."

"We're being shot at, sir. We've got to get out of here."

"I can't. My foot's stuck in the pedals. Can you get out?"

"I think so. I'm trying. The Monkey Strap and ammo belts have me tied up pretty good."

"Well, hurry the hell up. I don't want to burn to death."

"I'm trying, *dammit!*"

"Ok. Ok. Sorry, Mike."

"Me too, sir. Almost clear." For some reason I felt calm, even happy. I wasn't sure if it was because I was alive, or because Lieutenant Reese called me by my first name. Since I first met him, it was always "Mason." I didn't dwell on the thought as another burst of automatic gunfire riddled the engine compartment.

I began tearing the ammo belts into small strips. I was then able to reach the buckle on my Monkey Strap. It took a minute but I was finally clear. Sitting up was difficult and I felt sharp pains in my back and right leg. I let out a brief scream of pain.

"Mason, you ok?"

"Yes, sir. Just a few sore bones, that's all." I crawled out of the dead Loach, dragging belts of machine gun ammo with me. I fell head-first into the mud. I got up slowly, painfully, and limped over to my pilot. He was trying to free his right foot from the mangled, foot pedals. He winced in pain as I tried to pry his foot free. "Sorry," I whispered.

Working together, we managed to extricate his foot. I helped the Lieutenant from his seat and he grimmaced in pain when his bruised foot hit the ground. Just then, I heard a *thud*, and then a loud, "Oh, God!" I looked up and into the cockpit. Willie was gone. He had crawled out of the ship on his own. He was belly-crawling around the front of the shattered canopy.

I helped Lt. Reese hobble to the sparse cover of a nearby dike. I then went back to help Willie. He was in a prone position and wasn't moving. Blood was coming from his ears, nose, and mouth. He was whimpering. I grabbed him under the armpits and slowly dragged him over to the dike. He screamed in protest but there was no other way to get him out of the line of fire. I positioned him in a sitting position, his back against the three foot wall of dirt. Through the pain, he smiled at me. His teeth were red.

The VC knew we were alive and fired sporadically at our position. I knew they were Viet Cong because the NVA would have killed us almost immediately with accurate gunfire. They were much better marksmen than the poorly trained guerilla fighters.

The dike was only three feet high but afforded us cover from the sporadic, automatic weapons fire. We were lying almost prone behind the protection of the little ridge of dirt. The Cobra was circling and probably wondering if the crash was accidental or the result of hostile action.

Except for my 45, and knife, we were unarmed. I drew it from my holster, cocked it, and gave it to Lt. Reese. He looked at me with questioning eyes but gladly accepted the comforting, little weapon. Willie was too busted up to handle anything. He was still bleeding profusely and I noticed that his left side seemed to be crushed in. He lay there, moaning, with eyes that couldn't focus. He just stared. I knew that he would soon lose consciousness.

The *scrambled egg* was missing its tail section, front canopy, or bubble, the right skid, and three of its four rotor blades. I told Lt. Reese that I was going back to the Loach to search for our missing weapons. He didn't argue.

In a crouch, I ran back to the crumpled remains of the ship. A few shots rang out and bullets thudded in the mud around me. Reaching the ship, I looked in the back. My M60 was pinned under the ship. The muzzle was sticking out from under the left door frame. I crawled in and tried to free it. It wouldn't budge. The ammo belts were useless and the grenades were gone. I crawled back out and looked in the cockpit. Nothing. "*Damn!*"

I was feeling helpless when I noticed more smoke coming from the engine compartment. Fearing an explosion, I grabbed the fire extinguisher and sprayed the turbine. Bullets slammed into the Loach and I dropped the extinguisher and ran. That's when I saw the Lieutenant's AR15. The assault rifle was half-buried in the soft earth.

I picked it up and the stock came apart in my hands. The barrel was also slightly bent. Throwing it to the ground I muttered, "Well, this really sucks!" I ran back to the dike and joined the others. I pulled my knife and looked at Lt. Reese holding the Colt 45. Before either of us could say something stupid, we heard a familiar sound in the sky. We looked up. We witnessed salvation.

The Cobra was making a gunrun on the hammock. It let loose with rockets and I peeked over the ridge to see them obliterate the grassy island. The minigun sprayed the enemy hideaway before the gunship pulled out of its attack dive. Even if the VC had disappeared down a spider hole, they wouldn't be popping up anytime soon.

The aerial warship *whomped* loudly as its rotor blades bit the air on pullout. I sat back down and looked over at the remains of #384. It was then that I first noticed how far we had bounced, rolled, and slid after getting blown out of the sky. We were over 300 feet from the sniper's nest. No wonder they didn't pick us off.

I looked at the long, furrowing trail in the muddy field. Bits and pieces of #384 littered the ground. Here and there were the rotor blades, the engine compartment doors, the right skid, and my splintered grenade box. The trail of debris led back to a small crater, the point of impact. "*Damn!*" I thought, "We hit hard."

Lieutenant Reese and I relaxed a bit, and I thought I saw Willie smiling through his pain. I put my knife back in its sheath. It's a special commemoration blade with a silver eagle pommel. My dad sent it to me after I wrote him, asking for a knife. I didn't really need it. I just thought it would look good on my gun belt.

It seemed like we were on the ground for hours. The Gunship kept circling so we felt pretty safe. Reese pointed to the sky and said, "Look." I did, and a feeling of great joy swept through my mind, body, and soul. Coming in fast were two Hueys. The lead ship was a Slick. The other was a Gunship. It was the lethal, mighty Hog.

The ships each flared to a hover about fifty yards away. The slick landed but the Hog spun around and trained its powerful arsenal on the smoldering Hammock. Out of the Slick came a squad of infantry. The first boots to hit the ground belonged to Tom Donald. I'll never forget the look on his camouflage-painted face.

It was fierce, had a sneer, a look of resolve, and was totally tuned-in to the events around him. Tom was in killing mode. He was an all-together different person than the happy-go-lucky guy who entertained us in the hootch.

I watched my friend, the Buck Sergeant, command his squad. With just a few hand signals his squad dispersed. Two of the seven soldiers walked toward the hammock and stopped near the Hog. They kept their rifles trained on the target. I was glad for the rescue but thought it funny to see two soldiers with M16s backing up D Troop's battleship. Two others from the squad took positions on our flank. They watched the open fields for any signs of Charlie. Tom led the other two toward us.

"You guys ok, Lieutenant?"

"Willie's hurt bad, Tom. Mason and I are ok, though."

"Hey, Tom. You do a pretty good soldier." Sergeant Donald looked at me and cracked a smile. It lasted for a second, then he was all business.

Michael W. Mason

He told one of the two soldiers to get the stretcher from the Slick. The other soldier, a medic, was already working on Willie.

I helped Lieutenant Reese to his feet and he leaned on me as we made our way to the Slick. We waited outside the ship until Willie was put aboard. I looked up and noticed that the Cobra had left the AO. It needed to refuel and, besides, the Hog was here. The old Huey Gunship would stay and cover the infantry squad while it checked out the wasted hammock. Tay Ninh was only ten minutes away. The slick would return for Tom and the others after we were dusted-off to the hospital.

As we lifted off, the infantry squad fanned out and slowly advanced toward the smoking hammock. The Hog climbed to five-hundred feet. It would cover the soldiers until the Slick returned to dust them off. Loach #384 would be airlifted back to base. It would be stripped of any usable parts and studied by aircraft engineers. In its death, #384 might end up saving lives.

The Slick took a southeasterly heading toward Tay Ninh. Lieutenant Reese passed me the 45 and I removed the clip and ejected the chambered round. I put the bullet back in the clip and then slammed it into the butt of the Colt. I holstered the gun and placed the small, leather loop over the hammer. Reese looked at me and smiled through his pain. He bent over and untied his boot laces. I saw that his right foot was bruised and swollen.

Willie was stretched out on the deck and in great pain. I felt bad for him. This had been his virgin flight with the Baby Scouts and he never had a chance to learn the ropes. My 20th birthday wasn't supposed to turn out like this. Willie's suffering haunted me all the way to the hospital.

The Lieutenant and I were checked over quickly and then sent to the showers. My pilot was limping on his sprained foot but was otherwise ok. I had a strained back and a black and blue bruise on my right leg but was also given a clean bill of health. Willie was taken to surgery and went under the knife. The doctors did everything they could but his injuries were too severe. After two hours on the operating table, he died. His internal injuries were massive and his heart just stopped. Even if he had survived, the doctors said Willie would have been partially paralyzed and possibly a vegetable due to brain damage. Bill *Willie* Peters would be remembered for his name, and his courage, by the Baby Scouts.

I was given a couple of shots. One was for tetanus, the other, a sedative, for shock. I learned that the Cobra pilot saw me moving around on the ground and thought I was dazed or in shock. I wasn't, but couldn't convince the doctors. The second shot put me to sleep for hours.

The sun was setting when I woke. An orderly came in the sickbay with a couple of trays of food. Lieutenant Reese was right behind him. On one of the trays was a chocolate cupcake with a little candle in it.

"Happy birthday, Mike."

I smiled and said, "Yeah. Thanks, Lieutenant." I wasn't smiling. Turning 20 didn't exactly turn out like I thought it would.

"We're alive, Mike. We shouldn't be, but we are."

"Sorry, sir. You're right. I don't know how we survived the crash, either." I bit my lip, suddenly thinking of Willie.

"None of us should have walked away from that crash, but you and I did. Now, blow out the *damn* candle. That's an order."

"Yes, sir." I was feeling better about things and put out the tiny flame with a soft puff of air. The Loach pilot sat on the bed next to me and we ate our hospital food. I shared the cupcake with him and we talked about the crash. We both agreed that the next time we spotted anything suspicious, we'd shoot first and reconn later.

We also talked about Willie. He would be going home to Bucksport, Maine. When we got back to Cu Chi, the Lieutenant would have to inventory Willie's gear, then crate it for shipment home. I told him I'd help. This is a duty no one likes to do. Unfortunately, it happens all too often.

I was feeling drowsy. Lieutenant Reese saw this and said it was time for me to turn in. He had the bunk next to mine. There is no *officers country* in the hospital. A nurse came in and woke me up to give me a shot. She said it was to help me sleep. I asked her why she had to wake me up to give me a shot to make me do what I was already doing. She just smiled and said, "Doctor's orders." Lieutenant Reese was laughing but stopped abruptly when she turned to him and said, "Your turn. Roll over."

"Only in the Army," I said, laughing. Reese managed a weak smile, then grimaced as the needle jabbed his butt. I laughed again, and he laughed, too. The nurse shook her head and walked out of the room. I fell back on my pillow, happy in revenge, and fell asleep thinking how great it is to be 20 years old, and alive.

The next day a Loach arrived to take us back to the 3/4 Cav. Lt. Kerns was the pilot. Reese jumped into the observer's seat and I climbed into the back. It was my ship, #395. There was no M60 but my grenade box was there. This was just a milk run for Kerns and I didn't have to worry about Charlie as we'd be flying back to Cu Chi at 3,000 feet.

Lieutenant Kerns was talkative and wanted to know about the crash. While Reese filled him in, I dozed in the back. The drugs hadn't quite worn off. I relived the crash over and over again as I slipped in and out of consciousness. By the time we got back to Cu Chi, I was a nervous wreck. The pilots checked in at OPS. Lieutenant Reese had to be debriefed on what happened. I walked straight to the hootch and collapsed on my bunk. I slept through the day and most of the night.

I got up around two in the morning and lit a cigarette. Sitting in the darkness, my mind reeled with thoughts about the crash. I would later learn that all Willie wanted, was to be a soldier. He enlisted on his 18th birthday and was sent to 'Nam after infantry school. I would never know what made him volunteer for the Baby Scouts. He didn't seem nuts.

I stayed awake the rest of the morning. I put on my boots and walked outside the hootch. It was a hot, humid night and my shorts were soaked with perspiration. I pulled off my drenched undershirt and sat down on the walkway. It was a quiet night. A few stars winked through dark clouds and the crescent moon was a bright yellow. The war seemed far away. Off in the distance, high in the sky, my eyes caught a glimpse of slow-moving lights. I stared after them for a few minutes and then the war was back with an explosion of fire and light.

The lights in the sky was a Gunship and it lit up the darkness with its minigun. The tracers, firing at over 2,000 rounds a minute, looked like a solid stream of fire. When the sound reached me a few seconds later, I knew that I would never escape the sights and sounds of war. There is no place in Vietnam where you can hide from the reality of mortal conflict.

Even in darkness, in the sanctity of D Troop, war found me. It always seemed to have a way of seeking me out. For another minute I watched the light show. That's all the time it took for the Gunship to expend its ordinance. I got up and walked back into the hootch. I lay on my cot and daydreamed the rest of the morning.

After chow, I helped Lt. Reese inventory Willie's gear. His battered, green footlocker had his name on it. We emptied it, writing down the contents, and then put everything in a wood crate. On top of his clothes we placed pictures of his family and girlfriend. I covered them with a folded towel. The pine box would be shipped to his parents the following day.

BABY SCOUT

The dull thud of the empty locker's door, slamming shut, closed the chapter on Specialist 4th class, William Peters and his brief history with the Baby Scouts. That night, I went to the bar and got drunk on 3.2 beer.

I had a hangover in the morning and was relieved not to have dawn patrol. Sergeant Jenkins, always the opportunist, placed me on shit burning detail. I was pissed. It was the first time I had to pull this disgusting duty. The tough part about it, for me, is having to tug the heavy, steel cans out from beneath the latrine. I couldn't help but get my face right over the cans and it made me want to puke. Afterwards, I felt like getting drunk again but the bar was closed. My world, in a few short days, had literally turned to crap. One day I was blown out of the sky. The next, I was burning feces. There is no reprieve in the Vietnam War. You get up every morning and take what comes.

I took a shower. There were two mamasans doing laundry but I didn't care. They didn't seem to care, either. I was glad the crew chief with the giant penis didn't show up. I just wanted to be alone and to put the events of the last two days behind me.

I dried off and walked back to the hootch. I passed the Gunship crew chief on the way. By the time I got to the Baby Scout hootch, I had been passed by half a dozen, running mamasans, including Mei. She grinned at me and I laughed. "My God!" I thought, "What a war."

I walked through the Hootch door and went straight to my cot. While getting dressed, Hutch came over and asked me if I had heard the latest about our night on perimeter duty. I shook my head and he proceeded to tell me the strange, yet humorous, story. It is the only story of death that I ever found to be funny.

"Mike, do you remember the claymore mine that went off while we were sitting behind that dirtpile?"

"Yeah, Hutch. What about it?"

"Well," said Hutch, and he began to laugh, "this dumb-ass VC had penetrated the outer wire to the mine field. I guess he had never seen a claymore before because the moron picked it up and held it in front of his face."

"You're kidding?"

"No. He was probably trying to figure out what it was. Anyway, the dumb gook just kept looking at it. The guards in the machine gun bunker saw this and couldn't believe their eyes. They were still laughing as one of them hit the detonator switch. The gook was just standing there with no head."

Michael W. Mason

Hutch was laughing so hard he fell backwards onto my cot. I began laughing too and couldn't stop for almost a minute. A vision of the headless VC, just standing, motionless, entered my mind. I started laughing again and couldn't stop.

"His body," said Hutch, wiping tears from his eyes, "just stood there, without a head, for about five seconds before it toppled over." We laughed together for a long time. My eyes were watery and this was one of those times I laughed so hard that I cried.

I cried and Hutch stopped laughing. I got up, walked out the door, and ambled toward the road. War machines rumbled by as I relieved myself at the pisser pipe. My mind was in turmoil. My job as a Baby Scout crew chief, and gunner, is a thrilling one. I love every minute of it. The flying, the hunting, and even the killing is exciting. So, why was I feeling so disconsolate. I couldn't figure it out. I finished my business at the pipe and turned back toward the hootch. I ran into Mei on the way. She asked me what was wrong. I said nothing and kept walking, wiping the wetness from my face with the back of my hand. She ran past me and planted herself in my path.

"You tell Mei what wrong, My."

"Nothing. Really."

"You tell Mei now, My. I no tell." I looked into those soft, oval eyes and saw real emotion. She really cared. I had never seen this side of Mei before and it was almost as if my mom was trying to comfort me. I stopped trying to hide my tears and told her what had happened. I told her about Willie and about the VC on the perimeter. I told her that I laughed at a story about a man getting killed. She looked at me as I told her the story and we both sat down on the boardwalk in front of the Baby Scout hootch. Tears formed in her eyes but she didn't cry. She smiled.

"My, you no belong here. You go home."

"I can't go home, Mei. I have a job here for another five months."

"You go away Scouts."

"I can't leave the Scouts. I like flying with them."

"You no hiller, My. You only think you hiller. You stay Scouts, you die."

"No, Mei. I won't die. I'll go home when my tour is up."

"My be safe, yes?"

"Yes. My be safe. I promise."

She wiped her eyes and smiled. I smiled back and realized that my personal agony was over. I was myself again and I owed it to a little, sixteen year old Vietnamese girl who cared about me. Grinning, I asked her how the laundry was doing. She blushed, then hit me on the arm. She laughed and rose to her feet. I looked up at her and smiled with gratitude. She looked down at me, then bent over and hugged me and gave me a kiss on the cheek. I looked at her with wide-open eyes. She stared at me, smiling, then ran off. Mei was more than a good friend in this land of enemies. She was my confidant.

Death really could be funny in Vietnam. It is so commonplace that body count stories have happy, sad, bad, or funny endings. Bad endings related to you, or a buddy. Sad ones were about dying without a fighting chance.

The next month brought the monsoon season. It seemed to rain all the time and mostly in the afternoon. Little creeks became streams and streams became rivers where there were none the day before. The rainy season changed the look of the countryside and sometimes the way we flew our missions. We dodged the storms almost as much as the enemy's bullets.

The monsoon season is a good time for the villagers. The rice paddies are fertile with buffalo manure and water. The Vietnamese also use the paddies as a communal toilet.

I once saw an old mamasan squatting over a dike and then wipe herself with her hands. She then washed her hands in the paddy water and dried them on her clothes. Another time, I saw a mamasan pick up a large beetle and pop it in her mouth. She saw me staring at her, smiled, and between crunches she said, "Chop, chop." Many of the Vietnamese, mostly the old ones, had black teeth. I first thought it was from snacking on beetles and roaches. I later found out it was from eating the *Beetle Nut*. It is some kind of seed that turns their teeth and gums black.

Vietnam is filled with the strange and the exotic. To them, it's just custom and normalcy. Back home, our family dog ate the table scraps. In Vietnam, table scraps might very well be the family dog.

I was back in the war groove. The Baby Scouts were back at full strength and my Loach was still the best ship in the fleet. The pilots always like to fly #395 and I still had my reputation for being quick and deadly on the trigger.

Michael W. Mason

    I riddle the enemy, blow them up with frags and Willie Peter, and still my body count sucked. I always seemed to have the misfortune of killing without confirmation. It really bothered me that my kills were high but rarely proven. The pilots commiserated with me but loved my quick trigger finger just the same.

    I once commented out loud, and foolishly, that I wanted a medal, even a Purple Heart. This made the other scouts incredulous. They thought I was crazy and told me so. I thought about it and admitted they were right. It was a crazy thing to say.

    After making this *Freudian Slip*, I discovered the world of *Kevlar* and *Chicken Plates*. I was about to learn that Purple Hearts, like all medals, find you. You don't ever go looking to find them. Very soon I would learn this, and in a very painful way.

BABY SCOUT

Michael W. Mason

NINE

KILLING THE DEAD

Buck was gone. So were Hutch and Mr. Dunne. Their year was up and they went home. They left the best way possible. Alive! Hopefully, they wouldn't have to come back. Some career soldiers extend their tours or end up being sent back two or three more times. Some like it for the adventure. Most like it for the extra money you get for being in-country. You can save a lot of money in Vietnam, especially if you add on the bonuses you get for hazardous duty and flying. I hoped to go home after my year was up. OCS and a $10,000 reenlistment bonus weren't incentives enough to chance being returned to the cesspool of the Orient.

This isn't to say there aren't any good times here. I have the comraderie in the hootch, the bar, volleyball games, and the occasional milk runs to Saigon and China Beach. I also enjoy getting the care packages from home. There is the Armed Forces Radio Network, and there is even television. Sometimes, there's entertainment. Live entertainment. Hollywood entertainment.

I remember one show that came to the 3/4 Cav. It was billed as the *Mouseketeer* show. The headliner was Doreen, or Darla, or something like that. I never was good at remembering names. Anyway, she was billed as one of the original Mouseketeers. Now, though, she was all grown up.

The show was held in our huge maintenance hangar. The aircraft were moved to the far side and a stage was erected. A hundred chairs were set up with a section up front reserved for the officers. I sat near the back with some of the other Baby Scouts. I was curious about what a grown up Mouseketeer would look like.

The entertainment began with a Vietnamese rock and roll band. The musicians wore white shirts, black slacks, and pointy, black Italian shoes. They all had Beatle haircuts and played top forty rock tunes…badly. Imagine Vietnamese rock singers doing the *Beatles*, the *Association*, or *Elvis*. If it was memorable, it was because they were so bad.

A loudspeaker announced, "And now, here she is, Darla the Mouseketeer," or was it, "Doreen the Mouseketeer." I still can't remember the name. I sat back, applauded, and didn't recognize *Disney's* little girl at all. She was all grown up, in her mid-twenties, brunette, nicely built, and showing it all off in a tight, miniskirt outfit. The buxom Mouseketeer wore white *Nancy Sinatra Boots*, and her tight blouse was open, revealing large, round breasts. She sang and gyrated provacatively to the music. Every so often she would grab her breasts and lift them up to kiss and lick them. Most of the guys cheered and whistled when she did that. Some, like me, were more reserved and a little shocked.

Watching a former Mouseketeer perform like that was a jolt to my cultural upbringing. Everytime she licked her boobs, I was bombarded with images of the old *Mickey Mouse Club* tv show. I think a little bit of my childhood died that day. I would never again think of Cubby and Karen in the same way.

The Bob Hope show is the big one. He gets escorted around by Generals and an armada of Gunships. When it was announced that he was coming to Cu Chi, I was ecstatic. His is a great show and Ann Margaret would be with him. When the big day arrived, I got assigned to fly perimeter recon. I didn't think it was fair but I understood that his safety was paramount. I got some satisfaction knowing that the Baby Scouts, and #395, were assigned to protect Mr. Hope's butt.

After Buck went home I was promoted to Spec-5 and took over as Flight Line Chief. My duties included assigning crews to pilots and keeping the flight line in order. Nothing else much changed for me except that I got more pay and didn't have to pull the dreaded shit burning detail anymore. Sandbagging continued, though. Even some of the officers sandbagged. It is the one detail that none of us ever complain about.

I did a lot of flying with Lt. Kerns during the months of August and September. He was still a stickler for military protocol but I got used to his ways. In some respects, I admired him for being so military. He is secure in his ways, and knows that his life's work will be the Army.

The Lieutenant is also a good pilot. On dusk patrol one day we came upon a creek bed. My Loach was the low ship. I always assigned myself to the hunter role. I had a thing about looking for trouble before it found me, and killing was still fun.

In the shallow pool was the biggest crocodile I ever saw. It was also the first crocodile I ever saw. It was just resting there, minding its own business, snoozing in the cool water. We were bored and Lt. Kerns said, "Shoot it." Without hesitation, I fired a burst into the unwary giant. The beast roared in startlement, and pain, and thrashed about violently. I fired another burst. It just wouldn't die.

We went lower and I tossed a thermite on the writhing monster. It quickly burned into the Croc's belly. The twenty foot beast moved no more and I instantly regretted killing the animal. It wasn't doing anything or bothering anyone. It was just basking in the sun, oblivious to the human war. I wished I had left the peaceful, sleeping giant alone.

We followed the creek aways and it widened into a stream. The observer spotted something and the pilot headed for it. As we approached, Lt. Kerns kept the floating object to his right, under the cover of my machine gun. We weren't prepared for what we found.

It was a body, floating face up, and very bloated. Lt. Kerns and I noticed something very familiar about the corpse. He was dressed in American Army jungle fatigues and wore two bandoliers of M16 ammo clips. "Oh, my God!" I yelled into the intercom. "He's one of ours." Kerns pulled collective with forward cyclic and we rose into the sky at a ship-rattling rate of ascent. The G-Force held me frozen in my jumpseat.

Lt. Kerns leveled off at 500 feet. He radioed the high ship and we flew around the area to check for any signs of Charlie. We were still circling when OPS came up on the radio. I couldn't believe what I heard.

"Sink the body."

"*Damn!*" I said into the intercom.

"No way," said the observer.

"Knock it off," said Kerns. "I don't like this crap either but we got our orders." Apparently, the brass didn't want the enemy to find our boy or whatever he might be carrying. I was angry about the order but there was nothing else to do. Kerns was as mad as me but brought the Loach in and over the body. "Sorry, Mason," he said, "but this is your job. Make it quick."

"Sorry, man," I said as I opened up with the M60. The short burst ripped into the body and it exploded like a bomb. I could smell the ripe gasses from the decomposing corpse through the rotor wash. The dead soldier slowly sank below the surface of the still water. His face was the last to disappear into the watery tomb. I watched the slow-motion event as wide-open, lifeless eyes stared back at me. It gave me the creeps and I shuddered beneath my facade of war-hardened warrior.

We stayed on-scene for a few minutes and the observer marked the location on his map. Lieutenant Kerns said, "Let's get the hell out of

Michael W. Mason

here." He pulled stick and we slowly climbed to 500 feet to join up with our cover ship. On the way up I watched bubbles pop on the surface. Kerns radioed the other ship that dusk patrol was over. This was the first time a mission ended early and I didn't complain. As we headed south, back to Cu Chi, none of us spoke. For the first time, I hated my role in the war. The three of us would always remember this mission and would carry the scar on our souls forever.

Killing the dead killed something in me. I don't know exactly what I lost but something has been missing ever since. I drank heavily that evening. I thought about the KIA that I helped make an MIA. I also wondered if the brass would keep its promise and recover the dead American soldier and send him home. I thought, "Probably not." A family would never know what happened to their boy. I drank until I passed out.

The weeks passed and the world became normal again. Flying was still the thrill it always was, and even the killing was good again.

There were many new guys in the Baby Scouts. Most of them were draftees. The FNGs were assigned to the Baby Scouts whenever replacements were needed. The Baby Scouts wasn't a volunteer outfit anymore.

Most of the new guys were ok. A few were potheads. One was a mean bastard who resented being in the army, resented me, and hated authority. I was glad I never had to fly with him. One night his 45 went off in the hootch. The slug ripped through the wood partition that separated my cubicle space from the rest of the hootch. Being Flight Line Chief has its advantages.

The bullet missed me by inches and slammed into the hootch wall. The *SOB* claimed it was an accident. I wasn't convinced. We steered clear of each other out of mutual hatred. Some days I wanted to kill him more than I wanted to kill Charlie. I know he felt the same about me.

The only pothead I ever flew with was a big, lumbering, freckled 19-year-old. He was a hippie and a college student before he got drafted. His name is Ira Ritchfield. He's a friendly guy and smokes his weed whenever he can. We call him Ritchie and when he's straight, he makes for a pretty good crew chief. Soon, Ritchie and I would go hunting together on #395. It would be the first time I ever flew as observer on my own ship. It would also be the last.

There are few, happy, memorable highlights in Vietnam. During the rainy season, it's hard to find any. If there is one, it's the flooding of the new, freshly dug, underground bunker. It's a ten foot hole in the ground about forty by fifteen feet. The torrential rains filled it quickly and the new swimming pool became an instant hit with us troops.

During the monsoons of Southeast Asia, we went swimming. We were like boys at the old swimming hole. The water is a muddy brown but cool and refreshing. Some of us jumped in with clothes on. Others wore only shorts, or nothing at all. The mamasans would stand around and laugh. I, and a few other Scouts, showed off for Mei. We did cannonballs, flips, and silly belly-whoppers just for her. She knew it, appreciated the attention, and laughed at her Baby Scout boys.

A few officers even joined in the fun. Among them was our Scout leader, Nathaniel Reese. The Lieutenant told me, and two others, to go to his hootch and drag Lt. Kerns out to the pool. I balked at this but Reese said, "Go!"

We broke away and yelled, "Charge!" We hit the hootch door on the run. It swung open with a resounding crash, and a startled Hank Kerns didn't know what befell him. We had him by the arms and waist and were dragging him to the door. The other officers in the hootch were laughing at the preposterous scene. Kerns ordered us to stop, or else, and then Lt. Reese walked in. He was soaking wet and said, "Hank, you're going swimming with your men."

Lieutenant Reese grabbed the flustered Kerns by the arm and led him to the door. We followed behind to prevent any escape. Kerns protested all the way to the mud hole. The XO was there, acting as the unofficial lifeguard. He looked at us and just smiled. Kerns looked at the XO with pleading eyes but found no help there. The XO just grinned. Baby Scout business is Baby Scout business. At the edge of the rain-filled bunker we picked up the squirming Lieutenant and yelled, "One, two, three!"

We flung the Loach pilot high and far. He hit the water with a splat, flat on his back. He sank a few seconds later. When Kerns surfaced, he shook his head and laughed. Kerns, the man who would be General, was actually laughing. Even Lt. Reese was surprised at this. The man had a sense of humor after all.

He swam to the edge and climbed out. Still laughing, he grabbed the flight leader who, in turn, grabbed me. We tumbled into the muddy water. Officer bars and enlisted stripes were forgotten. We splashed and played like little boys. When I left for the showers, Reese and Kerns were still rough-housing like brothers.

In the days to follow, I noticed a change in Lt. Kerns. He was no longer the Army's poster boy. He didn't bug anyone about saluting anymore and he even socialized with the Scouts. Kerns was still miitary, just a better person. He came of age during a wilding time of boys running amok in Southeast Asia.

Lieutenant Kerns became one of my favorite pilots. We flew many missions together and, every once in a while, I'd throw him a salute in the hootch area. He would grin and toss one back. I think he appreciated that.

The days continued to be hot, humid, and very wet. Even though the bunker stayed filled with water due to the daily storms, few of us went swimming again. That one time was all we needed.

At the beginning of the monsoon season I inherited a pair of stray mutts from a homeward-bound, Gunship crewman. He was afraid the dogs might end up on a villager's dinner table. I adopted them and named the short, pudgy pooch, *LT*. The larger, friskier one, I called *Smokey*. He was white with large, brown spots. LT was black with white splotches. While the lithe Smokey was friendly with a perpetual wagging tail, LT was a solitary mutt with an attitude. They were *night and day* and always a much-needed diversion from the war.

I built a pen for them and a little, wood hootch. I even spent a few of my off-hours to sandbag it. Smokey and LT became our mascots and we all helped to take care of them. Once in a while, I even felt generous enough to share my dog bisquits. Uncle Rusty always sent enough to go around.

My Uncle Rusty would retire a *Bird* Colonel in the Air force. He was one of the pioneers in rocketry and missile development. His men liked him and even gave him a cool nickname, *Silver Fox*. He and Aunt Audrey raised three daughters and a son. Russ and Audrey have always been like second parents to me.

When it wasn't raining, I took in the evening, outdoor movies. Makeshift, wood bleachers were set up and an old 16mm movie projector dragged out from the supply hootch. One of my favorite movies was *The Good, The Bad, and the Ugly*. It was called a *spaghetti western* and was unlike any I'd ever seen. I liked it and identified with the *man with no name*.

Realism was rampant on the big screen but, of course, I hadn't seen *The Wild Bunch* yet, so I thought the Eastwood flick was as bloody as it gets.

The movies were becoming more and more realistic, and the *shoot 'em up* scenes were graphically accurate. I always wondered if the Vietnam War, or *TV War*, helped Hollywood get by the censors with their newly discovered realism.

The next day I was summoned to the maintenance hangar. All the helicopter crews were there and being issued something called *Kevlar*. It was white, an inch thick, and very heavy. These were the *Chicken Plates* we had heard about, or seen on crewmen of the 1st Air Cav. Before now, we only had the flack jackets. Unfortunately, they never did a good job at stopping bullets or shrapnel.

The heavy kevlar plates were placed in front and back pouches of flight vests that we slipped over our heads. This new, heavy garment was called a *bulletproof vest*. We just called them chicken plates and learned to love them. A few pilots, and myself, drew bullseyes on them. It seemed like a funny, rebellious thing to do. Mostly, it was a dare. We were saying, "Here you go, Charlie. Maybe now you can hit something." My chicken plate would soon be put to the test. It would literally save my life.

Michael W. Mason

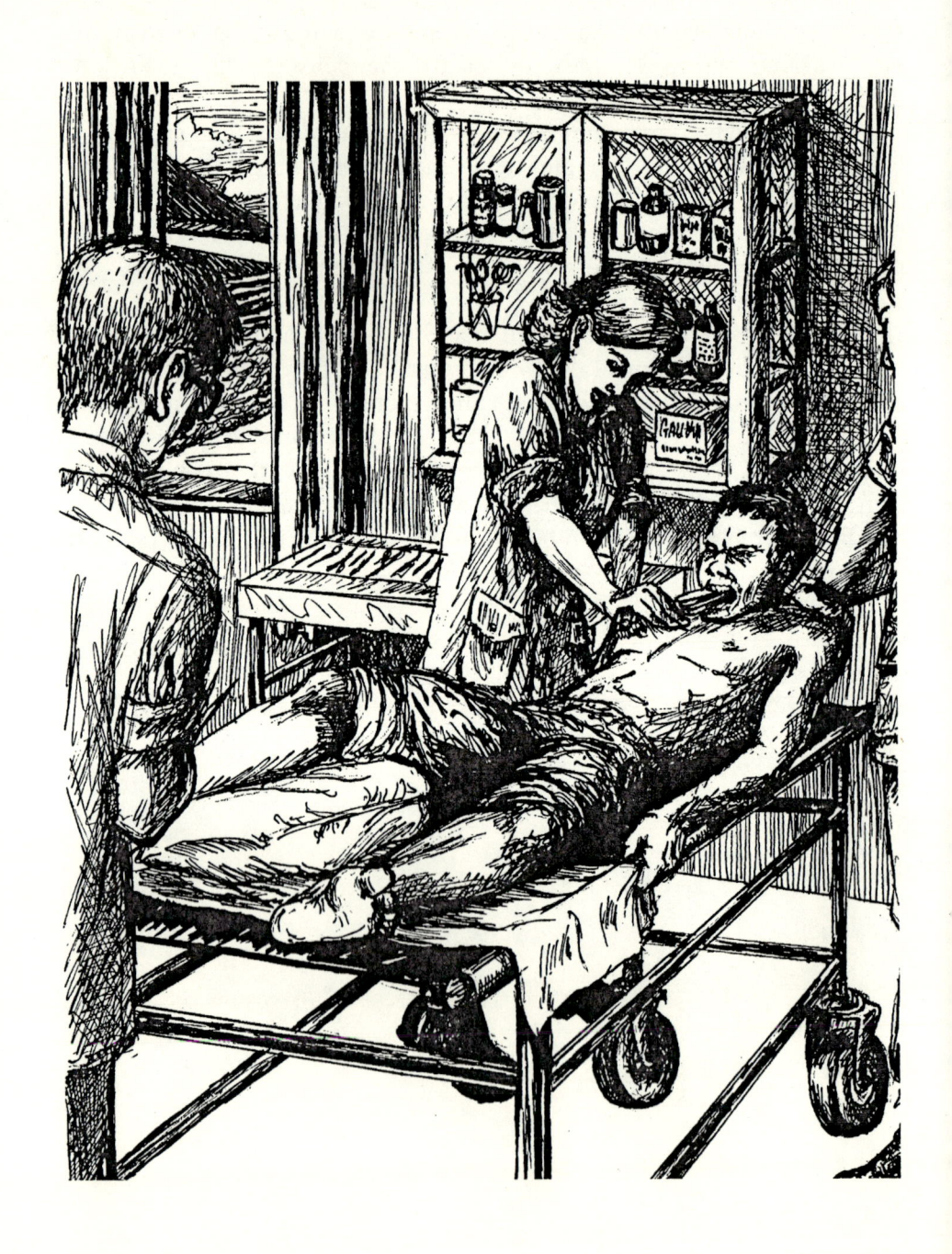

TEN

BULLETS AND BUTT PLATES

The Iron Triangle is a thick piece of jungle. We didn't fly there too often as it's out of our normal AO. Further south is a rubber tree plantation. We call it *The First Rubber*. One day, one of the snake drivers flew his Cobra straight into it. At the last moment he was able to pull collective and make a somewhat gentle landing onto the resilient, rubber trees.

The claxon sounded and the call went out, "Centaur down." We all scrambled to protect the downed flyers. The nimble Loaches were in the air first, followed by the powerful Gunships. The crash site was quickly secured and the rescue and recovery of men and machine went off without a hitch.

After a debriefing, it was determined that the pilot suffered from vertigo. Embarrassingly, it was the XO who plowed the Cobra into the rubber tree plantation. What made the accident even more embarrassing was that only a few days before, the XO had given a safety class on flying and vertigo. This crash, though not funny to the XO and his weapons officer, was amusing to the rest of us. It kept everyone smiling for days. When the Cobra was airlifted back to the airfield, it looked pretty beat up. It was repairable and the only Cobra casualty during my year in-country.

Lieutenant Reese, the observer, and myself were flying back to Cu Chi after a search and destroy mission over the Iron Triangle. We flew low and fast over the thick, green jungle canopy. My Loach, #395, was clipping along at 140 knots. No one flew the Triangle at less than *flat out*. The Iron Triangle is a favorite hiding place of the NVA and Charlie. It has dense foliage above and a myriad of hiding places below.

The jungle is a green blur as it races by the muzzle of my machine gun. I try to peek through the lush greenery but it's too thick and the Loach is moving too fast.

I was comfortable in my jumpseat, M60 cradled in my arms, and my right foot flying in the wind. I always fly with my right foot dangling out the door. It feels good and is a habit that makes me more flexible when firing the machine gun.

Michael W. Mason

My eyes were getting tired when the jungle erupted in gunfire. Reacting instinctively, my M60 came alive. I returned fire before seeing the tell-tale puffs of smoke. Tracers filled the air and the Loach seemed to be flying through a storm of green rain. I leaned out and looked back at the visible muzzle flashes. The glowing embers spitting from my machine gun blanketed the enemy's hiding place. In the middle of this long burst from my M60, my flying foot was slammed upward and over my head. I thought I raked the rotor blades as I tumbled onto my back. The Loach began to weave erratically and I yelled, I'm hit! I'm hit." The observer looked back at my contorted body. His eyes were wide in surprise.

"Wait a minute," I said. "I'm ok. I'm not hit." My right foot was throbbing but I wasn't sure if I was shot or not. I regained my seating and composure and looked down at my aching foot. It was still attached to my leg and already I felt better. The boot, though, had a couple of small holes in it. My foot hurt when I tried to wiggle my toes. It also felt like my toes were sloshing in water. I then saw the blood dripping from the sole of the boot.

"Lieutenant," I yelled into the intercom, "I'm hit. There's blood coming out of my right boot."

"Hang on, Mason," he said. "We'll be back at the corral soon." Lt. Reese radioed the information to the high ship and then climbed to five hundred feet. He gave #395 all the forward cyclic she could handle and the airspeed indicator redlined past 140 knots. On the way to Cu Chi, I wondered why my butt hurt more than my injured, flying foot.

The killer in the sky made a single gunrun on the enemy position while we sped for home. The Loach seemed to have picked up even more speed and I could tell from the sound of the wind rushing by that #395 was beyond its redline. Reese would later claim that he broke the 160 knot barrier. I believed him. The Cobra caught up to us fifteen minutes later. Its pilot radioed the Lieutenant that he didn't think a Loach could go that fast.

Once out of the Triangle, everyone breathed easier. I didn't think my wound was that serious. Never-the-less, dark thoughts of amputation raced through my mind. My butt was numb and I wondered if it might be related to the foot wound. I thought about removing the boot, however I figured it was acting like a tourniquet. My biggest fear was that my foot would come off with the boot. The pain was subsiding but a throbbing numbness remained. I thought, "Well, my stupid medal wish has come true." I didn't feel brave and never in my life had I felt so stupid. Further more, my butt was beginning to throb.

Something wasn't quite right with #395. Even through the slight numbness, and pain, my crew chief's sensitive butt felt a vibration that shouldn't have been there. With increasing horror, it dawned on me. I had shot my own ship. I looked out, and up at the blur of rotor blades. I concentrated and slowly it came to me. My ears heard a slight whistle, the kind you associate with bullet holes. Only the pain in my foot, and butt, kept me from launching into a tirade of surly invectives.

"Cu Chi tower, Centaur one-six requesting emergency landing. Wounded on board, over."

"Roger, one-six. You are cleared for a straight-in approach. Medics have been alerted and will be standing-by, over."

"Roger, Cu Chi. Centaur one-six on final." Reese landed in front of the hangar.

A jeep, with a stretcher, was parked in front. The base hospital was only a few hundred yards away so at least the bumpy ride would be a short one. The medics came up to me as I was stowing the M60 and removing my flight helmet. One of them said, "Remove your boot." I tried but it wouldn't budge. My foot was too swollen. One of the medics produced a pocket knife and cut the laces. He pulled slowly and the boot slid off, spilling a crimson waterfall of blood. Lieutenant Reese was at my side and helped the medics carry me to the stretcher. The observer waked over to the jeep and jokingly said, "Don't worry, Mason, you've still got another foot left." It was a bad joke and Reese gave him a dirty look. The Lieutenant said, "Sorry, Mike, but it doesn't look bad enough for a ticket back to the world." I felt a little better as the jeep left my partners behind in a cloud of dust. I think the Lieutenant wanted to go with me but the XO had cornered him for a debriefing.

On the ride to the hospital, I sat upright and looked at my foot. Most of the pain was coming from my right, big toe. I was able to hop into the emergency room with the help of a medic's shoulder. I was placed on a shiny, aluminum gurney in a very sterile-looking room. The metal table was cold and foreboding. A doctor came over and started to examine my foot. He asked, "Does it hurt anywhere else?"

"Just my butt, doc." A nearby nurse laughed and the tall, young looking doctor smiled.

"Well, let's see. Unbutton your pants and turn on your side." The blonde nurse walked over and stood by the doctor. I followed orders but felt uncomfortable in front of the pretty Lieutenant. I slipped my pants and shorts down and guessed that my face was as red as my foot.

The doctor prodded my butt and said, "You're bruised but you'll live. It looks like you got hit with a paddle or something. Any ideas, Mason?" The doctor had read my name tag.

"Beats me, doc," I said, managing a weak smile through the pain.

"Funny, Mason. Ok, you can pull your pants up and roll over on your back."

The nurse went to work and rolled up my right pants leg. She then washed my leg with antiseptic soap from knee to toes. It hurt but I tried not to show it. The doctor called for a *local* and the nurse passed him a syringe. In my mind, it was the biggest needle I ever saw. The doc stuck me in the big toe and the excruciating pain almost sent me flying off the small operating table. Imagine pouring alcohol over an open wound. That was the kind of pain that shot through my body.

I blurted out some very colorful verbiage and then remembered the nurse. I looked at her and saw that she was giggling.

"Sorry, doc."

"That's ok, Mason. I've heard worse." After two more shots I was still feeling pain. I told the doctor that I had a high tolerance to pain killers. He nodded and said that he couldn't waste any more of the valuable medicine on me.

"Can you put me under?"

"Nope. Sorry. That's only for life-threatening injuries."

"Well, what's going to happen, then?" I saw the answer to my question before I finished asking it. The nurse was taping a dozen tongue depressors together. This wasn't the answer I was looking for.

The nurse placed the wad of wood sticks between my teeth and said, "It's ok to scream." Looking at her with wide, unbelieving eyes I thought, "In front of you? I don't think so." It was like a scene out of an old war movie or western. The only thing missing was the bottle of whiskey.

The doctor went to work on my foot. Electric pain shot up my body and erupted as a growl from my throat. With each passing minute I bit deeper into the sticks. Through watery eyes I saw the nurse glance at me and shake her head. The look she gave me said, "You boys are always so brave when a woman is around." She was right. As much as I wanted to, I wasn't going to scream in front of a woman.

The doctor pulled sharp bits of shrapnel out of my foot and big toe. The surgery took fifteen minutes though it seemed like hours. When it was over, the nurse removed the sticks from between my teeth. She held them up and showed the doctor. They were completely bitten in half. The doctor looked down at me and saw blood coming from my lower lip.

"Strong teeth, Mason. You trying to get a second Purple Heart?" He smiled as he said it and the nurse laughed as she put antiseptic on my teeth-bitten lip. She followed-up with a band-aid and said I could remove it after a few hours. After cleaning and bandaging my foot, the doctor gave me the damage report.

He said I was a lucky boy and that I would get to keep my foot and all its toes. As he explained it, I was hit in the boot by bullet shrapnel. Apparently, the copper-jacketed round had ricocheted off the skid, sending pieces of it through the boot sole and the soft leather on the right side. Small bits of copper went into my foot and a large, ragged shard had lodged in my big toe, blowing off the nail. The doc said the sliver of metal went in straight, like a spear. He said, "Had it gone in sideways your toe would be in your sock."

The nurse gave me a tetanus shot and then showed me the boot. It had some rips in it but, other than that, looked to be in pretty good shape. A medic brought over some wooden crutches and a pair of rubber flip-flops. The doctor said to stay off the foot for a week. He gave me some dressing and said to change the bandage in two days.

"Come back in a week for a checkup."

"Ok, doc." I looked down at my injured foot for a second and when I looked back up, the doc was walking away.

The nurse smiled and said, "Keep your foot inside the helicopter from now on, ok?" I laughed as she helped me off the table. She smelled of antiseptic but a whiff of woman got through. I thought, "God! I miss girls."

Stepping outside, my sudden blindness in the Asian sunlight cured itself in seconds. I hobbled on my crutches back to the hangar where the injured Loach was being looked at by mechanics and the curious. Everyone was happy to see me and a little amazed that I was back so soon. Some had passed rumors that my foot was shot off. Others believed my foot had been

Michael W. Mason

amputated. It would take a few days for all the rumors about my injury to stop.

Lieutenants Reese and Kerns both asked how I was doing. I answered that all was fine and asked how my Loach was. Reese said the TI (Technical Inspector), was still assessing the damage. He then pointed to a rotor blade. There was a hole in it. Reese pointed to another blade. "*Damn!*" I muttered aloud, then thought in anger, "I shot my own ship. I must have riddled the blades when I was knocked on my back." The Lieutenants looked at me but didn't say anything.

The hangar chief took me on a tour and pointed out the battle damage. The right side was peppered with bullet holes, most of them in the tail boom. He said, "Take a look under your seat." I bent down and craned my neck to look under the jumpseat.

"Wow! No wonder my butt hurts."

"What's that, Mason?"

"Nothing, Sarge. Nothing at all."

A bullet had struck the kevlar plate that I had put under the seat. It was cracked, almost into two separate pieces. The converted chicken plate had literally saved my butt, the family jewels, and probably my life. All I could say was, "I guess I need a new chicken plate."

When the kevlar vests first came in, I took out the back plate and put it under my seat. Most of us did. It seemed the smart thing to do as enemy fire always came up at us from the ground. I painted a red bullseye on mine, thinking it was funny. I wasn't laughing anymore.

My gimpy foot put me out of action for a week. However, I still helped out on the flight line. My ship was patched up and got two, new **rotor blades. Lieutenant Reese made sure that a new chicken plate** went under my jumpseat.

I spent most of the week on the flight line. One day while I was cleaning M60s, I was startled by a *whoosh* further up the line. A Gunship rocket had been accidently launched and it streaked across the airfield, slamming into a Slick. The rocket didn't explode but caused a lot of damage as it sliced through the ship's tail boom and thudded into the heavily-sandbagged bunker. I thought, "Some pilot, or crew chief, is going before the old man for that *snafu*." I wondered if a pilot could be put on shit burning detail.

Another time, a Loach gunner was clearing the minigun and forgot to remove the breech plate. He twirled the barrels of the modern-day gatling gun and it fired a round across the road and into a culvert, just missing a tank. The gunner got the nasty detail for two weeks. None of us thought much about the incident. *Shit* happens!

Being grounded, there wasn't much for me to do except clean weapons and watch the ships fly in and out. I began to think about R & R. It was almost time for me to take my two weeks of carnal pleasures and I had pretty much settled on Thailand. My dream was shattered, though, when one of the Scout pilots begged me to let him go in my place. He said he wanted to meet his wife in Hawaii and see his baby boy for the first time. What could I do. I let him have my two weeks, but Lt. Reese said I still had to get some R & R for myself. The Lieutenant said I was going to Saigon for a weekend and not to argue.

"Another Scout is going with you, Mike. You need the time off." I didn't argue. You always visited Saigon in groups, never alone. The Scout going with me was Ernie. He was being rewarded for having consistently-high body counts.

The mini-vacation would turn out to be very enlightening and the highlight of my tour in-country. It would also be anything but restful. *Rest and Relaxation* is all in the mind. Besides, how could I rest with all those exotic, Asian girls just waiting for the gunslinging terror of the Iron Triangle.

Michael W. Mason

ELEVEN

THE EXOTIC WHORES OF SAIGON

The week on crutches went by slowly. Eventually, though, I got back in the war. My boot still wouldn't fit over my swollen foot, so I wore a sock and a leather *Jesus sandal*. It felt good to be flying again, even though Lt. Reese had some minor objections about me coming back too soon, and the Jesus sandal. I assured him that all was fine and he grudgingly gave in. Flying missions again made me feel more like a Baby Scout. The rushing wind felt good as it passed through my sock and briskly massaged my flying foot.

The first week back was spent shooting up the river banks and sampans. We stitched the little, wood canoes with minigun and M60. Once, we spotted a whole stack hidden under some palm fronds. I dropped a Willie Peter on the sampans and we left a huge, raging bonfire behind us. In only a few weeks, we destroyed hundreds of those little boats. Unfortunately, most of the time there weren't any VC to send to the bottom with the little, wood canoes.

Another week went by and my boot was back on my tender foot. I had kept the battle-scarred boot for good luck. I figured lightning wouldn't strike twice. Lieutenant Reese finally got my R & R cleared with OPS. He said, "You and Ernie leave in the morning."

"Great, sir," I said, "We can't wait."

"One of our new pilots will fly you guys to Saigon. Also, you know you're not supposed to take weapons with you, right?"

"Yeah," I said. "Right, sir." He smiled, knowingly, then walked away with a grin, a wave, and a, "Have fun, boys." Reese knew we would be carrying armament to Saigon. I knew that he knew and he knew that I knew that he knew. He was just being a good officer by telling us the rules. It was a rule, though, that no one obeyed.

Lieutenant Reese knew that I, in particular, would never leave base camp without my beloved Colt 45. It was also common knowledge that I slept with it under my pillow. My Colt is as important to me as the minigun is to a pilot. For an instant I wondered what kind of weapon Ernie would bring along. I shrugged and went about packing my necessities for the trip into a clean, canvas sandbag.

Michael W. Mason

Excited, we skipped formation in the morning and went straight to the flight line. we wore our jungle fatigues. However, we had a change of *civvies* in our sandbags. My makeshift luggage also carried my Colt 45 and an extra ammo clip. I didn't know what kind of weapon Ernie was packing. I was only certain that he was bringing one.

The pilot was waiting for us by #395. The Loach was patched up. However, it had a slight tracking problem with the new rotor blades. I made a mental note to fix the problem when I got back from R & R.

Even though weekends mean nothing in 'Nam, we left for R & R on a Saturday morning. War is the same every day, but American tradition demanded we take our vacation on a weekend.

The new pilot was Chief Warrant Officer Jimmy Latham. The W1 was fresh out of *Mother Rucker* (Fort Rucker Flight School), in Dothan, Alabama. He's a year younger than me and had only been in-country for a few months.

Jimmy Latham is tall and skinny. He has a few freckles about the nose and a shock of curly, straw-colored hair. The W1 was trying to grow a mustache but failing miserably at it. I sported a thick, wide handlebar and it matched my dark, brown hair perfectly.

I volunteered to check the ship out. Mr. Latham started his preflight and Ernie yelled, "Dibs on the left seat." Ernie is a crew chief, also, and he helped me out with the inspection. He's a *good old boy* from the *Volunteer* state of Tennessee. His accent isn't too thick and he always seems to be smiling. He reminded me a lot of Hutch. They didn't look alike, but they both have smart-ass mouths. Ernie is a little shorter than me, but stockier. Most of it is in his chest and belly. He's powerfully built with rounded shoulders and huge legs. He didn't look strong but he could crush your hand during a friendly handshake. Everyone who met Ernie Bledsoe for the first time always ended up with a courteous, "Pleased to meet ya," and a bruised right hand.

Ernie has a round head with big, pink ears. Whenever his body count stories got exaggerated, they would turn red along with his freckled cheeks. His smile is all buck teeth. He couldn't crack a smile without me thinking of a beaver. His front teeth are inordinately large and prominent with every smile. He brushes them three times a day and I have to admit, they are the whitest, brightest teeth in the 3/4 Cav. They are also very sharp. Ernie would always oblige us if we needed help in opening a care package from home. His huge, buck teeth can cut through any string, twine, or narrow rope like butter. All-in-all, Ernie Bledsoe is a good guy.

    The Loach checked out and I grabbed the fire extinguisher. Ernie wasted no time climbing into the front, left seat. The pilot yelled, "Clear!" The ignitor began to pop and the turbine *whooshed* to life. In just a few minutes we were making a left bank over the main gate. I looked down and saw the line of mamasans, and papasans, getting searched by the sentries. American soldiers searched the men. A trusted Vietnamese woman searched the women. The same procedure occured at night when the *domestic help* went home. A lone figure, wearing a conical, straw hat and black pajamas waved at us as we flew overhead. I waved back, recognizing the tiny figure as Mei. I laughed and I could tell that she was smiling. I would miss her while I was gone. She was always a cheerful sight to come back to after a long, tiring day of search and destroy.

    The village of Cu Chi became a blur of dull colors as it passed below the ship. It always looked the same…drab, archaic, a little town that never progressed out of the 19th century.

    Cu Chi village is like most others in 'Nam. It never embraced the industrial revolution, and remained forever destined to repeat history of the agrarian kind. Labor is done by hand, tools are made by hand, crops are planted and harvested by hand, and the closest thing the Vietnamese have to a machine is the Water Buffalo.

    The large beasts pull the axe-hewn, wooden carts and supply manure for fertilizer and for the cooking stoves. The buffalo is a much revered animal in Vietnam, though not deified. When it dies, it is eaten.

    The village is made mostly of bamboo, straw, and wood. Here-and-there were signs of an American influence; some of the hootches were made almost entirely from aluminum beer cans. The villagers scoured the base dump every day and would cart away tons of refuse. Some of it was left-over food, blood-stained clothes, and aluminum cans. The natives seemed to prefer the colorful *Budweiser* beer cans for building hootches. I don't know why. Maybe it's because the soldiers drank more beer than soda.

    I settled in my jumpseat and tried to get comfortable. My box of grenades was there, however the M60 was back in the ammo locker. I felt under the seat and was pacified by the chauky touch of kevlar.

Michael W. Mason

The night before, Tom Donald asked me if I had ever had an Asian girl. I said no and he grinned and said, "It's in a different place, you know."

"What are you talking about?" I looked at him with a puzzled expression.

"Their pussy, Mike. It's not where you think it is."

"Come on. Its got to be there."

"Nope. Not Asian girls. It's, well, it's back-a-ways."

"What do you mean, back-a-ways?"

"Their pussy is further back between their legs. You can't see it unless they're on their back with their legs in the air."

"You're kidding me."

"Nope. This is for real, Mike. You know how American women have a lot of hair down there?"

"Yeah. So what?"

"Well, Vietnamese women don't have any hair in that spot. They're just like the Japanese, Chinese, Koreans, and the rest."

"Ok. So what?"

"So, they aren't well protected. I don't know why it happened, maybe some Darwin thing or something. You know, evolution. For protection, their genitals somehow developed in a different spot than American or European women."

"You're kidding."

"Hey, I've been there. I learned it when I went on R & R four months ago."

"So, what's the difference?"

"Not much. It's still a pussy, just further back and closer to the ass."

"I still don't believe it. You're so full of it."

"Ok. Whatever. Just remember what I told you when you find out for yourself."

"Yeah. Ok, Tom."

"Another thing."

"What?"

"The gooks are the best lovers in the world. You won't want to leave Vietnam if you can get a lot of R & R."

"Thanks, Tom. It'll be fun."

Tom was so serious that I half-believed him. I'd heard the old joke about Asian pussy going sideways, like the eyes, but never this. Being quite gullible, I didn't fully discount the story. It seemed possible...evolution and all.

Lieutenant Reese had asked me to help break in the new pilot. On the flight to Saigon I pointed out some landmarks. I told Mr. Latham to remember them and to use them as reference points. I would fly with W1 Latham all next week. The first few days would be on dawn and dusk patrols. Jimmy Latham was eager and wanted to impress the other pilots. He was much like me when I first came over...big jewels and little common sense. A near fatal and stupid mistake would envelope the young pilot very soon. It would end a promising career and destroy the best little Scout ship in the fleet.

Mr. Latham dropped us off and headed back to Cu Chi. A seasoned pilot would have found the time to goof-off in Saigon and visit the PX (Post Exchange). The PX is the military version of a department store. You can load up on clothes, jewelry, stereos, food, liquor, and cigarettes. The prices are incredibly low, and Ernie and I decided we'd go shopping before leaving Saigon.

We grabbed a cab into the city and then just walked around. There were people everywhere. Most of them seemed to be in a hurry. There weren't many cars but the streets were a flurry of bicycles, mopeds, and scooters.

The women wore ankle-length, white dresses. The *Ao dai* is a very tight, form-fitting garment and accentuates the slender figures of the young Vietnamese women. I couldn't believe how beautiful they were. Most had long, black hair, or wore it tucked up into conical, straw hats.

The older men and women looked aged beyond their years. There was no spring in their steps and no smiles. They had a look in their eyes that the young had yet to acquire. It was a reflection of many years of war, personal loss, and despair.

Also in large numbers on the street were South Vietnamese soldiers. They patrolled the sidewalks and were stationed at every street corner. United States Army MPs (Military Police), were also about, mostly in jeeps.

Ernie and I stopped in at a few bars. One was huge and designed like a movie theater. There was a concession, or bar, and behind it were many rows of soft, plush, folding chairs. A few tables were scattered about, but they were occupied by soldiers and civilians who came in with escorts or girlfriends. The bar girls were all beautiful. They wore the traditional and brightly colored, Ao dai. The ankle-length dresses were worn very tight and accentuated their small but supple breasts. Some of the red, white, blue, and pink Ao dai were sequined or embroidered with gold dragons.

The girls were all young, maybe sixteen to twenty years of age. They had black hair but none wore it past their shoulders. The overhead track lighting made their onyx tresses shine like a polished, black Camaro under a street lamp. The girls were small but vocal and very forward. They were anything but shy.

As soon as Ernie and I walked in, there were girls at our side. My friend was escorted off to a table with two chairs. Ernie is anything but shy and I wondered if the unsuspecting girl knew what she was in for. The girl at my side took my hand and led me to a row of plush, red-velvet, folding chairs. I could have sworn the seats were identical to those of my neighborhood movie theater. They even had cup holders and ashtrays in the armrests.

The girl sat next to me, grabbed my crotch and squeezed. I jumped with a start, then settled down. I looked over at a giggling, smiling face.

"Buy me drink, yes?" Excited, I would have bought her almost anything. She ordered a champagne cocktail and, for me, a rum and coke. In less than a minute, she had her cocktail and I was stirring my drink with a *swizzle stick.*

"My name, Trinh."

"Hi. I'm Mike."

"My. Nice name. You live Saigon?"

"No. Cu Chi."

"Oh. Cu Chi. Army base. What you do, My?"

"Crew chief on helicopters. I fly 'em and fix 'em." I began to wonder where the conversation was headed. I knew that there wasn't much else I could tell the girl without giving up information she didn't really need to know about. Then, the questions changed.

"My, where you from?"

"New York."

"My have girl, New Yor?" Trinh couldn't pronounce the word, but it was cute, kind of like Mei, the babysan.

"No. Not anymore."

"Trinh be My's girl today, ohay?"

"Ok, Trinh," I said, laughing.

"Buy me drink, yes?" She grabbed me by the crotch again and squeezed…and that's how the next hour went. I got half-looped on rum, and Trinh put a *vise-grip* on the family jewels whenever she wanted another cocktail. Being a little slow on the uptake, it took me about three rum and cokes and six champagne cocktails to realize Trinh's drinks were just colored water.

I began to slow-up on my drinking and the pretty bar girl gave me more than a squeeze. She began to caress and rub me until I gave in and bought her a drink. I was fully aroused and wondering if this was going to go any further than just sitting in the bar. When she grabbed me again, I responded by taking her left breast into my hand and gently squeezing it. She calmly removed my hand and said, "No allow touch girl." She smiled, then asked for another drink.

"No, Trinh. No more drinks."

"My, you buy one more, Trinh."

"No. No more." She looked at me, smiled, then pulled her hand off my crotch and bolted. I watched her greet another customer at the bar. She sat down with the soldier and grabbed his crotch. She said, "Buy me drink, yes?" I watched her seduce the young soldier and discovered that I didn't really care. I wasn't angry, or sad, only a bit wistful and a lot wiser in the ways of bar girls in Saigon.

I looked around for Ernie. He was off in a dark corner of the bar and having a great time. He had two girls with him. To his enjoyment, both of them took turns playing with him. He was a lot more *buzzed* than me and the girls were taking him for everything he had.

Feeling brotherly, I got up to save Ernie from an empty wallet. That's when the severe pain hit me. I was suffering from over-stimulation of the family jewels. I quickly sat down and waited another ten minutes. By the time I finally got Ernie out of the bar, I was limping slightly and my stomach was growling.

We hailed a cab and told the driver to take us to a nice hotel; preferably one with a good restaurant. During the ride I took the Colt 45 out of the sandbag and tucked it into my waistband. I didn't know what Ernie was carrying, but I knew he had a weapon hidden on him somewhere.

The cab dropped us off in front of a white, five story building. A big marquee on the roof said, "Sun Hotel." To the right of the entrance was a large picture window. Through it I saw a few people seated at tables and a waitress. I was instantly reminded of how hungry I was. We walked through the double doors and up to the reception counter. A small, elderly man, wearing fragile, wire-rimmed glasses, looked up and smiled.

Michael W. Mason

During the check-in, the old man asked if we had any weapons. I said, "No," and he looked at us with a slight grin. On his face I saw a look that said, "Sure you don't."

We paid in advance and the clerk asked if we would like companionship for the evening. Ernie blurted, "Yeah! Yeah!" I sheepishly agreed, still feeling the pain from the ordeal in the bar. The old man said he would take care of everything and then asked if there was anything else he could do for us.

"How about dinner?" I was really hungry.

"Follow me," he said. The clerk led us into the dining room and seated us at a table by the front picture window. He said a waiter would take care of us.

The dining room was small with a polished, wood floor. A glass chandelier hung from the ceiling, its candle-design lighting glowing softly. The entire room was wallpapered in a green and red mosaic. The tablecloths were of the same color and design. The dining room was reminiscent of my grandmother's house in Newport, Rhode Island…Victorian.

She would have felt right at home. I, however, felt a litlle out of place and out of time.

A waitress entered the room through the kitchen's swinging doors. She was young, slender, and wore a white Ao dai. Her hair was tucked up under a small, white cap and an apron protected the front of her dress. She had a heart-shaped face and her lips were full and somewhat pouty. Instantly, I knew that she was the prettiest girl I had ever seen.

She walked to a table that seated four Vietnamese. The young girl talked to the two elderly couples and bowed. She suddenly turned around and caught me staring at her. I looked away, embarrassed, and thought I saw her smiling out of the corner of my eye. As she walked toward the swinging doors, my eyes watched every, graceful movement. She seemed to float as she walked. I didn't think it could get any better until she reached up and removed her cap. Long, ebony tresses fell to below her swaying buttocks. Incandescent light from the chandelier gave her raven-black hair a luxurious sheen.

Then, she was gone. The kitchen doors engulfed her and the dining room seemed so empty. I hoped she would return. She didn't. I sat back in my chair and lit up. My mind reeled with the vision. The young Vietnamese girl was tall, maybe five-seven or eight. Her hair was shiny black and straight. It hung almost to the backs of her knees. Her face was oval, almost heart-shaped, with not a trace of freckles or blemishes. She had an upturned, tiny nose and it sat above a pair of the most sensuous, full lips I had ever seen. The girl's eyes were very large and seemed out of proportion to her cherub face. They reminded me of baby eyes...the kind that look so big on such a small face. I sighed and looked up at the male waiter who walked up to take our order.

We knew not to drink the water so we ordered a couple of beers. Ernie got some fish dish and I asked for a cheeseburger and a bowl of Vietnamese *noodle ball* soup. The burger was good, but I would pay dearly, for the soup, in a couple of days. Ernie, though, had seconds.

After dinner, we went to our rooms. Mine was not much bigger than my bedroom back home. It was rectangular with light-green walls and no window. There was a queen-sized bed with fresh linen, and one bedside table with a small, brass lamp. The bathroom was also small but had a sink and a fairly large shower.

I started to unpack my sandbag when there was a knock on the door. I walked across the worn, grey carpet and asked, "Who's there?"

"Ernie. Open up." I unlocked the door and opened it. Standing behind Ernie was the old clerk. He said, "Come." We followed him down the hallway and up two flights of stairs. On the fourth floor we entered a large room. It had nice, beige carpeting, sofas, and tables with lamps. Three ceiling fans whirred softly above. We were in a parlor, of sorts. It was dimly lit and smelled of incense and perfume. The old man walked ahead of us and toward the main reason we took R & R.

Sitting, or standing, were about twenty girls. They were all attractive, young, and most were wearing American-style clothes...miniskirts and blouses. Some of them wore the popular, white *Nancy Sinatra Boots*. All the girls had black, shoulder-length hair, or longer, and wore eye makeup and lipstick. A few looked as if they couldn't be any older than fourteen. The rest were in their late teens or early twenties. They all had one thing in common. They were prostitutes. Whores, whose only job is to please young soldiers like me.

The clerk clapped his hands and the girls lined up against the far wall. He turned to face us and said, "Choose, please." Ernie, the brash guy that he is, quickly took up the challenge. He walked up and down the line of living, beautiful, female flesh. Ernie looked each one over as if he was examining some animal at an auction. At any moment I expected him to examine the teeth of one of the girls.

Ernie took his time and eventually stopped in front of the smallest girl in the line. She also looked the youngest. I doubted she was even fourteen. The Vietnamese *Lolita* wore a black miniskirt, white boots, and a pink blouse that couldn't hide a pair of surprisingly large breasts. It was obvious to me why Ernie picked her. She was an exotic *woman-child* who had matured before her years.

"I'll take her."

"Very good, sir," said the clerk. "She'll be at your door with any beverage of your choice."

"Jack Daniels?"

"Yes. We have Jack Daniels." There was an exchange of American currency and then Ernie walked back toward me. He was all smiles and said, "Your turn." I looked at the clerk who was beckoning me to join him. I moved forward but not toward the old man. My eyes directed me to the girl I had noticed when we first entered the parlor.

The girl I wanted was the one who looked different from the others. She was tall, about five-eight, had black hair that hung straight and to her knees, and had an oval face with large eyes and full, pouty lips. She was the waitress I had first seen in the dining room. The young woman wore a red Ao dai decorated with yellow suns and gold embroidery. It fit her snuggly and accentuated her lithe figure. Her waist was tiny, yet her hips were rounded, as were her breasts that seemed too large for her slender frame.

Her full lips were a lightly painted scarlett and her full cheeks had a trace of blush. The girl's eyes were truly Asian…oval, yet large, and hiding behind tiny slits of eyelashes. I stood in front of her and stared into those wonderous eyes. She looked down for a moment, then looked back up at me with a darkened expression. She was blushing. The girl managed a weak smile, then looked down again. She seemed embarrassed and a little shy. The old man walked over to me and I told him, "She's the one."

"Are you sure, sir?"

"Yes. I'm sure."

"You haven't looked at the others."

"No need. I want her. I want the girl in the red Ao dai, please."

The clerk looked at me for a few seconds. I thought he was going to say no. He seemed to be studying me. Slowly, he nodded his head and said, "All right. She is yours for the evening." I was surprised by his sudden propriety. I also noticed, for the first time, that his English was as good, no, better than mine. I said, "I'd like to order a bottle of champagne." A smile came to his face and he said, "Will *Korbel* be satisfactory?"

"Korbel will be fine." I never heard of Korbel before but figured it had to be good champagne.

"This girl," he said, "is special. You are correct in ordering champagne."

"Thank you." I was puzzled by his compliment.

"That will be forty dollars which includes the champagne." I didn't know if that was a fair price, or not, but I didn't argue. The clerk said he would personally escort the young woman to my room. I looked back at the beautiful Vietnamese girl and she smiled at me. I smiled back and she looked down again. I never knew that a prostitute could be shy. The clerk led us out of the Parlor and guided Ernie and me back to our rooms. On the way I wondered what he meant by *special*. I thought, "Why is this girl special and why is the old clerk so protective of her?" The thought left me as my hotel room door closed behind me.

I unpacked and then washed my hands and face. My teeth also got a good brushing, as did my hair and mustache. A knock on the door came as I was slapping on some after-shave. Nervously, I walked over and opened it. She was standing there, holding a large paper bag. The old clerk stood behind her and stared at me. I smiled at him. He bowed, then walked away.

"Hello," I said. She smiled, meekly, and I moved aside to let her enter. She passed me the bag as she walked by. My eyes followed her rythmic movement as she walked over to the bed, sat down, and began to unlace her black, ankle-top shoes. Opening the bag, I removed the large champagne bottle and was happily surprised to find an ice bucket and two champagne glasses.

When I turned back around, the girl was unbuttoning her dress. She slipped it down over her shoulders, stood up, and it fell to the floor. She wore only pink panties. Her breasts were a nice, round shape and ended in very large and pointed nipples. Gathering courage, I walked over to the night table and put down the ice bucket, champagne, and glasses. As I twirled the bottle into the ice, she lay back on the bed, on her side, with her head in her hand. It was the most provocative sight I had ever seen. I stood there, frozen, not knowing what to do.

A year after this awkward moment I would see the movie, *The Graduate*. The film would instantly transport me back to Saigon and the hotel room with the beautiful girl on the bed. The only difference was, this lovely, young girl wasn't Mrs. Robinson.

The leggy, long-haired siren was waving bye-bye to me. In Vietnamese the gesture means hello or come here. I grabbed the bottle of champagne, the glasses, and sat down on the bed. She smiled and took the bottle from my hand. She undid the wire but couldn't pop the cork. Not giving up, the persistant young woman placed the bottle between her thighs and tried again, but to no avail. She just didn't have the strength. I put my hand on her shoulder and said, "Please." She passed me the bottle and I began to work the cork with my fingers. The girl sat up behind me and grabbed me around the chest. I felt cold, hard nipples pressing into my back as she began to unbutton my shirt. Then, it hit me. The Colt. I still had the pistol in my waistband. Before I could think of anything she was already unfastening the bottom button.

"*POP!*" The cork went flying across the room and bounced off the wall. Bubbly froth spilled out and down the bottle, splashing her hands and my lap. She was laughing as I jumped up, keeping my back to her. I pulled the 45 from the waistband and covertly slipped it under the mattress. As I turned to face her, she took the foaming bottle from my hand. She put it to her lips and took a sip. A little stream ran down her chin.

She giggled and patted the bed. I sat down next to her. She passed me the bottle and I took a drink. The champagne was cool and the bubbles tickled my nose. The young woman looked me in the eyes and unfastened the last shirt button. I placed the bottle of Korbel on the night table and then she removed my shirt. She held it over the floor, then dropped it on top of her Ao dai.

Playfully, she pushed me down on the bed and unbuckled my belt. Her large, brown nipples swayed over my face and I couldn't resist the urge to kiss them. She purred in pleasure and then began to unbutton my champagne-soaked pants. I still had my boots on so she sat up and unlaced them. With some effort, she pulled them off and removed my socks. A puzzled look came to her face, then a frown, as she stared at my right foot. The big toe, without a nail, and the other scars from battle confused her. She looked at me and I said, "Bullet wound. It's ok." She smiled and began to remove my pants. She dropped them on top of my shirt.

She worked her way up my body, slowly massaging my legs as she went. As she brushed over my ever-increasing hardness, she noticed and smiled at me. She continued her trek and stopped at my chest. I had never felt so relaxed, and excited, at the same time. She rested her cheek on my shoulder and began to rub my sparse chest hairs. Two large eyes stared into mine as delicate fingers began to play with my handlebar mustache. She twirled the ends between her fingers and softly giggled. She kissed my cheek, then sat up. Reaching across me, her hand grabbed the bottle of champagne. I sat up and picked up the two glasses. She poured and then placed the bottle back on the night table.

I passed her a glass and said, "Cheers!" She smiled, we *clinked* glasses, and sipped. Her nose wrinkled and I could tell that the bubbles were having the same effect on her. She looked at me, pointed to her chest, and said, "Su Lei." (Sue-Lee).

"Su Lei," I repeated. "Your name is Su Lei?"

"Su Lei," she said again, pointing, "Su Lei." I patted my chest and replied, "Mike."

"My."

"No," I said, "Mike. Mike."

"My. My." I laughed, saying, "Close enough."

We finished the champagne in silence and Su Lei put the empty glasses on the table. The incandescent light from the lamp created a sparkling effect on the remaining drops in the glasses. It was a splash of rainbow that spilled over onto the bed and half-covered our bodies. Su Lei noticed the light show and laughed. Her chest was freckled with tiny dots of light. I slowly touched each one with the tips of my fingers. She threw her head back and a cascade of hair fell like a waterfall. Most of it fell behind her shoulders, but a long shock fell over the front of her left shoulder. It covered my hand and it felt like the soft touch of silk.

Su Lei gently pushed me down on my back and lay half on top of me, pressing a smooth leg into my groin. I returned the favor and cupped a firm, round breast. I then kissed her on the lips. She purred and responded by pressing her warm, soft body closer to mine. We hugged and carressed each other for minutes. Our hands went places that aroused our bodies to a heightened sensitivity. Her nipples were rock-hard and pointing up about half an inch. I took turns with them, gently rolling the long, brown tips between my fingers and lips. Her hand moved down and found my hardness protruding above the waistband of my shorts. She quickly, and deftly, removed them, and then slowly went to gentle work on my physical and emotional excitement.

Michael W. Mason

Electricity shot through me as Su Lei carressed me into an even higher and *harder* state of arousal. She slowly moved her nails up and down my erection. If there was a heaven on earth, I had found it in a small, antiquated hotel in Saigon, South Vietnam.

My hand moved between her thighs and up to her wet panties. I slipped them off and her *woman scent* enticed me. I found her crotch to be surprisingly smooth and hairless. My fingers slowly, and gently, massaged her, and when she arched her back, a finger slipped into her. Su Lei began to move up and down as I took an erect, hard nipple into my mouth. I tickled it between my teeth, with my tongue, and she went into spasms.

Our bodies were glistening with perspiration and we sparkeled under the light of the lamp. She pulled me on top of her, reached down, and guided my hardness into her. She thrust upwards and I entered her slowly and smoothly.

I looked at her face and saw that her eyes were closed. She had a slight smile and her moans began to build in magnitude. My head dropped to the side of her face and I kissed her ear. She moaned louder, thrusted harder and faster, and we moved as one. It was a synchronous ballet of two bodies moving in unison.

As hard as I tried, I knew this time of rapture was about to end. I was building to a climactic finish when, suddenly, Su Lei stopped moving, and constricted herself around my swelling excitement.

It was at that moment that she took command of this night of passion and erotica. I was a passenger on a ride that wouldn't stop. This encounter was one that I had only imagined in my boyhood dreams. Su Lei prodded me, massaged me, stroked me, and tickled me. She found spots on my pliable body that, when manipulated, sent shivers down my spine. Here I was, the Baby Scout gunslinger, and helpless in the arms of a sensuous, young woman. Being in control has always been important to me, yet I let myself be led in the ways of exotic love. In a scout ship I was invincible. Here, in this hotel room, I let myself be controlled. It made sense. I was being taught a lesson in love-making that I would never forget.

We held each other and rolled about the bed. We knelt, stood, sat, kneeled, and lay on our sides, stomachs, and backs. There was no position we didn't try. Su Lei used her long hair to sweep the length of my body. She did this slow and purred in Vietnamese as she went. I didn't understand a word but loved every brush stroke of her glistening, raven-black hair.

All the while, the tenderness remained. The sex was never rough or awkward. One moment flowed into another. Our love-making never escalated beyond gentle. It was strong but always soft. When I held her in my arms I had no fantasies. She was real. My world was Su Lei, and her passion and mine became the love of a lifetime.

We came together three times in three hours. The things she did to me would never be believed in *hometown* America. We explored each other's bodies. Hers was slender, smooth, and almost golden in color. Her hair smelled fresh and its extreme length was always wrapped around her body in some erotic fashion. Su Lei's large eyes were as black as her hair, and they peeked at me through slanted, oval slits of long eyelashes. Her lips were full and pouty. At times she seemed older, maybe twenty five. Using our fingers to communicate, I learned that she was nineteen.

I slowly moved down her soft, smooth body. Her nipples were always hard and her stomach, flat. There wasn't a hair on her and her buttocks were round and firm. I wondered how she would look in ten or fifteen years. The Vietnamese didn't seem to age very well at all.

Su Lei looked taller than her five-foot, eight inches. She was perfectly proportioned, right down to her toes. During our exploration of bodies, I discovered that everything was where it was supposed to be. *It wasn't further back* as Tom Donald had told me. I felt like an idiot for half-believing him.

Su Lei slid out of bed and beckoned me with a glance over her shoulder. I watched her enter the bathroom, then heard the shower come alive with a rattle of old plumbing. I got up and walked into clouds of steam. Su Lei grabbed me around the waist as I joined her in the steamy shower.

We stayed in the shower for a long time. She was thrilled to use my *Prell* shampoo and conditioner. She let me wash her hair as well as her body. She returned the favor and I immediately got excited. She noticed and then laughed as she looked into my pleading eyes. She jumped up and wrapped her legs around my waist. She slowly lowered herself onto me and we rocked together, slowly, under the warm spray of water. We came together in a soapy embrace of kisses.

My knees buckled and I slowly lowered us to the tile floor. She sat on my lap, legs wrapped around me, long after my physical enhancement had waned. We stayed like this for half an hour, just kissing and holding each other. She seemed to need, to want the holding more than I. Her eyes were also her betrayer. Even in the shower I could tell tears from the trickling water that ran down her cheeks in rivulets. Su Lei was crying.

    I put my hand behind her head and gently forced her cheek to my shoulder. She sobbed and her tears ran down my chest. I patted her head and stroked her. She looked up at me and forced a smile. I kissed a tear away. She buried her face into the crook of my neck and shoulder, and just cried. I whispered her name a few times and patted her back. She squeezed me tight and just held on as she got whatever was bothering her out of her system.

    It was at this moment that I discovered I had real feelings for this amazing, sensitive girl. I truly felt for her, and cared for her deeply. I found myself falling in love with a Saigon prostitute during what was supposed to be…just a *one night stand*.

    Su Lei lifted her head and looked into my eyes. The shower spray cleansed her tear-stained face and I kissed her on the forehead. Her sobbing slowly subsided and I gave her a little tickle to her ribs. She managed a slight smile and we sat there, in the swirling, soapy water until it turned clear and whirlpooled down the drain.

    Slowly, she stood and offered me a hand. I took it and she pulled me up. I was amazed at her strength. We exited the shower and left Su Lei's troubles, whatever they were, behind.

    I stood behind her, in front of the bathroom mirror. She let me comb her damp hair and it hung straight down to just below her knees. It was longer than I first thought. We stared at each other in the mirror and she pointed to the comb, then my hair and mustache. I gave her the pocket comb and she shaped my mustache into a handlebar. She then combed my hair and seemed amazed at how black it looked when wet. She held a handful of her own hair up to mine to compare the color. She giggled and I noticed that a few of my hairs were prominently grey. Premature grey runs in the family. Fortunately, baldness does not.

    Su Lei put on her panties and one of my green undershirts. Never in my life had I seen a *T-Shirt* worn so well. I put on a pair of *Levi* cutoffs. We lay on the bed, her head resting on my chest. I didn't smoke the entire evening. I didn't feel the need.

    The only word she spoke the entire evening was "My." I guessed she knew more English but didn't pressure her to speak. If she had wanted to speak to me in English, she would have.

Whenever I spoke to her, she smiled. I got the impression she understood a lot more than she let on. Although she didn't talk, her eyes and facial expressions spoke volumes. When she wasn't smiling, her lips seemed to be pouting. I thought it cute and very sexy. Su Lei seemed to have similar thoughts about my body hair and speckled, blue eyes.

"*Bam! Bam! Bam!*" The loud pounding on the door startled us and Su Lei hugged me tight.

"Mason, you in there? Open up!" I sighed. It was Ernie. A laughing, squeaky voice also betrayed his young, female accomplice. I shrugged to Su Lei, got up, and opened the door. The young girl rushed in and jumped on the bed with Su Lei. She began to jabber in Vietnamese and Su Lei laughed at whatever the tiny girl was saying. The talkative child was wearing one of Ernie's green, jungle shirts and nothing else. It had ridden up to her waist and Su Lei caught me gawking. I looked away, embarrassed, and she laughed at my red-faced guilt. Su Lei, still laughing, helped her young friend become more modest.

Ernie staggered in, half-a-bottle of Jack Daniels in his hand. He took a swig, then passed the square, glass bottle to me. I took a gulp and coughed. Su Lei looked at me but didn't laugh. I never could drink whiskey straight out of the bottle. Ernie laughed and said, "What a night, huh?" He walked over and collapsed on the bed. Su Lei and her girlfriend (I found out she was fourteen), laughed and started talking again. The little girl suddenly got sad and Su Lei hugged her and whispered something in her ear. The adolescent prostitute wiped away a tear and smiled. I had just witnessed a kind of *Mother-Daughter* talk.

The little girl was cuter without makeup, and had a body that was too developed for her years. She reminded me of the mature girl in sixth grade that none of us boys could figure out. Her name was Marsha and she was a female anomaly. Her mind was young, but her body looked fully developed. We boys teased her a lot because she had very large breasts. Most of our mothers, or older sisters, didn't have breasts that big. Neither did any of the teachers.

It was a confusing time of sexual discovery and Marsha bore the brunt of boyish ignorance and cruelty. I didn't understand that Marsha was on the threshold of becoming a young woman. She was developing into something we would eventually desire.

I couldn't pronounce her name so I called her babysan. She reminded me a little of Mei, the Baby Scout hootch girl. Babysan was very short, maybe four-six or eight, and had black hair that hung to just below her shoulders. Her cheeks were puffy and her eyes were tiny, oval slits. I didn't know, at the time, if Ernie knew how old she was. She had an *hourglass* figure, like Marsha, and I think Ernie chose her because of her breasts. Babysan was a fourteen year old prostitute, for reasons unknown to me. I never asked and never found out why.

For an hour, Ernie rambled on about his night and prowess in bed. Su Lei saw my polite torture and would pat me on the leg ever so often. Ernie chugged the rest of the whiskey and dropped the empty bottle on the floor. He was blitzed but still frisky enough to tackle his young consort and start wrestling with her on the bed. As the two rolled about, something shiny went flying through the air. It landed on the floor with a dull thud. Su Lei saw it and immediately turned and gave me a sad looking pout. I shrugged and frowned back. Now I knew what kind of weapon Ernie had brought with him to Saigon.

The shiny, nickel plated, over-under derringer gleamed in the low incandescence of the table lamp. It looked just like the *Mattel Shooting Shell* toy gun that I had as a kid. I reached over Su Lei to pick it up. She grabbed the waist of my cutoffs to keep me from falling off the bed. The derringer was heavier than it looked and I knew it was loaded. Su Lei opened the night table drawer and I put it in. She didn't close it.

She stared at me, with a pout, and put her hands up as if to say, "Ok, Mike. Where is it?" I knew what she meant. If Ernie had a gun, well, I probably had one, too. I shrugged, got up, and reached under the mattress. I pulled out the Colt 45 and tried a weak smile on Su Lei. She wasn't buying it. She pouted and pointed to the drawer. I placed the Colt next to the tiny derringer. Su Lei closed the drawer and waved a finger at me. I must have really looked like the proberbial *kid in the cookie jar* because her pout slowly formed into a smile. She then hugged me as if to say, "It's ok, My. This happens all the time."

A few minutes later, Babysan was helping an incoherent Ernie to the door. I was amazed that he was still conscious and able to walk. I grabbed his derringer and slipped it into his back pocket. Babysan saw me do it and simply smiled as she navigated an inebriated Ernie out the door. I watched until they safely reached their room.

I locked the door and turned back to Su Lei. She smiled and pulled off the undershirt. I dropped my cutoffs, forgetting I was not wearing any underwear. I felt embarrassed, again, and Su Lei laughed as I jumped into her outstretched arms. Apparently, I was forgiven for the indiscretion with the Colt 45.

I slipped under the sheet and she joined me, wrapping an arm and leg around me. I kissed her and she saw how tired I was. She rubbed my inner thigh and soon I was fully aroused. Her hand came out from beneath the sheet and I saw pink panties go sailing across the room.

Su Lei moved on top of me and rode me slow and steady. As she ground her pelvis into mine, her hands went up and through her hair. Sounds erupted from her throat that echoed like melodic humming. I just lay there and let her do all the work. Her breasts were slowly heaving and the nipples were fully erect. I held them, one in each hand, and her moaning got louder. I was mesmerized, half-asleep, and half-aware of what was happening.

For half an hour she worked her magic on me. When we came, it was an explosion that rocked us to the very core. She screamed and collapsed on top of me. I reached out and hugged her to me. Her woman-scent enveloped both of us and I sadly realized that this night was never again to be repeated.

I hugged her tight and grew smaller inside her. I stroked her hair and for the first time, she seemed fragile, almost delicate. Su Lei fell asleep on top of me. We were still as one and her breathing tickled my chest hairs. I held her close until I, too, fell asleep. My last thoughts were of flying into war and how unimportant it now seemed.

The dream came to me and it was very puzzling. I saw myself swimming through a dark sea of cigarettes and sampans. The dream ended with a pair of coal-black eyes beckoning me.

"My, come for me."

"Where are you?"

"I don't know. Find me. Don't forget me, My."

"What happened? Where are you, Su Lei?"

"Find me, My."

"Where are you, Su Lei? Where are you? Where are you?"

The dream slowly faded to black, but not before I saw a heart-shaped face staring up at me from below. Long, black hair partially covered the young woman's features. Dark, red blood streamed from her eyes. Quivering full lips asked, "Why, My. Why you kill me?"

I woke with a start. Only the weight of Su Lei's body kept me from rolling out of bed. Beads of perspiration covered my body and I was shaking. I tried to settle down and it was only Su Lei's steady breathing, and closeness, that helped me to regain my composure. After about fifteen minutes, I drifted back to sleep. This dream, or vision, would confound me for weeks. After that, it would terrify me.

I woke in the morning with the table lamp still burning. It had a low wattage bulb and it had never occured to me to turn it off. Su Lei was asleep, on her side, and I had an arm around her. She was facing me and had an arm around my waist.

My Seiko watch said it was six a.m. Drunk, or sober, I always woke at six. The Army had trained me well. Su Lei woke to my movements and yawned. We lay there for half an hour, just holding each other. She got up first and waved at me to join her in the shower. We lazily took our time and made love standing up, covered in shampoo bubbles. I didn't know how I managed to rise to the occasion again, but Su Lei's ministrations were not to be denied.

In silence, we dried each other and dressed. I put on civvies and she, the red Ao dai with golden suns. We hugged for a long minute before I reluctantly let her go. She walked to the door and opened it. I said, "Su Lei, wait." Taking out my wallet, I took out a twenty and placed it in her hand. She hesitated but took it. She hugged, then kissed me before running out the door. Halfway down the hall she stopped and turned around. She was pouting and I almost laughed during the sadness of this moment.

"My," she said, "see me later, please."

"*Damn!*" I said aloud. "You can talk." She turned, and then she was gone. I went back in my room and instantly felt alone. I opened the night table, grabbed my Colt 45 and tucked it into my waistband. After packing and turning off the lamp, the creaky, wood door closed on a very empty room.

My slight hangover and growling stomach led me straight to the hotel dining room. A few guests (soldiers), were nursing their own hangovers with *Bloody Marys* and *Screwdrivers*. The window table was vacant and I sat there. The sun was low on the horizon and the rays of light coming through the glass cast my shadow across the room. The sudden darkening caused heads to turn in my direction. Even the lone waiter stopped to witness the cause of the sun's eclipse. I shrugged my shoulders and scooted the chair back a few inches. The room lightened and the curious went back to their morning chores of serving and being served.

The menu had an English translation and I was happy to see a *bacon and eggs* special. The waiter poured me a cup of steaming coffee and took my order. Sitting back, I lit up and the wicker chair protested with its familiar, scratchy sound. The smoke-rings floated across the room and came under attack by the incoming rays of sunlight. It was a reminder of the war that raged on with or without a lone Baby Scout gunslinger. My mind was in a melancholic state as I watched the smoke-rings dissipate in the tracers of sunfire. Even during rare, wistful interludes, the reality of war persisted. In Vietnam, it was the one truth that I could never escape. It always followed me with a vengeance.

The waiter returned all too quickly with my repaste. I should have known that *lighting up* would hasten the morning feast. With smoke slowly streaming from my nose, I snubbed out the cigarette and reached for the green, linen napkin.

The hotel clerk entered the room, stopped just inside the doors, and slowly moved his head in a 180-degree sweep. A smile came to his face as his eyes locked on mine. He walked toward me and all I could think of was, "Uh Oh!"

His stride was purposeful and I wondered what it was that I did. He stopped in front of me and in perfect English asked, "How was your evening, sir?" There was a slight smile on his lips, so I figured there wasn't anything to worry about.

"Fine, sir. It was a nice time."

"May I sit?"

"Uh, sure." I stood without hesitation. It was more instinct than manners. I was taught early, and often, that you always stood for ladies and the elderly.

"Mr. Mason, what do you know about Su Lei?"

"I was going to ask you that question."

"Yes, of course," he said. He got comfortable in his chair and then proceeded to tell me a story…a tale of sorrow that brought sadness to his eyes.

"Su Lei is my niece," he said. "Her family, and my sister, were killed last March in My Lai."

"My Lai. That's a village, right?"

"Yes. Su Lei was visiting me here, in Saigon, when American soldiers attacked and burned the village. Many died. Su Lei went back the next day and saw the carnage. Friends who survived the slaughter told her how her parents died. They also told her to leave as the Americans were rounding up survivors for questioning."

The waiter returned to refill my coffee cup and the old man paused. He removed his wire-rimmed glasses and wiped them with a green, linen napkin. I thanked the waiter and he left. Su Lei's uncle put his glasses back on and picked up where he left off. The story got more interesting and brought me into the middle of a secret, government conspiracy.

"My niece returned here and told me what happened. I believe we are the only ones, outside of My Lai, who know what happened. Now, I'm sorry to say, you know."

"Why are you telling me this?" I dropped my fork and swallowed a piece of egg-soaked toast with a painful gulp. His eyes bore through me and never blinked.

"Am I going to get in trouble? Will the Army come looking for me?"

"No, Mr. Mason. Not as long as you say nothing. Su Lei, me, and you, are the only ones who know about this. It must be kept secret. Can you imagine what would happen to Su Lei, or you, if the American government discovered that we knew what happened at My Lai?"

"I guess we'd probably be put away somewhere…prison or something?"

"That's right, or something. Prison or worse. I suspect it would be worse for Su Lei."

"Mr. Uh…"

"Phuoc. My name is Phuoc."

"Ok, Mr. Phuoc. Why did you seek me out? I saw you come in here looking for me. It wasn't just to tell me this, was it?"

The old man smiled and said, "No. I was going to tell you that Su Lei likes you. She wants to see you again." I sat straight up when I heard that.

"Why? I mean, why does she want to see me?" The old man smiled as he saw my look of eager anticipation.

"You're different from the others. I watch over Su Lei and make sure that only the right men choose her. Your brash friend, for instance. I never would have let him take her. You, however, were different. There was a shyness about you, especially when it came to the girls. I saw your *lack of experience* with women. Your innocence showed through, Mr. Mason."

"*Damn*! Was it that obvious?"

"Yes, Mr. Mason. Su Lei knew it, too."

"Where is she now?"

Phuoc smiled and said, "Su Lei no longer works here. She told me as soon as she left your room. She'll continue to live here, though, waitress, and will continue her studies. My niece is trying to save enough money to go to the United States. That's why she was whoring here. I didn't like it but she said she'd do it elsewhere if she had to. I gave in, thinking she'd be safer with me than in some other brothel."

"Will the hotel manager allow her to stay here without, well, you know?"

"Whoring? Yes, Mr. Mason. I'm the manager, and the owner."

"I see. What about Su Lei's village? Her family? What really happened?"

"I only know what my niece told me. Why the people were killed, I don't know. Now, there's just me, a few friends, and you."

"That's what I don't understand. Why me? You could have just ignored Su Lei's request and let me leave. You and your niece would never have to see me again. Why even involve me in this?"

"It was her wish, Mr. Mason. Yes, I could have let you go, without telling you, but she made it clear that she wanted to see you again. It was my idea to tell you about the slaughter at My Lai."

"You figured it would involve me in something that I couldn't just walk away from."

"Something like that. I'm sorry for the deception." Mr. Phuoc bowed slightly and stared at me, waiting for an answer. I didn't hesitate, as there could be only one answer.

"Tell Su Lei, I'll be back. I want to see her again, too." With these words, I surpassed the *crime* of just knowing about My Lai. I became directly involved. Mr. Phuoc and Su Lei were wanted criminals, even if the American government didn't know who they were, or what they knew. Now, a naive gunslinger would be added to the *wanted poster*.

The hotel owner looked at me, then began to rise. "Wait," I said, "What about Su Lei? You said she wanted to see me." Mr. Phuoc produced a pen and wrote on a napkin.

"Here is the hotel's address and phone number. Call when you can come back. I'll see to it that Su Lei is here." He passed me the napkin and waited for an answer.

"Tell her, I'll be back as soon as possible. Ok?"

The old man smiled. "Yes. I'll tell her. Remember our secret, too. Above all, Su Lei must be protected. No one can ever know what she knows about My Lai."

"I understand. Tell me, Mr. Phuoc, how did you learn to speak English so well?"

"School, Mr. Mason. Like you, I went to school. Not all Vietnamese plow rice paddies behind a water buffalo."

"Sorry. I didn't mean…"

"I know you didn't. I apologize." He bowed slightly and told me about his schooling in Saigon and how, after graduating high school, he traveled to Europe and took classes at various universities in Paris, Munich, and Zurich. He never got a degree but learned three languages and English. He studied economics and business, and eventually opened the Sun Hotel. He met his future wife in Paris. She was Chinese and an art student. They had no children of their own. Mrs. Phuoc died on the bloody streets of Saigon during the early days of the American occupation of the city. She was in the wrong place at the wrong time…a hapless victim of a VC grenade attack on a popular outdoor market. Since the tragedy, Su Lei became the daughter he never had and, to some extent, the wife he sorely missed.

We both stood and shook hands. His grip was surprisingly strong.

"I'll keep the secret, Mr. Phuoc."

"You'll have to, Mr. Mason. Su Lei's life, our lives, depend on it." He bowed, turned, and walked away.

"Mr. Phuoc," I yelled after him. "Tell Su Lei…My will be back. My will come back, soon."

He laughed over his shoulder and replied, "I will." He walked out of the dining room, still laughing.

My breakfast was cold but I was too hungry to care. I ate slowly and digested my food, and everything the old man had told me. I didn't think I was in big trouble but I worried about what might happen to Su Lei if the American government was trying to cover-up a major *SNAFU*. I sopped up the remaining yellow egg residue with a scrap of toast and wolfed it down. Chasing it with coffee, I sat back and felt better about the morning and its strange tidings.

I lit up and inhaled deeply. My mind calmed and the only thought I had was, "How do I get back to Saigon to visit the girl who was causing me so much wonderful anxiety?" I thought of flying my next mission, and

Su Lei entered my mind. My thoughts turned to home, and the beautiful prostitute was there, again. I had it bad.

Ernie walked in the dining room as I was thinking about Su Lei and ways to wrangle milk runs to Saigon. He sat down and began to regale me with the exploits of his evening. I listened patiently for ten minutes and then told him my night was also a good one. Ernie had a terrible hangover, so he ordered a screwdriver with his pancakes and eggs. He didn't remember coming to my room. He didn't even remember the name of his adolescent companion.

I went up to the register to pay the bill. The waiter said that breakfast was on the house, courtesy of the hotel manager. After tipping the waiter a few dollars, I walked out of the Saigon Sun Hotel. The street was noisy with scooters, mopeds, and rusty chains of old bicycles. Few eyes locked with mine. Americans were a familiar sight in downtown Saigon.

"Wait up," said Ernie. I hailed a cab and we were picked up in an old Ford sedan. Ernie told the driver to take us to the PX. On the way, the cabbie begged us for the use of our *PX Cards*. We both said, "No!" He wouldn't let up until we agreed to buy him a carton of *Kool* cigarettes. American tobacco is a hot item on the black market. The cabbie would sell them for many times the actual price.

It was about ten, Sunday morning, when we arrived at the Post Exchange. It was crowded with people, mostly soldiers, some sailors, and a few civilians. They were looking for bargains to either drink, smoke, wear, or send home.

We bought cigarettes and watches. *Seiko* watches were all the rage with the American servicemen. The Vietnam War probably did more for that particular watch company than a million dollars worth of advertising ever could. The American soldier put the Seiko Watch Company on the map. I would keep my new watch for twenty years. It ran great, up until the day I lost it at a South Florida beach. It's probably still ticking somewhere in a hundred feet of water.

I also bought a cheap *Kodak* movie camera and a charm bracelet for Su Lei. In my mind there was no doubt that I would see her again. Ernie bought two bottles of Jack Daniels and a small holster. I asked him sarcastically, "What's that for, Ernie?" He didn't get the sarcasm and told me about the derringer. He had no memory of the night in my room.

"Why a derringer, man? It's more useless than my Colt."

"I bought it from a Slick crewman. He only wanted thirty bucks for it. Besides, you never know what might happen."

Michael W. Mason

"What are you talking about?"

"Mike, why do you think that *Slicker* had it?"

"I don't know. Up close fighting, like with a knife?"

"Get real, Mason. Don't you know what the VC do to captured Americans?"

"I don't plan on getting captured."

"That's the point. I don't either. The derringer is my way out."

"You're kidding, Ernie?"

"Nope. I'm not going to let some slant cut my jewels off and stick-em in my mouth. The derringer goes where I go."

"Well, I've thought about that, too. I don't think I'd ever shoot myself, though."

"What, then? Blow yourself up with a frag or a Willie?"

"Well, yeah. Something like that. Might as well take some of them with me."

"You and your Cowboy holster. You're living in a movie."

"Maybe. But, it's my movie and I'm the good guy."

"Mike, you're the kind of guy who doesn't go home."

"You don't know that, Ernie."

"Hell, I don't. Gunslingers usually don't live to ride, or fly, into the sunset. You don't retire to the ranch and you don't get the girl."

"What are you talking about, you idiot."

"I don't know. You just seem to live differently from the rest of us, like you're always in a romantic, dream world. I'm not the only one who's noticed it."

"Oh, yeah. Like who?"

"Well, Lieutenant Reese for one. Mei has mentioned it, too."

"Mei? Our babysan?"

"Yep. She's worried about you. She thinks you're going to die here because you're a dreamer in a nightmare world."

"You're kidding?"

"Nope. That's what she said. You know her better than me. You should know."

"She never told me."

"I'm surprised. You two are almost like brother and sister." Most of us would be jealous but we know you're just friends."

"I wonder why she never told me?"

"Because she loves you, you moron, like a big brother."

"That's funny. She takes care of us like we were her kids."

"I know. With you it's different, though. She's afraid to jinx you, I think. Anyway, that's all I know."

"Ok. Thanks, Ernie."

"Just keep this gunslinging crap in reality, ok"

"I'll think about it. You keep that derringer out of your mouth."

"We'll see. That'll depend on Charlie, I guess."

"Yeah. Everything over here depends on Charlie."

We screwed around in the giant store for an hour. It reminded me of home. All the while, I couldn't forget what Ernie had told me. It had never occured to me that the other Baby Scouts were worried about my mental status. I was also upset that Mei thought I was going to die. For the first time, I had doubts about my self-proclaimed role as a hired gunslinger in Southeast Asia.

The cab was waiting for us when we left the PX. We gave the driver his carton of cigarettes and told him to take us to the airfield. He was a slow driver and it took twenty minutes to get there. I tipped him in dollars instead of military script or Vietnamese money. He was ecstatic. I never used the military *Monopoly* Money. American green got me more service and greater respect.

The cabbie dropped us off, gunned the engine, and rumbled down the road, leaving behind clouds of black smoke. We showed our *temporary duty passes* to the guard and he passed us through the gate. We walked to the airfield and sat under the only tree by the terminal. We sat in silence and waited for our return-flight to the war.

A Slick, bearing the Centaur emblem, flared to a hover fifty yards away. As usual, the Army was punctual. We grabbed our sandbags and ran to the Huey. The pilot got us airborne in seconds.

I left Saigon feeling good about myself. It was a refreshing diversion, but I was ready to rejoin the war. There was also a little sadness. As Saigon disappeared from view, my thoughts turned to a vision of a beautiful, Vietnamese girl. Somehow, some way, I would get a milk run back to the big city and the Sun Hotel. After all, being the Flight Line Chief of the Baby Scouts has its perks.

The terrible secret that Mr. Phuoc shared with me, gave new meaning to my life in Vietnam. The butchery at My Lai wasn't just ordinary gossip to spread around.

This was dangerous, covert stuff. Stuff that could get me hurt or even killed. I vowed silently, to myself, never to mention the subject of My Lai again. The deaths of the villagers, Su Lei's family...it made me wonder why she wanted to continue a relationship with me, an American. After her life was turned upside down, you'd think her attitude would be anything but understanding and friendly. I thought about it all the way back to Cu Chi.

Ernie was playing with his derringer and new holster. "Another new gunslinger," I thought to myself.

"Ernie!" I yelled. He looked at me with that red, freckled face of his.

"We're both a piece of work, you know."

"*Fucking-A*," he said.

I laughed. Ernie had a way of making profanity sound funny. I looked past the starboard gunner and saw Cu Chi on the horizon. Soon, I would have my hands wrapped around the familiar stock of my M60. For a fleeting moment, thoughts of R & R, and Su Lei, were absent. Something inside me clicked on. I was in Baby Scout mode and ready for doing what I loved best...hunting my prey! God help me. I missed the killing.

BABY SCOUT

Michael W. Mason

TWELVE

THE LAST FLIGHT OF #395

As soon as my feet hit the dirt of the flight line, I lost my lust for battle. Instead of assigning myself to hunter-killer missions, I checked on squadron milk runs to Saigon. There was a scheduled Slick flight to the harbor on the following week. I bribed the door gunner with a carton of cigarettes to take his place. I also had to take his next shift on guard duty. The crew chief ok'd it because he knew of my reputation with weapons and because I was a Baby Scout. I couldn't have been happier as I got back in the war.

I assigned myself to dawn and dusk patrols. It felt good to be in the air again and to cradle my M60. The notches I carved in the stock numbered seven. Seven kills. Most of them were unconfirmed but you never forget when you kill a man. You never forget and it weighs on your soul like a millstone.

I would have had more kills but I stopped carving up the machine gun. I did my job but I wasn't the same anymore. The love of fighting and killing was gone. The thrill of flying and the hunt, however, was still there. So was the killing. It just wasn't fun anymore.

Dawn and dusk patrols were uneventful. At least I got to test-fire my M60. After one such day, Tom Donald came over to my bunk and asked how my R & R was.

I said, "Great. Best time I ever had."

"No. No," he said, "How were the women?" I smiled at him.

"Just one, and she was the best." Tom sat down. He looked confused.

"Mike, the Saigon girls are the worst lovers in Asia. They just lie there. I was joking with you before you left, about them being good."

"Tom, I guess I found the only good girl in the city." He pressed me for details but I didn't tell him much.

As he walked away I said, "You know, Tom, it's in the right place and it doesn't go sideways." He laughed.

"Next time, Mason, I might not save your ass in the Triangle." He kept walking back to his bunk, laughing all the way. I went back to cleaning my Colt and shining the holster.

Michael W. Mason

The next morning I painted a little shark's mouth with sharp, white teeth on my Loach. It seemed appropriate as the Cobras were flying with the Baby Scouts more often. The following day there was an awards ceremony. I received a Purple Heart and My third Air medal. Tom got the DFC (Distinguished Flying Cross). We all congratulated him. You never got kudos for getting a Purple Heart. There is no pride in receiving one; only memories of pain and horror.

The following week I had a search and destroy mission in the Go Dau Ha Province. I flew as observer since I was still breaking in W1 Jimmy Latham. The rear gunner was Ritchie Ritchfield. He was a relatively new Scout and a pothead. He showed up on the flight line singing, and reeking of weed. I sighed and said aloud, "*Hell*! This mission is off to a great start." I took the box of grenades out of the back and put it in front. Ritchie looked at me, smiled, and didn't say a word. As we took off, I thought, "*Damn*! I should have grounded him."

The flight was going well. Mr. Latham was pretty good and loved to go fast. I pointed out things for him to look for and he said, "Ok. Ok." Just outside the village is the Go Dau Ha bridge. It's a small, steel, expansion bridge built by Army engineers. It arched over the narrow river and had communication wires strung under the half-moon curve of the span.

I watched the river bank as it blurred-by at 90 knots. We were going way too fast and I looked up to tell the pilot to slow to forty. I never got the chance. In front of the ship was the looming, grey structure of the bridge.

It happened so fast I never had a chance to feel terror consume my gut and soul. I yelled, "No! No!" as we flew under the span and into the commo wires at 100 miles an hour.

The Loach was *clotheslined* under the main rotor hub. The baby warbird struggled vainly against the wires. They snapped and whipped about the rotor blades and control linkage.

"No, God! Not like this," I screamed in my mind as we hit the concrete-hard water at almost a hundred miles an hour. The Loach hit skids-first, then pitchpoled end over end. The front canopy and tail boom were ripped away in an ear-piercing screech of tearing metal. I kept a death-grip on the seatbelt portion of my safety harness. The Loach flipped over and over. I waited for the life-ending explosion that never came.

The ship went into a roll and then began to skip down the river like a stone. Rushing water slammed into me and the box of grenades became a missile launcher, sending frags and Willies ricocheting off my chicken plate and flight helmet. My yellow-tinted visor cracked as it absorbed a direct hit from one of the grenades. The ruined, metal remains of #395 continued its slide down the black, opaque water of the unforgiving river.

The shattered Loach slowed and came to an abrupt halt. For the better part of a second, #395 floated on top of the muddy water. I got out half a, "*Damn!*" before my mouth filled with dirty water and the cracked shell of the finest aeroscout ship in the fleet sank like a rock.

My hands struggled with the safety harness as we sank into the murky abyss of leech infested water. Daylight became twilight and the yellow sun, like the crew of the doomed warbird, was swallowed up by the liquid blackness. I reached for my knife, but it was gone. Panic was beginning to claim the last of my rational thoughts when the harness buckle opened.

Before I could shed the restraint, the pilot tried to climb over me. He was as disoriented as I. His mistake in direction, though, gave us both knowledge as to which way to go. What we didn't realize was that the ship was on the bottom, upside down. I climbed out of the cockpit, my hand hitting the slimy river bottom. In an instant the upside-down world made sense. I had my bearings and kicked for the surface.

It was black as a starless night and I couldn't see my flailing hands in front of me. I kicked harder and reached with cupped hands, keeping my fingers together for more power. My lungs were on the verge of bursting from the pressure and felt like they were on fire. I exhaled a few bubbles to relieve the pressure and the intense, searing pain. The minor relief spured me on. I kicked harder and was rewarded with a visible layer of light.

"Light," I thought. "I see light." My hands grabbed for it but the light seemed to back away from my searching, pleading fingertips. I was falling. Falling back down into the total darkness of a watery oblivion. For the second time of this ill-fated flight, I thought I was going to die. Giving up, I slowly sank toward the bottom. Time slowed and the light ebbed back into nothingness. Then, it hit me. "The chicken vest. The helmet." I was a human paperweight…an anchor. Frantically, I struggled with the helmet strap. It seemed like an eternity but the metal clasp opened. I pulled off the helmet and visualized it falling to the bottom. The vest came off easy and followed the flight helmet into watery limbo.

Almost immediately, my mind cleared and death didn't seem to be the only option. With strong kicks and a new, desperate resolve, I clawed my way back toward the surface.

I saw light, and then a small, yellow dot. Vision came to me in a blurred, surreal sort of way. My hands were shadows, reaching for the cause of their dark reflection. Despair became hope, and a grasping hand enveloped the sun. My body broke the surface with open eyes, fire in my chest, and a powerful, painful exhale of stale air and toxic water.

I coughed and gasped for air. My lungs hurt with every breath and my foggy mind began to slowly clear. Treading water, my eyes searched for the missing crewmen. I was alone on the surface. Suddenly, the water exploded in front of me. Mr. Latham broke the surface in a frenzy of flailing arms. He also gasped loudly as fresh, humid air filled his oxygen-depleted lungs.

"Where's the gunner?" I yelled. We looked around and still no Ritchie.

"*Dammit*! He's still down there," replied Latham.

I took a deep breath and dived for the bottom. My feet were still above the water when a large, passing shadow scared the wits out of me. Surfacing, I found the tardy pothead breathing heavily. He was still wearing his chicken plate and flight helmet.

The three of us treaded water and asked if each was ok. The pilot's eyes got real big and he said, "We've got to get out of here, now." I turned and saw a flotilla of sampans bearing down on us from the village. They were filled with men, all wearing black pajamas and conical, straw hats.

"We're dead," said Latham as we swam for the riverbank. He had forgotten about the Hog. Our killer ship was waiting for us, in a hover, all guns and rockets trained on the approaching armada.

"*Ouch*! *Dammit*! Now what?" Something had hit me in the head as I was swimming to shore. It was a folding, wood, beach chair. My head ached with confusion, and pain, as I resumed my course toward the waiting Gunship. My hand came down on something hard, but pliable. I stopped again and found myself being torpedoed by cartons of *Lucky Strike* cigarettes.

The sampans were closing in and Mr. Latham yelled at me from the river bank. "Mason, what the hell are you doing? Get your ass over here." Befuddled, I swam on and crawled up onto the muddy riverbank.

The floating merchandise was carried downstream with the current. Latham extended a hand and pulled me out of the soggy quagmire that was the shoreline. "Like quicksand," I thought, as we ran for the safety of the waiting Gunship. As we climbed in, the pothead complained, "My belly hurts."

The Hog lifted off and streaked over the river. It dipped its nose into the water and for an instant I wondered if I was going for another swim in the Go Dau Ha River. The pilot pulled back on the cyclic stick and the nose lifted out of the water. We shot upward and cleared the fleet of sampans by only a few feet. Several of them blew over from the Hog's powerful rotor wash. The Hog gunners kept their M60s trained on the menacing-looking men in black pajamas.

As it were, the Vietnamese turned out to be *friendlies* from Go Dau Ha Village; they saw the crash and were coming to rescue us. As we left the AO, I watched the small armada give chase to the floating cartons of cigarettes. Rubbing my bruised head, I wondered, "Where the heck did that stuff come from?" The Hog climbed slowly and I saw a slick of JP-4 (jet fuel), and red hydraulic fluid, forming on the surface of the water. Underneath were the remains of #395, once the finest scout ship in the fleet.

Sitting back, my hand rubbed the bump on my head. The pothead complained again about his belly. He finally thought to unbutton his wet jungle shirt and inspect his aching stomach. It was immediately clear what was causing Ritchie's pain. A long, fat, disgusting, black leech had attached itself to his bellybutton. I didn't know whether to laugh or try like hell not to laugh. Either way, it was ridiculously funny and, for a minute, took our minds off the horror that almost took our lives.

One of the Hog's gunners passed over a *Zippo* lighter. Mr. Latham burned the black creature until it writhed and released its bloodsucking grip. I grabbed it and flung the tiny monster out the door. I waited for the imaginary scream that never came.

A drop of blood rolled down Ritchie's stomach. He looked up and stared at me with wide, unbelieving eyes. His face was strangly contorted and when I thought he was going to scream, all he said was, "Far out." The gunners laughed, as did I, and Mr. Latham just turned away with a slight smile. It became apparent to me that Ritchie had done more than just a little pot before we began the mission. I don't know what he took, but he was clearly in *Wonderland.*

We all settled-in for the long flight back to Cu Chi. Ritchie played with his bellybutton, Mr. Latham sat quietly and probably thought about his career, now in jeopardy, and I was beginning to remember my cigarette and sampan dream from my night with Su Lei.

I, too, sat quietly on the flight back to the 3/4 cavalry. The meaning of the dream, if there was one, eluded me. It was a mystery. The cause of the crash wasn't. The pilot screwed up. For some reason, I felt partly responsible. I should have kept a closer watch on the *FNG* scout pilot. I also felt that I had let down Lieutenant Reese.

As the Hog crossed the base camp perimeter, I saw an outbound liftship. The Huey was, undoubtedly, going to salvage the remains of #395. I sighed and thought about what else had been lost in the senseless crash: the chicken plates, flight helmets, minigun, one M16, the box of frag and Willie Peter grenades, and my knife. Dad would be mad when I told him that I lost his eagle head, commemorative blade. In solace, I patted my holster and felt some comfort in the fact that my Colt was still there. In all, we survived the crash with little more than our lives.

I never thought #395 would die like that. It was senseless. It was supposed to be me and her, together, going down in the middle of a firefight. That's how I always imagined the end would come…with bullets, blood, fire, and lots of glory. After getting blown out of the sky during the battle for Tay Ninh, I never doubted I'd leave Vietnam in a flag-draped, aluminum casket. I just figured it would be a glorious gunslinger's death.

There was no ceremony when the Hog landed at the corral. The other scout ships were off on missions, as were most of the other Gunships. Jimmy Latham silently exited the Hog and walked toward OPS. I watched him go. He walked with head low and shoulders slumped. It was like he was going off to the principal's office, or to the wood shed for a well-deserved beating. The pothead had to be helped out by one of the gunners. He stumbled his way back to the Baby Scout hootch and collapsed on the first bunk he came to. Thankfully, it wasn't mine.

I, too, walked to the hootch, though more in a straight line than the pothead. I grabbed my towel off the nail and kept going until I got to the showers. The water was cool and cleansing. Slowly, I undressed and let the mud-soaked clothes hit where they fell. I forgot the soap but didn't care. The water was more for therapeutic and mental cleansing than it was for the body.

"My." A soft voice spoke my name. For a second, I thought it was Su Lei.

"My." Looking around, my eyes got wide as they landed on Mei, the babysan.

"Mei, what are you doing here?" I looked around for the Gunship crew chief, then realized she was only looking at me. Embarrassed, I quickly wrapped myself in my towel.

"Mei, you shouldn't be here. What do you want?"

"I hear My crash. I worry."

"I'm ok."

"You crash much, My."

"Yeah, well, it happens, My."

"You crash no more. Mei say so." I was astounded. This little girl was giving me an order. Before I could answer her, she was gone. I removed the towel and got back under the soothing water. Mei was something else. She was my friend, a confidant, a little sister, and, sometimes, like today, my mother. The tears came and I cried like a baby.

The next day a debriefing was held in OPS. I was questioned about the crash by the investigating officer; a Major from headquarters. "What happened? What did you see? How fast were you going?" The Q & A session seemed more like a witch hunt, or an inquisition, than an impartial hearing.

Everything was leading toward the pilot and there was nothing I could do to bail out Jimmy Latham. The Major warned me not to cover for him and said that only the truth mattered. I wasn't going to lie but I wanted it on the record that I was responsible for breaking him in.

"*Bull!*" The investigator looked at me and added, "The Lieutenant's a big boy who made a big, stupid mistake. Mason, Chief Warrant Officer Latham was showing off and wanted to brag about flying under the bridge. Other pilots have done it, kind of like an initiation for green pilots. That, however, was before commo wires were strung underneath it. His ignorance doesn't excuse him from responsibility."

"What's going to happen to him, sir?"

"I don't know, Mason. Most likely, because of his age, he'll be disciplined back in the states and then sent through flight school again."

"Court Martial is more like it," I thought.

"Anyway, you and Ritchfield are cleared of any wrongdoing. Nothing about this incident will appear in your records. You may go, Mason."

"Yes, sir." I saluted and walked out the door.

I never saw Jimmy Latham again. He was shipped out the next day to the states and to whatever fate awaited him. Although I felt sorry for him, a part of me hated him for what he did to #395. My ship was gone, forever, and it was due to the recklessness of a young pilot who, one day, tried to prove his mettle by impressing the Chief of Scouts.

The pothead never knew what happened. Ritchie was just happy to be alive. During his debriefing, the Major learned that he was more concerned with his missing beach chair and cigarettes than the crash. At least I finally learned where those floating torpedoes came from.

Ritchie had gone shopping the day before at the Tay Ninh base exchange. He stowed the goods in the back of #395 and covered them with a small tarp. Being *high*, as usual, he forgot to remove the stuff before the Go Dau Ha mission. After the near-drowning in the river, Ritchie never-again got high before a mission. He actually turned out to be a pretty good crew chief.

Lieutenant Reese took me out to the flight line. Near the hangar was the crushed shell of #395. We walked around the remains and the Baby Scout leader whistled and asked, "How the hell did you survive this?"

"Lucky, I guess, sir...like the crash you and I walked away from." Luck really didn't have much to do with it. The tiny Loach is built around a steel *A-Frame*. It, and the rubber, fuel-bladder design saved our lives. If the Loach landed right, it was resilient and explosion-proof. Jimmy Latham also helped to save our skins by fighting the controls to keep the ship level as it hit the water. I will admit, though, that luck was with us as we tumbled down the murky river at 100 miles an hour.

The Lieutenant and I stared at the wreckage. The entire rotor assembly was missing, and the front canopy was sheared off. The tail boom was gone and probably still resting on the bottom of the river. Both skids were gone as was, of course, the side-mounted minigun. I walked around the little metal shell and stopped in front of the aerial identification number that was painted on the dog house. There were two scratches, like an X, through the last three numbers...395. The little ship that could...wouldn't, anymore. Her days of hunting were over. Little did I know, that my future was just as bleak.

"Sorry, Mike," said Lt. Reese. "I know what she meant to you." There was genuine sadness in his voice. He patted my shoulder, then walked away. Loach #395 was his favorite ship, too.

If there was any consolation at all it was that, "I went down with my ship." It was a weird feeling, but that's how I felt. It wasn't the glorious ending that I had envisioned many times before, but there was a modicum of satisfaction. Also, I was still alive.

A friend took a black and white *Polaroid* of Lt. Reese and me standing by the wreckage. I would carry it always, in my wallet. Every now and then, I look at it and think how wonderful it is to be among the living.

Life in Vietnam was beginning to make sense to me. Dying a glorious, gunslinger's death wouldn't have been glorious at all. It would have been a damn shame and a pity. I turned from the casualty of war and headed toward the Baby Scout hootch. I thought about getting drunk but didn't. In the morning a Huey would be flying to Saigon. A beautiful, black-haired girl was there, waiting for me. I would be on that milk run to keep my date with Su Lei.

The Slick landed on a helipad near the city docks. The crew was going to barter with the Navy for some steaks and real American beer. The helicopter crew had brought with them, captured AK-47s, NVA flags, and even some crossbows and arrows. Most of the stuff was taken from dead bodies. The crew chief said I had six hours and to be back on time. I agreed and then went hunting for a cab.

The cabbie dropped me off in front of the Saigon Sun Hotel. I went in and walked up to the registration desk. Mr. Phuoc looked up, squinted his eyes, then smiled.

"Mr. Mason, you came back." He really didn't think I would.

"Yes, sir. I had to. Is Su Lei here?"

He gestured toward the dining room. "In there."

"Thanks." The old man quickly turned and disappeared into the back office. I did what he told me and took a seat by the large, picture window. I felt that I owned that little table by the window, much like owning that regular barstool in your favorite tavern.

I looked around the room. There were few customers…a black Corporal and an elderly Vietnamese couple. I lit up and looked at the soldier. He was eating noodle ball soup. I smiled inwardly, knowing all too well what he would go through in the next few days. It wouldn't seem funny to him, though, when the latrine would become his best friend.

My ears perked at the familiar sound of the squeaky, swinging, kitchen doors. My eyes turned and focused on the pretty waitress carrying a tray of food and a bulbous, ceramic teapot. Her Ao dai was covered by an

Michael W. Mason

apron and her hair was tucked under a white cap. Even if I hadn't seen her face, I would have known it was Su Lei.

I snubbed out my cigarette, sat back in the wicker chair and said, "Miss, coffee please."

Su Lei turned and froze. I was afraid she would drop the teapot. Gently, she placed the tray on the table and then walked slowly toward me. Her face had that cute pout and I stood up, laughing. She stopped in front of me and said, "My, I knew you would come back." In an instant my arms were filled with the soft warmth of a sobbing, Vietnamese girl. We embraced for minutes. She wouldn't let go and I didn't want to. The tears came and I felt wet eyelashes on my cheek. In my ear she whispered, "I know you come."

"Su Lei," I answered, "you can talk." She looked up at me with tear-tracked cheeks and laughed as she cried. "Uncle Phuoc no think you come. I know you come back. Su Lei know." I kissed her and the war went away. Her lips were salty as the tears continued to flow. I stroked her back and looked up to see a most captive audience. The customers were staring and the corporal gave me a gold-toothed smile and a thumbs up. I meekly returned the smile with a wave of my hand.

Su Lei's fluttering eyelashes were like *butterfly kisses.* She had spent her tears and the streams that went from cheek to neck to chest had soaked the front of my green, jungle shirt. I held her tight and hoped the moment would become an eternity.

She looked up and I gazed into a pair of coal-black eyes that floated behind a thin veil of liquid glass. Su Lei smiled and told me to sit down. She walked toward the kitchen, wiping her eyes with the back of her hand. She went through the swinging doors and shortly emerged with a pot of coffee and a mug. After casting a smile in my direction, she walked over to the elderly couple. She spoke Vietnamese to them and I couldn't understand a word. The man and woman turned their heads and stared at me. They appeared happy. The Corporal got up, left a dollar tip, and waved at me as he walked toward the exit. I waved back. He wore the distinctive, 1st Air Cav shoulder patch and silver wings adorned his jungle hat. I thought, "He probably deserves a little R & R."

Mr. Phuoc came in the room and joined in the discussion with Su Lei and the old couple. It was obvious they were talking about me and I was anxious to know what was being said. Su Lei bowed to the couple and walked back to me.

"My uncle friends say thang you." I smiled at the compliment and the cute way she pronounced certain words.

"Why, Su Lei?"

"Uncle friends say you help me come good girl."

"I think I know what you mean. My is happy, too, that you're a good girl."

"Yes, My. I no whore, now. Su Lei happy."

I didn't know what to say to that. Apparently, to her uncle and his friends, this Baby Scout gunslinger was Su Lei's salvation.

Su Lei patted me on the shoulder and darted her eyes toward the distant table. The elderly couple and her uncle were nodding at me with big smiles. Su Lei grabbed my collar and tugged. It seemed that I was expected to do something. I wasn't sure what, but I stood, looked at Su Lei, then smiled and bowed to the three *Cheshire* Vietnamese. In unison, their smiles got bigger and they returned the bow.

Su Lei laughed and asked, "How you know to do that?"

"Just smart, I guess." She looked at me and shook her head. Sitting down, she wiped her tear-stained face with the back of her sleeve. I took a sip of coffee and when I looked up, a key with a plastic tag was dangling in front of my face. On the white tag were black letters and a number…PH4. She said her uncle had given her the rest of the day off and the key to the Penthouse.

We stopped by the Vietnamese couple's table on the way out. Su Lei kissed them, and her uncle, on their cheeks. I bowed again, though this time less dramatically. We headed off toward the stairs with the key to the Penthouse.

As we walked the five flights of stairs, Su Lei said that one of the four Penthouses would be mine anytime I visited.

"They for rich men, government people, and Generals."

"Generals come here?"

"Yes, My."

"Which Army?"

"Both. Vietnamese and American."

"Did you, uh, I mean…"

"No, My. Su Lei no sleep with men. Uncle Phuoc no allow."

"Why? I mean, I'm glad, I guess, but why weren't you allowed to uh, you know?"

Michael W. Mason

"Uncle no like these men. They old and mean. He no trust Generals who come here."

I just nodded and we continued our climb up the stairs in silence. By the time we reached the fifth floor, I was wondering which Generals visited the Saigon Sun Hotel. Su Lei led me by the hand down the long, dark, dimly lit hallway. We stopped in front of a door that had a brass placard. It read, "Penthouse 4." Su Lei passed me the key and smiled. I unlocked the door and followed her into the room where Generals played and slept.

The room was enormous. The floor was covered with wall to wall, beige, shag carpeting. In a corner was a small bar with refrigerator. Across from it was a sofa, coffee table, and an old *Philco* console television set. The opposite wall was mirrored and in front sat two wicker chairs with a wooden, round table between them. On the table was an ashtray, a table lighter, and a cigar-filled, glass humidor. I was tempted to light up but Su Lei grabbed me by the hand and led me into another room. My feet froze and my eyes couldn't fathom, muchless believe, what they were seeing. It was the bedroom. A bedroom unlike any I had ever seen, not counting Hugh Hefner's bedroom that I had seen pictures-of in *Playboy* magazine. Three of the four walls were mirrored, as was the ceiling. The unmirrored wall was covered by a sheer, white curtain that rippled from the breeze the came from the hidden, open window.

The centerpiece of the room was the bed. It was round, king-sized, and covered with a comforter, the same color as the shag carpeting. At least a dozen, small pillows of different colors decorated the head of the giant bed. The huge, polished headboard was half wood, half mirror. A night table was covered with a red cloth and on it sat bottles of bourbon, scotch, vodka, and gin. Soft music came from speakers that were recessed into the headboard. The eight-track tape player was enclosed in a hidden compartment. Su Lei saw the wonderment in my eyes, laughed, and pulled me further into the room where the rich and the mighty played.

We walked slowly across the room. At any moment I expected Mr. Hefner and a bevy of bunnies to magically appear. Su Lei led me through the decadent bedroom and into the bathroom. It, too, was large and ornate. There was a Roman tub big enough for four people. The faucet was gold-plated and the hot/cold knobs were ivory.

Next to the toilet was a commode, but without a seat. I thought it was a urinal. Su Lei giggled and called it a *Bidet*. When she told me what it was for I said, "You're kidding?" She laughed at my ignorance and guided me back to the bedroom.

"Look on bar, My." I walked over and saw the bottle of Korbel Champagne sitting in an ice bucket. Also on the bar were two crystal champagne glasses. I unwired the cork and pried it out with a resounding "*POP!*" With bottle in one hand, glasses in the other, I turned around just in time to see the turquoise Ao dai fall gently to the floor.

Su Lei was wearing only a smile. Light, filtering in through the translucent curtains, bathed her in a golden aura. I had only seen her naked in the glow of a 15 watt light bulb. I stared and remembered her round, upturned breasts with large nipples. Memories returned and I recognized the flat stomach and cute bellybutton. Her body was smooth, virtually hairless, and my mind remembered it all. However, there was something missing.

I put down the bottle, and glasses, and walked over to her. She looked into my eyes as my hands went to the little, white bonnet that covered her head. While I removed it, and the hair pins, her hands began to unbutton my shirt.

When the last pin was out, I let go. Her silky, black hair cascaded down over her shoulders and fell to just below her knees. The ebony tresses covered her body except for two, pointed, protruding nipples. I stared, mesmerized by the erotic vision that my eyes couldn't turn away from. Su Lei laughed and made a joke about those not being her eyes that I was looking at. I grinned and took her hair and placed it behind her back. She removed my shirt, took a step back and said, "My, My, My."

I looked down and saw the butt of my Colt 45 sticking out of my waistband. She saw the "I'm sorry" look on my face and shook her head, laughing. She walked to the bar, grabbed the champagne, and glasses, and came back with a big smile on her face. She nodded toward the night table and I knew, from experience, what she wanted me to do. I carefully took the Colt from my pants and placed it in the drawer of the night table.

She felt light as a feather as I picked her up and carried her to the bed. We sprawled in a heap, her hair flying everywhere. My face was covered with the long, silky strands. Miraculously, not a drop of champagne was spilled.

Su Lei giggled as she placed the bottle, and glasses, on the night table. She was still laughing as she went to work, removing my jungle boots, green socks, and my green, jungle pants. Su Lei moved back up to face me and said, "My. You no ever go." The only answer I gave her was a hug. I squeezed her tight, stroked her hair, and then rolled on top of her. My lips branded her forehead, nose, lips, and then I began to work my way south. Her large, protruding nipples were hard and I kissed them. Resuming my journey, I kissed her bellybutton. By this time, she was quivering, moaning, and anticipating what my destination would be.

I moved on and discovered her inner thighs. Her hands went up to her face. The frequent moans became soft purring as I reached the end of my purposeful quest. Her throaty sounds increased in magnitude and her body began to slowly move up and down. The moans returned and Su Lei's body began to convulse. She was building to an orgasm that would launch our time together in the room where Generals played.

It was better than the first time. I can't explain it. What Su Lei taught me the first time was amazing. The little I knew, and taught her, seemed to excite Su Lei beyond all measure. We now shared knowledge and could take turns as the agressor. She was no longer my teacher. When I took charge, she screamed her pleasure at being the student.

During the few hours we had together, we consummated our love twice. I would learn that, while a tigress in bed, out of the sack she was the girlfriend I needed to get through a lonely and chaotic time in my life. Because of my time with Su Lei, I would never again think about dying in a blaze of gunfire. Not the crashes, nor the wounds, but the tender ministrations of a Saigon harlot brought me back to the harsh world of reality. Slowly, I began to think that dying in Vietnam wasn't such a glorious end for a twenty year old Baby Scout. A lot of living was ahead of me and I began to realize that it could be a good life, but only if Su Lei could live it with me. On a disheveled bed, in an old Saigon hotel, I held a body that had mated with mine. The war was far away and I thought, "If there is a God, he'll help me find a way to bring Su Lei home with me." We were both exhausted. I asked if she wanted to go for a walk with me. A few hours remained before my ride would leave…with or without me.

"No, My. I want bath with you."

"Well," I thought, "that's a better plan than going for a walk."

The Roman tub was as big as a kid's wading pool and twice as deep. It came with hot water and a lavander-scent bubble bath. We tried to make love again but I couldn't answer the call to action. Su Lei was sympathetic and understanding. She said, "My, you tired. Su Lei also tired. It ok." I felt better and we played in the tub for an hour. When we finally got out, we looked like human prunes.

We left the room where Generals slept. Su Lei walked with me out to the street. I had half an hour to make my flight. She said, "My, here come soon?" I laughed and discovered that I was learning to understand her every word.

"Yes, sweetheart. I'll be back as soon as I can." I held her with one arm around her waist as I hailed a cab. As the old Ford pulled up to the curb, I remembered the gift that I had bought her at the Saigon PX.

I took out my wallet and carefully pulled out the little charm bracelet. There were two, tiny gold hearts on it. On one heart was engraved, *My*, and on the other, *Su*. She cried as I fastened the bracelet around her fragile wrist.

"Bye, Su Lei. I love you." She pulled me to her and hugged me tight. Her lips gave me a long kiss on the cheek.

"I love you, My," she sobbed as I climbed into the back of the rusted, white, fifteen year old Ford sedan. The cab rumbled off and as I watched Su Lei grow smaller through the rear window she yelled, "My. You no die."

Those words haunted me until I saw her again. They were the longest two weeks of my life. I wrangled an overnighter on a Loach that had to deliver a *Bird* Colonel to Army Headquarters. It cost me twenty dollars and a night of guard duty, but nothing could have kept me away from Su Lei.

We went on a picnic. She took me to a park and we just relaxed on a blanket for most of the afternoon. The wicker picnic basket was filled with pork sandwiches, potato chips, and a bottle of red wine. We wrestled on the blanket and she discovered how ticklish I was. Eager to learn everything she could about me, and America, I taught her *hide and seek*, *tag*, and how to skip stones across the glass-like surface of the small pond. Tired, we sat on the blanket and tossed bread crumbs to the ducks.

"My," she said, looking at me with wet, glistening eyes, "you no go back."

"What?"

"You no go. My go, My die." I was startled by her frank concern, and a little frightened of her prophetic-sounding words.

"I won't die, Su Lei. I'll always come back to you."

"No. You die. My a Baby Scout. You like war too much."

"*Damn*, Su Lei! I didn't mean to scare you with my stories."

"No stories. You fight all time. You get shot, you crash three times, you always get big trouble."

"It's my job. I can't quit the Army."

"No leave Army. You leave war. Come live in hotel."

"I'd be AWOL (Absent Without Leave), and in war that's like being a traitor. The Army can shoot me for that."

"No. Su Lei hide you." I looked at her and saw well-meaning sincerety on her small, pouting face.

"You know I can't. I want to, but I can't."

"One day you go. Never come to Su Lei."

"Always to Su Lei. I will never, ever, leave you."

"My, I scared for you. You no scared but Su Lei scared."

"Don't be. I'll always be with you."

"You have luh no more. You say to me…no more luh."

"Luh? Oh. You mean, luck. I never said that."

"You tell me stories of Go Dau Ha River, Iron Triangle, Tay Ninh. You no have luh no more."

"Worse things have happened to others, Su Lei. Besides, it's what I do. I like flying. I like the Baby Scouts."

"The Baby Scouts kill My."

"No. Stop it. I chose the Scouts. It was my decision. I can't just up and quit. That's not how it works in the Army." For the first time, I lost my temper with Su Lei. Instantly, I regretted it.

Tears welled up in her eyes and her pouting lips quivered in fear and remorse. I reached over and hugged her close. She cried and the tears rolled down her cheeks.

She shook in my arms and I comforted her by patting her back. The bag of bread crumbs fell from my fingers and together we cried, surrounded by a dozen, hungry, quacking ducks. The commotion drowned out the mechanized sounds of the city. Strangers, passing by, stared and pointed at what must have been a ludicrous sight. The platoon of invading ducks captured the blanket and nipped at anything that looked like food, including Su Lei's toes. She squealed and began to laugh between the sniffles. We both scooted off the blanket and watched the victorious ducks claim their spoils of war.

A sigh came from Su Lei's lips and I saw that she was almost smiling.

"Are you alright?" I asked.

"My," she answered, "Su Lei sorry." She began to giggle in-between the sniffles.

"Su Lei, are you laughing?"

"Quah," she said. "Quah, quah."

"Quack, quack," I answered, laughing, looking into her eyes with a smile on my face.

"My, duhs tickle feet." I looked down and saw three ducks nipping at her toes. I laughed and shooed them away. The brave ducks returned, probably bolstered by their recent victory over the invading, human horde. Flailing my arms, and shouting, did nothing to discourage the attacking squad of ducks. Su Lei tucked her feet up under her and laughed at my ineffective defense.

It was time to go on the offensive. I got up and the ducks froze in their tracks. They stared at me and one of them quacked. A black jungle boot moved slowly forward and the feathered recon patrol began to retreat. My other boot came forward and landed on the edge of the blanket. The ducks ceased their retreat and it appeared that they were going to make a last stand. It was now or never. I raced forward, the ducks scattered, and Su Lei began to laugh uncontrollably at the ridiculous sight of man versus ducks. Seeing the almost empty bag of bread crumbs, I picked it up and threw the prize into the pond. In full retreat, the ducks quickly waddled after the shower of bread crumbs that sprayed from the torn paper bag. Never had I laughed so hard as my eyes watched the floating fowl turn on each other with vigorous nips and raucous, threatening quacks. From behind, a small, soft hand touched my cheek and turned my head. Red, bloodshot eyes looked into mine. Smiling lips seemed on the verge of speaking. I looked at her and as the words formed in my mind…she spoke them first.

"I love you, My."

"I love you, Su Lei." We lay down together, embraced, and shut out the world of sputtering cars, whining scooters, and quacking ducks. For the moment, only our own little world mattered. Saigon went about its business of Capitalism and war. War was never far away. Above, helicopters often announced their presence with their loud, wind-beating rotor blades. Su Lei snuggled into the crook of my arm and I stroked her hair while she slept. Distant, muffled explosions were another grim reminder of the beckoning holocaust that is the Vietnam War.

Michael W. Mason

Su Lei awoke as twilight turned to night. Only a few stars twinkled through the dark layer of clouds. Silently, we cleaned up the mess that was the result of the *Great Saigon Duck Battle of 1968*. Su Lei took the picnic basket and I carried the blanket. We walked around the pond and toward the street. On the far side of the pond, a dozen pair of eyes watched us depart the battlefield. A lone "Quack" let us know that the feathered army was still there. Like the battered VC, they were never going to go away. The pond was theirs, and they were never going to give it up without a fight.

On the half-mile walk to the hotel my hand, unconsciously, went to my waistband several times. The Colt wasn't there. Su Lei wouldn't let me bring it on the picnic. I didn't feel too threatened as there were many soldiers on street corners. We passed several bars and intermittant sounds of music escaped through opening and closing doors.

I silently wondered if the partying American soldiers were gulping watered-down whiskey in exchange for a lot of groping from the always-smiling bargirls. I winced as I remembered the painful encounter on my first trip to Saigon. Su Lei squeezed my hand and I looked down into shiny, reflective, black eyes that sparkled in the rays of light that escaped from the curtained-windows that we passed.

Saigon was a dark city. Few lights burned, except from behind barricaded, or blocked, doors and windows. Even the cars that travelled by night, did so without headlights. Though pretty much over, the Tet offensive was not quickly forgotten.

Saigon prostitutes came out at night. The working girls hung around the nightclubs and offered themselves to anyone who passed by. We must have walked by these scantily-dressed solicitors half a dozen times on the way to the hotel. Each time we passed, Su Lei gave my hand a squeeze and looked up at me with a sad face. The street girls were a sad reminder of what the war had made her. We walked on and all the way to the hotel I thought about our strange and bewildering relationship.

I was a trained killer, a soldier who wontonly rained down death from above. Su Lei was the hapless victim of such killers and lost her family, and innocence, to the very same soldiers who forged her destiny of orphan and prostitute. My feelings for her were understandable. Yet, her fondness for me was inexplicable. The only rational answer I came up with, was that We both found each other at similar turning points in our lives. Su Lei was looking for a new beginning at life, and a war-weary gunslinger was searching for a better way to live it. Our answers were found in the unlikely companionship that we forged out of the horrors of war.

The Penthouse was a welcomed respite after the long walk from the park. We left a trail of clothes across the floor and into the bathroom. The Roman tub was relaxing and we just lay there and talked about our day, our lives, and the war. Always the war.

I saw Su Lei once more after that. We picked up where we left off…snuggling in the huge, oval bed of the penthouse. We talked about love, war, American girls, and my hometown. She said it sounded like a nice place to live. "Hun-tee-ton," she said. She couldn't quite manage to pronounce, Long Island, New York. Su Lei was most interested in the girls of the United States. She smiled when I said they were much like her…smart and pretty.

"My, you have girl you home?"

"No. Not anymore. Do you have a boyfriend?"

"Yes." I looked at her with wide eyes, not expecting that answer.

Laughing, she said, "You, My. You Su Lei boyfriend."

"Come on. You know what I mean." Her face turned to one of sadness.

"He die in war, My. He die three years ago when he sixteen. He Viet Cong and die by Vietnamese soldiers." I was shocked at what I heard.

"Were you VC, too?" I hated asking the question and tried to look sad.

"No, My. I hate war. No ever fight in war. It bad, but people not all bad. Uncle Phuoc teach me that." She looked me in the eyes and added, "Su Lei love My. You no die war. No die."

"Ok, Su Lei. I promise." I looked at her and asked, "Is Su Lei my girlfriend?"

"Yes, My," she said with a brightness of eyes. "My always Su Lei boyfriend." She held up her wrist and showed me the charm bracet to emphasize her vow. "I no tay off. I wear always. Su Lei promise."

Again, making love with Su Lei was better than the time before. It always got better. The night passed quickly and morning arrived too soon. As before, I left her teary-eyed on the curb. The war welcomed me back with a vengeance. There were many missions and many firefights. Through it all, I plotted ways to get Su Lei home to the states.

During these days of lonely warfare, Army Intelligence discovered the hiding place of Su Lei. While I was flying missions over the Iron Triangle,

Michael W. Mason

the best thing in my life was taken away. It was weeks before I was able to get to the MARS facility to call the Saigon Sun Hotel. Barney was at my side and placed the call for me.

Mr. Phuoc answered and, with great sorrow, explained what had happened. He said the Military Police showed up at the hotel and simply escorted her out to a waiting, black sedan. A man in a dark suit, wearing sunglasses, warned him not to speak of the incident, or of the atrocities at My Lai. The *government man* warned the old man to be discreet or he'd disappear too. Su Lei's uncle was sobbing as I hung up the phone.

I thanked Barney and he saw the sadness on my face, and the tears. I said I was alright and that my girlfriend in Saigon was going to be away longer than I had days left in Vietnam. He looked at me and probably didn't believe a word of it. I walked out the door and into the harsh world of heat, dust, killing, and inhumanity.

Very alone, I began my long walk back to the Cav. For the second time in just a few weeks, tears came and I cried amidst the rolling thunder of steel, mechanized chariots. The warriors aboard the mighty dreadnauts ignored me as they rode through thick clouds of dust.

The anger came but it was not directed at the Army. I remembered what Su Lei had told me on our last night together. It wasn't the people. It was the war. I would keep that remembrance with me, always.

The gunslinging days were over. I learned the hard way that there was no need for make-believe heroes. Not me. Not anyone. On the walk back to the Baby Scouts I grew up a little. No. A lot! The Vietnam War was bigger than both opposing armies put together. Who was I to think that the conflict would leave me and Su Lei untouched. She was right when she said, "No people bad, My. War bad."

I emerged from the dust storm and into the white light of the blinding, midday sun. The Cav, and D troop, was just ahead. The tears had stopped and I wiped the moist dust streaks from my face. I loved the girl from Saigon. She was central to my life and the sole reason I was changing into a pragmatic citizen of a crazy world. I walked into camp knowing that I was still in love with a girl, like no other. Su Lei would always be with me. Maybe some day we would meet again. And, maybe the love between us would still be there, just waiting to be rekindled. Those were a lot of maybes. For the present, though, I was home. "It is good to be a Baby Scout," I thought, as the hootch door slammed behind me.

BABY SCOUT

The rainy season ended and, almost overnight, creeks and streams dried up and disappeared. The landscape took on a familiarity that was like the back of my hand. The hunting continued but I had to assign myself to other ships. My Loach, #395, was gone and sent to wherever destroyed warbirds go. I later heard, through the rumor mill, that the little chopper was shipped back to the states for study by aircraft engineers. I wondered if those people knew, or cared, if anyone was hurt or killed in the crash.

My days in-country were many and I was getting close to becoming a shortimer. Only 49 more days to go before boarding the *Silver Bird* for the *Freedom Flight* to the *world*. Playing *hide and seek* with Charlie is fun, but not enough to keep me off the plane. Only one thing could do that, and she no longer was part of my life.

I was the last of the original Baby Scouts. All the others from the days of the old, sputtering Ravens were gone. They left behind their own contributions to the war effort. Some also left behind flesh, blood, and their lives.

Lieutenant Reese was still here. So was Lt. Kerns. In the Baby Scout hootch, though, only I remained of the original volunteers. I, alone, had the memories of what it was like to be a skidrider on the slow, lethargic Ravens. It was a time when the Baby Scouts, standing on skids, fired their M60s at an enemy who had the advantage of hearing us before we could see them. The flack jacket, the monkey strap, the skid-mounted M60…they were all a part of my history with D Troop of the 3/4 Cavalry. There were few cares and fewer distractions. To me, the war was everything and the flying made it the thrillride of a lifetime. The Loaches changed that. Life got more complicated, as did the war. Everything moved at a faster pace. It became easier to kill and seemed easier to get shot down. Also, without the Loach, there probably would have been no trip to Saigon, and no Su Lei. Life, I learned, does sometimes become a paradox.

Ten and a half months have gone by and I consider myself fortunate. During this time in-country, I had survived numerous rocket attacks, been shot at many times, wounded, shot down twice, crashed into a leech-infested river, and considered myself lucky.

I had met Su Lei and was still alive. Nothing else seemed to matter. Now, with her out of my life, staying alive became paramount. Though bittersweet, the memories of my short romance with the Saigon prostitute would always be imprinted on my soul. No one, myself included, ever

Michael W. Mason

returned home from Vietnam without a few scars...physical, mental, or both. I would go home with both.

Tom Donald went home to St. Louis to run his dad's grocery business. Hutch went back to the farm in Kansas. Buck was in Brooklyn and owned an auto repair shop. He had a girl and a cherry '57 Chevy Belair convertible. I was glad that Buck had found paradise. LT and Danny Narvone were sent to stateside hospitals to recover from their gunshot wounds. I never found out if Lieutenant Larry Tinder survived his wounds.

The new guys were different. They had an attitude unlike the original Scouts. Most were anti-war and were drafted after high school or while in college. After a mission, however, they would brag about their body counts and how they cut Charlie in half. They probably thought I was different, too. One thing, however, kept us together. We were Baby Scouts. Whether volunteer or draftee, we all shared that proud, common bond.

Even though I only had 45 days to go, in-country, I continued to fly often. It was still an aerial roller coaster ride and, besides, it kept my mind off of Su Lei. As Flight Line Chief, I assigned myself to the low ship as often as possible. When flying with a Gunship, my little Scout ship was always the low, or recon ship.

Lieutenant Kerns and I were flying low, over some scrub brush near Trang Bang Village. Suddenly, the two lower bubble ports exploded from incoming AK-47 fire. The rounds went straight up and through the upper ports, but not before severing the minigun's gunsight assembly. Kerns whipped the Loach around in a flat 180 degree spin, and we were face to face with an angry man in black pajamas.

Charlie took aim and fired his Russian-made assault rifle at us. I don't know how he missed and didn't care. I opened up with the M60 a split second before the pilot engaged the awesome power of the minigun. Hundreds of bullets shredded the contorting body of the VC rebel. The rag doll corpse sailed ten feet through the air and landed in a grotesque pile of severed limbs and mangled flesh. My darting eyes spotted another VC running across the open field. "Come right!" I yelled. Kerns gave chase and I followed the fleeing prey with a stream of machine gun tracers. The bullets plowed the ground behind him and then stitched him up the back. He was flung into a clump of sawgrass. We saw much blood and I tossed a Willie Peter grenade into the dense, dry sawgrass. It erupted in sparks and flame. "Over there! Over there!" yelled the observer. The Loach tacked to port and the hunt continued. I couldn't see the quarry as he was on the left side of the aircraft. The lone VC crossed under the ship and appeared on the right side. He was running fast and carried an AK-47 in one hand. His life was now mine to take away.

I brought my M60 up for an easy kill. There was no joy, no remorse about it. I was just doing my job and the M60 was unsympathetic and uncaring. It would only do what my trigger finger forced it to do.

"Back off, Mason. He's mine." Lieutenant Kerns wanted the kill for himself. I lifted my head and got a good look at the terrified victim. He had a young face and eyes that were big and filled with fear. Long, black hair trailed behind the running man. It whipped through the air in rythmic motion with his stride. The body was small, lithly built, and, for some reason, just didn't look right. Then it hit me. "Oh my God! It's a girl."

The roar of the minigun drowned out my yell. The young militant was riddled by dozens of rounds as she turned to bravely face her killers. For the first time in my life, I watched death unfold in slow-motion. The young girl was lifted off her feet and carried backward by the tiny, lead missiles. Her straw hat flew off her head and long strands of black hair seemed to float in the air. The rifle turned end over end, much like a Majorette's baton. The body landed on short, brown grass, arms flung to the side. She, like a crucifix, lay still, blood pouring from her viscerated body. The rifle landed a few feet above her head, muzzle first, then slowly fell to land on her left shoulder. The straw hat was carried by the wind and, like a tumbleweed, rolled across the open field.

The pilot circled the small, bloodied body. I stared at what would be a memory never to be cleansed from my soul. The girl's shirt was shredded where the bullets had slammed into her. Small, bloodstained breasts protruded through the disheveled, black garment. I looked into open eyes that seemed to stare into mine. "We killed a little girl," I said to myself, aloud. "We killed a little girl."

The lifeless girl seemed to rotate in a circle as Kerns slowly hovered around her. My eyes locked with hers and they followed me, much like those in a painting. The long hair was spread out like a black cloud about her head. I guessed her age to be about twelve, maybe thirteen. I tried not to think that she might even be younger. Time slowed as we circled the human effigy. The distant gunfire and explosions were only dull echoes in the back of my mind. We killed a little girl. I killed a little girl. The pilot killed the little girl. In truth, the three of us, as a team, had snuffed out her

Michael W. Mason

life. It didn't matter who pulled the trigger. We were one ship, one crew. A little girl's blood would forever stain us all.

Slowly, the small, elfin face moved away. The ship was rising and the girl's body became smaller in the sea of wet, red sawgrass. Eerily, her eyes followed me until the violent rotor wash blew her hair over her face like a death shroud. The Loach picked up speed and returned to the ongoing battle, leaving behind a small human sacrifice to the impartiality of war.

A Cobra gunship was attacking a small encampment of Viet Cong. Lieutenant Kerns joined up with it and the battle resumed. The body count was going to be big this day. Yet, I didn't care. I didn't care anymore at all.

Everyone was partying after the gunfight at Trang Bang. Everyone but me. No one seemed to remember that a little girl lay dead, alone, in an empty field of sawgrass and mud. She may have been the enemy, but her killing went against everything I was taught as a young boy. I tried to console myself with the thought, "Well, at least it wasn't me who pulled the trigger." It didn't work. I would have shot her in the back if the pilot hadn't stopped me. I rationalized and drank all night in the bar. After many mind-numbing beers, I staggered back to the hootch and collapsed on my bunk. Sleep came quickly and so did the dream.

The nightmare was of a young girl lying dead in a red ocean of grass. Hallowed eyes stared into mine and full, pouting, blood-smeared lips were asking, "My, what you done? What have you done?"

"I didn't mean to."

"Yes, you did." The lips moved but the eyes remained vacant, void of life.

"No. I didn't know you were a girl."

"I would have shot you, My."

"You knew I was on the ship?"

"Yes, My, and I would have killed you."

"I hate this *damn* war."

"I hate it, too, but I still would have killed you."

"Why?"

"It is war, My."

"You know my name.":

"Yes, My. I know everyone's name."

"Then, you are not Su Lei?"

"No, My. I am the war she told you about. I will kill you if I can."

"You're just a little girl."

"I am a girl, and a boy, and a woman, and a man. I am all that lives and dies in war: the bodies, the blood, the remorseful, and the innocent. Look into my eyes.

"I am. I can't see anything there."

"Look closer."

"Nothing. Just blackness and my reflection looking back."

"Exactly, My. You are seeing war; what war really is."

"Me? I'm war."

"Yes, My. You and all the others. When you look into the eyes of the dead, you always see the cause."

"I don't understand."

"Yes, you do. You just can't see it with living eyes. You only see yourselves as the reflection, not the cause."

"If that's true, why does war continue century after century?"

"Because only a few look into the eyes of death. Until everyone sees their reflection in the eyes of a little girl, I will be with you, always."

"Forever? You will never go away?"

"No. I will be with you, always."

"What about the future?"

"Always, My. Always."

I bolted upright, sweat flying from my sweat-soaked hair. Lieutenant Reese was beside my bunk, his hand on my shoulder.

"Are you alright, Mason? I heard you tied one on last night."

"Yeah. I'm fine, sir." He looked at me, doubting my words, but said to be on the flight line in an hour.

"What's going on?"

"We have another mission near Trang Bang."

"Yes, sir. I'll be ready." Reese nodded and walked away. The light, flooding in from the swinging door, hurt my eyes.

Somehow, I forced my mentally-drained body to stagger to the showers. The cool water rinsed the stains of the horrible night off my aching body. It couldn't, however, cleanse my mind. The nightmare would stay with me forever. Many times it would come to me, and the dialogue was always puzzling, much like a riddle. The little girl always asked me about war and always told me that the answer was in myself. In the weeks ahead, I learned to accept the dreams as part of my hellish life in Vietnam.

I headed out to the flight line, Colt 45 strapped to my leg and flight helmet in hand. Little did I know that another Purple Heart was looming

Michael W. Mason

on the horizon. I flew observer this time and cradled an M79 grenade launcher. It was Ernie's ship and he flew in the rear gunner's seat.

There was no clue that this would be my last mission as a true Baby Scout. After this day, I would just do my duty. There would be no fun, no thrills, no enjoyment of the hunt. Whatever fire used to burn in my eyes was now just a fading spark. Death, truly was in my eyes. Of all the Scouts, only I had it. What made it even more terrible was that our hootch girl, Mei, had noticed it. She told me, "My, you no look good no more."

I felt like a Black Horse among the Centaurs. Months earlier I had flown joint missions with Black Horse for the salvation of Tay Ninh. Those Aeroscouts all seemed to have death in their eyes. Now, I was fit to be one of them.

My remaining days in-country would be worse than anything suffered so far. I was on the way out of the war and the Baby Scouts, forever.

BABY SCOUT

Michael W. Mason

THIRTEEN

DEAD SCOUT WALKING

Lieutenant Reese was the pilot, Ernie the crew chief and rear gunner, and I flew as observer. We proceeded northwest to Trang Bang. A Cobra flew high cover. The brass wanted us back in the area to scout for signs of enemy resurgence. The infantry had swept the AO after our gunfight on the previous day, but HQ wanted us to look for stragglers or any signs of incursion from nearby Cambodia.

We neared the AO and Lt. Reese dropped to tree-top level. The Cobra was at a thousand feet and hungrily waited for us to flush out its prey. The search took us over many square miles of brush and grassy fields. The battlefield of the previous day was scarred with craters, burnt grass, and scorched, splintered trees. There was also a bloody patch of brown sawgrass. The indentation in the thatch looked like a cross. It was the empty death bed of the little Vietnamese girl that we, I, had killed. A path, from the killing spot, led off into the muddy field. Boot prints were visible. The girl was taken by either Americans or Viet Cong. I couldn't tell. There were heel marks in the soft mud. She was dragged away. I hoped it was by her own people, figuring that she would at least have a proper burial. Somehow, the thought consoled me.

I grimaced as the vision of her dead eyes appeared in my mind. Those eyes would always be with me. Those large, wide eyes of a child would be imprinted on my brain for a lifetime.

The Loach picked up speed and my eyes tried to refocus on the blur of tree tops that passed by. The girl became a memory and was replaced by the needs of the mission. The war returned in the form of a running man in black pajamas. Lieutenant Reese spotted the VC running toward a large mound of dirt covered with old tires. He gave chase but the man disappeared down a square hole at the base of the mountain of dirt and rubber.

We hovered around the opening. The inside of the tunnel seemed to be supported by a wood framework. A single shot rang out and Reese backed off the target. He radioed the Cobra, then told me to fire a frag grenade into the tunnel. The 40mm shotgun-like weapon was already loaded and ready to fire. Lt. Reese banked left so I would have a clear shot at the target. I fired and watched the large shell fly into the tunnel. It exploded and sent

Michael W. Mason

dirt, wood splinters, and smoke, blasting out of the opening. I quickly reloaded and the pilot moved the Loach a little closer to the underground fortress of earth and tires. From about twenty feet away, and ten feet off the ground, I fired. The grenade exploded on a wooden pillar. Debris and shrapnel ricocheted and peppered the Loach all along the left side, including my arm and face. The left plexiglass port cracked and shrapnel punched holes in the tail boom.

"*Damn*! Mason, why did you fire that round?" Lt. Reese was furious.

"Sorry, sir. I thought I had a clear shot."

"I wasn't ready, Mason. I wanted a fly-by, first, to check it out. You should have waited."

"I didn't know, sir."

"*Hell*! You should have known we were too close for that cannon. What's wrong with you, anyway?" Reese spun the loach in a flat spin.

"Do it, Ernie," he said over the intercom.

The crew chief opened up with the M60 and sent hundreds of rounds into the tunnel. He finished the job by tossing in a Willie Peter. He yelled, "Go!" Lieutenant Reese kicked the Loach in the ass and we screamed out of harms way. The nastiest of all grenades sent fire and smoke into the sky. Just to be sure, Reese called in the Cobra. We cleared the AO and watched the rocket attack from a safe distance. The mound exploded into bits of dust, splinters, and burning rubber. Some of the smaller tires flew a hundred feet into the air. The mound collapsed and I was sure that nothing could have survived the four exploding rockets. The Cobra's rotor blades *whomped* loudly as the mighty Gunship pulled out of its attack dive.

There was no sign of a tunnel opening, muchless anything. The infantry would check it out later and probably employ a *tunnel rat* to search the hidden labyrinth.

We limped back to base in our wounded ship. Lieutenant Reese said the pedals felt funny. Ernie probably guessed, as I did, that shrapnel had damaged the tail rotor. The Cobra kept a close watch over us and it wasn't until blood started dripping down my left cheek and onto my lap that I realized that I had been hit with shrapnel. My left arm was also bleeding with shrapnel wounds. Metal shards and wood splinters were sticking in my red-stained skin. It was only then that I felt the pain. I reached up and felt my left cheek. My hand came away bloody.

The trip back to Cu Chi was spent pulling shards of metal and wood splinters out of my face and arm. I used my fingernails, like tweezers, to extract the small, sharp splinters. Lieutenant Reese seemed amused by this. "Only you, Mason," he said, laughing.

I never reported the injuries. They seemed unimportant and another Purple Heart, especially for these injuries, would have been embarrassing. Reese and Ernie were unscathed. We refueld the Loach before putting her to bed in the corral.

Ernie was angry that he had to red-X his ship. The shrapnel holes would have to be patched and the tail rotor assembly replaced before the Loach could fly again. Lieutenant Reese chewed me out for firing the grenade launcher without orders. He walked away saying, "Hit the showers, Mason. You're a mess." I smiled as I heard him chuckling to himself. Shrapnel wounds were not uncommon in the Baby Scouts.

I helped Ernie inspect and clean the ship. I also plucked shrapnel from my flight helmet and mopped up my blood from the cockpit.

Ernie wasn't happy about the holes in his ship, but the resulting gun action had made up for my mistake. Any kind of gun action made Ernie happy.

"Hey, Mike. Let me ride shotgun with the cannon next time, ok?"

"Sure, Ernie. It's your ship."

"Yeah, but you're the chief. You could have flown as gunner if you wanted."

"I know, but it's still your ship. I won't take over someone's ship, Ernie."

"Mike, I just want to ride shotgun when Reese brings the M79."

"Ok, Ernie. Next time, the grenade launcher is yours."

He slapped me on my sore arm and said, *"Fucking-A!"*

I held my sore arm all the way to the Baby Scout hootch. More than a few stares came my way as I trudged down the flight line. I had forgotten all about the blood that was beginning to dry on my face and arm.

When I entered the hootch it was empty except for Mei. She was busy polishing boots. I said, "Hi, Mei." The babysan turned with a smile that quickly dissolved into a grotesque mask of sheer horror. Her eyes got real big, her brow wrinkled, then she screamed.

A minute passed before she got up off the bunk and walked over to me. I managed a weak smile. She hugged me and cried. Mei held on to me for minutes. I didn't know why. With tears running down her face, she looked up at me and said, "My, you go shower. Mei wait for you. Mei here for My." I was a little confused.

She released me and I went into my sleeping cubicle. Looking at me from the mirror was a face I hardly recognized. The left cheek was covered with red, dried blood. A piece of metal was sticking out of my eyebrow and my eye was swollen half-shut. No wonder Mei reacted as she did. I looked like a walking casualty of war. With sore fingers, I plucked out the tiny sliver of metal. It hurt real bad and a trickle of blood trailed down the side of my face.

I sat on my bunk and slowly unlaced my boots. I had inherited Buck's cubicle and was appreciative of the privacy. The boots came off with a bit of effort, and then the green socks. My arm hurt with every movement of my fingers. Undressed, and with a towel wrapped around my waist, I headed for the showers. Mei watched me as I flip-flopped through the hootch. She was pouting. It reminded me of Su lei.

I scrubbed hard at my face and arm. It hurt bad and I worried about infection. I thought about going on sick call for a tetanus shot but, since arriving in the Cav, I had already gotten two of them. There was probably no need for another.

There was no way I could shave so I just brushed my teeth and combed my hair. Mei was waiting for me when I got back to the hootch. She told me to sit. Her words came out like an order. She produced a bottle of Merthiolate and I cringed.

"My, you baby."

"Mei, not that."

"You baby. My big baby."

"It hurts."

"You baby, My." I laughed at the irony and thought about how this young girl was like maid, mother, and nurse to the Baby Scouts. I winced as she dabbed my cuts with the stinging antiseptic. I almost screamed when she smeared the orange solution over my left eyebrow. Mei whispered to me in Vietnamese. I didn't understand a word, but knew she was talking to me as if she was trying to comfort a small child. That's what I was to her, or so I thought. I was her injured child.

Mei produced a gauze bandage from the hootch's first aid kit. After smearing my arm with Merthiolate, she wrapped the gauze around it. Except for the band-aid she placed over my cut eyebrow, my face was left uncovered.

BABY SCOUT

"All done, My."

"Thanks, Mei."

"You no go shot no more. Mei say so." She turned to walk away, then looked back with a sad expression.

"My," she said, "You dying. Mei see in eyes. You dying, My."

"I'm fine, Mei."

"No, My. You die. You no same no more. You dying." I looked at her with my one good eye. It was very unsettling to hear what she was saying. She looked at me with a sad, pouting face that was reminiscent of a girl I still loved, but would never see again.

"You dying, My." She turned away, crying, and ran out of the hootch. I felt like crying, myself. I knew that she knew about Su Lei. Mei, Ernie, and Lt. Reese, I suspected, knew of my frequent milk runs to Saigon. Only Mei had realized what the loss had done to me; the change it had made in me. Mei was the first girl, or young woman, who taught me that intuition was an inherent gift of the female gender. I still believe it to this day.

Mei had learned of my Saigon girlfriend through evesdropping. I talk in my sleep and she discovered my secret by listening to my frequent outbursts during midday naps. During one such episode, she woke me up and demanded the details.

Everytime I returned from Saigon she pestered me for information. I told her we had nice picnics, dinners together, and went to the movies.

"No. No," she would sigh in exasperation. "What you do later? Bang, bang, yes?" My face would turn red and she would laugh.

"Mei, that's kind of private."

"No. You tell Mei. I have boyfriend in Cu Chi. Mei know about bang-bang. You tell Mei."

"You're only sixteen, Mei. I can't tell you about this. Besides, like I said, it's a private thing."

"My, you nineteen."

"Twenty."

"Mei almost seventeen. I woman. You tell Mei what you do in Saigon with girl."

"You might not understand. It's more than just bang-bang." She looked at me with a devilish grin and I knew that I had lost the argument. I told her everything.

"Mei know. Mei know all time. My talk in sleep. You make noise, you moan, you move all around bed. Mei know everything, now. You and Su Lei bang-bang much."

"Mei, it's more than that. You just don't understand."

"My love Su Lei. You die for Su Lei." She looked at me with a smile and a slow nod of her head. I realized that she did understand. Mei knew that our relationship was much more than passionate nights in the penthouse.

"Yes, Mei. That's how it is. It's more than just bang-bang."

"Mei know, now. Mei keep My's secret." She really did understand. The young girl in her only wanted the juicy details, but the woman-side of her understood the intimacy of the relationship.

"I keep secret, My, and you always tell Mei everything."

"Ok," I relented. "It's a deal." She smiled at me with rapidly blinking eyes. It became apparent that I was played like a fiddle. Mei had, somehow, managed to get me to open up about personal matters of the heart. She was going to grow into quite a woman. Of that, I had no doubt. Even now, there was a maturity about her. Maybe it was the war. The children, like the adults, seemed to age prematurely. In Vietnam you had to mature quickly, and not just the Vietnamese. Boys quickly become men in combat, or they pay the ultimate price. I wondered why I was still alive.

The rest of the day was spent sleeping. I woke at sunset and played with Smokey and LT. The dog bisquits were gone so I fed them some scraps from the mess tent. I tired quickly and returned to my bed, still sore and aching from the morning mission. Ernie, loud and boisterous as usual, was regaling the other Baby Scouts with the story of our sortie at Trang Bang. One of the newer Scouts asked, "Isn't this the second time the chief shot up his own ship?" I blacked out and dreamed.

The nightmare transported me back to every mission, every dawn and dusk patrol, and every gunfight and crash. My sleeping eyes witnessed the dead and the dying. I slept helplessly through the terrifying visions: bullets slamming into bloodied bodies, screaming men as they burned in a pyre of flesh and white phosphorous, and worst of all, the wide-eyed faces of stark terror, just before death sent these men to meet their god.

I relived the crash in the Iron Triangle…every vivid scene and every ear-piercing shriek of tearing metal. My eyes looked upon Willie's dying face and they witnessed the thick, oozing blood that gushed from Danny Narvone's shattered leg.

The visions kept changing. My ship, #395, was skipping down the Go Dau Ha River like a smooth stone across a glass, watery surface. Total darkness came and I found myself underwater with near-exploding lungs and terror that was slowly gaining control of my mind. My body slowly sank into the dark realm while my eyes watched the beckoning sun back away from my outstretched, frantically reaching fingers.

The small sun erupted into white light and I found myself looking down into the face of an American soldier. He floated on his back and stared at me with eyes that couldn't see.

Tracer bullets impacted the floating corpse and it imploded from within. The smell of decaying flesh penetrated the powerful rotor wash of the warbird, and it only went away when the desecrated body sank below the surface of a non-descript stream. Bubbles popping on the surface was the only epitaph this lost American would ever receive.

The death flight continued and the passing, beautiful, green countryside turned ugly. Muddy fields and sawgrass blurred past the muzzle of my M60 and I knew that I was, again, flying near Trang Bang Village.

Eyes! It was always the eyes! I knew what was coming. This nighmare wasn't going to end until I was looking into the lifeless eyes of the worst demon of all.

"Where are you? I know you're there." SILENCE.

"Come on. Face me. I'm here." SILENCE.

"What more do you want of me? Face me and get it over with." SILENCE.

My world of flying and dealing indescriminate death suddenly culminated into a replay of the first mission to Trang Bang. All over again I had to witness the slaughter, the running figure in black pajamas, the sound of the uncaring minigun, and the tiny body that crumpled into a horrible facade of crucifix and blood.

"You're here."

"Yes, My. I'm here. You know I always will be."

"Why did you wait so long?"

"You had to see the war."

"I've already seen the war. I've seen as much as anyone."

"No, My. Few have seen war and you're not one of them."

"I don't understand."

"I know. You look into my eyes and you don't see. You are blind."

"I see my reflection. Am I death?"

"No. You are only a cause of death. You must look beyond the reflection that is you."

"When I looked into the eyes of the Black Horse crewmen, there was no reflection. Something else was in their eyes. I thought it might be death."

"Yes, My. You were close to the secret of death, but you never went beyond what you perceived as the *living dead*."

"I saw it and, yet, my eyes didn't see."

"Yes, My. You came close. Those Black Horse men were, indeed, the walking dead. They knew, without reservation, that they would never go home. You only thought that you wouldn't."

"I understand."

"Do you? Look into my eyes." The blood-spattered body zoomed closer and only black, unblinking eyes floated before me.

"I don't see my reflection."

"That's right. What do you see?"

"I see nothing. Only blackness."

"Look closer." I stared into two, dark orbs of total blackness. It was like knocking on the door of an empty house. You knew it was devoid of life but you knocked anyway with an expectation of someone opening the door and letting you in.

"Futility. I see futility. It's like knowing there's someone there but you're not sure. So, you knock a second time even though your mind tells you there's no one home."

"That's what you see?"

"Yes."

"My, you now have seen death."

"You are death, aren't you?"

"Yes, My. I am. I am every person you killed and every lifeless body you've ever seen, or will see."

"You aren't just this dead girl."

"You know that, now."

"What about me? Lieutenant Reese, Mei, and even Su Lei have all mentioned that I'm not quite right. Mei and Su Lei both have said that they saw death in my eyes."

"They did."

"What? Am I going to die?"

"You might. I don't know. I'm only death, not fate."

"So, they see only the probability, not the certainty."

"Yes, My. Those Black Horse men were a certainty. You are a probability."

"Were? You mean…"

"Yes. They're dead."

"And, I could still die."

"Yes. You can still die."

"Then, you do know when death comes."

"Yes, My, because it is me."

"Am I going to die?"

"I said I knew when death was coming. I didn't say that I knew if it would take you. Even when I, death, approaches, it's not an absolute."

"Is Su Lei alive?"

"Yes, My. I am not coming for her."

"Can you tell me where she is?"

"No. I am here only for you."

"You are coming for me?"

"Yes, My. I have been coming for you for a long time. Some day, I will take you."

"Not now?"

"No. Not now. Soon, though, maybe. It's your choice."

"My choice? What do you mean?"

"I have to go."

"No! Wait! Tell me what you mean. Am I going to kill myself? Tell me!"

"Good bye, My. You know me, now, and I will always be with you."

The eyes dissolved into a tiny face which, in turn, dissolved into the cross-like figure that lay sprawled in a red swath of grass. Long strands of black hair blew *helter skelter* in the ship's rotor wash and then slowly fell to cover the face I would never forget. Everything turned black and out of the nothingness came a rocket propelled grenade. It streaked toward me and I lowered my weapon in recognition of futility and death. I watched the fireball approach and, for some reason, abruptly sat up and aimed my M60 at the ball of flame. My finger engaged the trigger and tracers flew toward the fiery death that was going to claim me. I laughed hysterically as small darts of fire met up with the monstrous, fiery face of death. "So this is what it's like," I thought, as the cataclysmic explosion consummated my nightmare in a painful brilliance of blinding light.

I awoke with eyes that saw only darkness and, for a moment, my mind fought the nothingness that it believed to be death. Quickly, rational thought took over and my deluded mind cleared and recognized life. I was alive.

My body was completely beaded with perspiration and I was in a state of physical and mental shock. The war had caught up to me and the terror of its grim reality had set-in with an unforgiving vengeance.

My hair was soaked and the bunk was a soggy pond. I breathed hard and fast. It was a scary few minutes of living-darkness, and I lay there, paralyzed, with unseeing eyes. Sunrise was hours away and it was at that moment that I knew the inevitable. My days of flying as a gunslinging Baby Scout were over.

I sat up and reached for my 45. It always felt cold in my hands, even in 100 degree weather. I couldn't see it, but could feel the familiar cold steel in my left hand.

Without thinking, my right hand pulled back the slide, then let go. It slammed shut, chambering a 45 caliber round in the breech. It was loaded, cocked, and lethal. Slowly, as if some unseen force was guiding the weapon, my hand rose and placed the barrel in my mouth. The steel was cold and it tasted of cleaning oil. My tongue found the muzzle and the large caliber opening. The hammer was cocked. The bullet waited patiently. All I had to do was pull the trigger.

In the dark I sat on my bunk, gun in mouth. My finger slowly rested on the thin metal fulcrum that would launch the powerful lead missile. Everything would end in a split-second. There would be no memories of war, no more horror, and no more hunting for the sheer excitement of killing. I could end my personal misery with a simple, quick pull on the trigger.

I closed my eyes, thinking the nightmares would finally be over. A face appeared in front of my clouded mind. It was Su Lei. Out there, in the world, somewhere, she was alive. Images came to me in rapid succession. I saw mom, dad, my sisters, and a few former girlfriends. Even Mei was there with her cute, pouting face. The *slide show* continued and it was becoming obvious that it was not the time to die. The gun barrel came out of my mouth and the front sight scraped against a front tooth. The odd sensation startled me, but also helped to clear my mind. I dropped the gun to my lap and carefully eased the hammer forward to its resting place.

My racing heart slowed and breathing came easier. I sat alone, in darkness, and began to cry. At the same time, strange, humorous thoughts infiltrated my healing brain.

"The shot would have woken the Scouts. Mei would have to clean up the mess. No one would be around to take care of Smokey and LT. Who would fly in my place?" Almost immediately, the shakes took over my body. I had the answer to my suicidal delerium. Flying! I was scared of flying.

I was going to die if I kept flying. I was sure of it. The gunfights weren't the problem. It was the flying. My mind searched for alternative answers but found none. There was no doubt in my convoluted mind that if I continued my role as a hunter, my journey home would be in an aluminum box.

"What could I do?" The prime directive of the Baby Scouts was search and destroy. My duty was to hunt and kill. I volunteered for it.

I thought, "Maybe I could fly high ship all the time. I'm the Flight Line Chief. I can schedule myself into any slot I want." The rationalizing continued and did me no good at all. A meeting would have to take place with Lieutenant Reese. He would understand.

As I walked to the showers, the sun was on time and Cu Chi was waking to another day of war. The cool water rinsed away the filth of the night, but not the permanent stain that crippled my soul. I slumped to the concrete floor and sat in the dirty, soapy water that welled-up around my legs. Surprisingly, no tears came. Thoughts of Su Lei, and what might have been, overwhelmed me. A scared ex-gunslinger sat under the cool spray and waited for the rays of morning sunlight. I thought, "The new day should bring a new beginning." I was wrong.

Lieutenant Reese was sympathetic but firm.

"You fly or you leave the Scouts." He added that I could fly high ship but only half the time.

"Well," I thought, "at least the odds are better than they were before." Reese said to meet him on the flight line in half an hour.

He said, "Tay Ninh is active, again. We're going to the Cambodian border."

"This is not good," I thought to myself as Lt. Reese walked out the door. Cambodian missions were among the most dangerous. We often crossed the border in search of enemy base camps and weapon caches. It was done without orders and the brass looked the other way. It was just another part of the war, though covert. A year later, President Richard Nixon would go on network television and announce that American forces were beginning to engage the enemy in Cambodia. Thousands of Vietnam veterans probably got a good laugh out of that.

I was very nervous and prepared to shoot anything on sight as we flew toward Tay Ninh. The M60 was comforting and helped me deal with the terror of flying. When we reached the AO, our Loach went low and the Cobra climbed to 1500-feet. The brass wanted us to skirt the Cambodian border to look for enemy trails. Having a Cobra for cover made it easier for me, but I was still nervous, jumpy, and scared. I was never scared on a mission before. It was a new and strange sensation. It was also a horrible one. For the first time, since arriving in-country, I felt fear. It was gut-wrenching, soul-wrenching fear. I didn't like it and my finger began to tap on the trigger of my machine gun.

Lieutenant Reese flew slower than usual and we scoured the thick brush for signs of NVA incursion. The jungle was so thick that it reminded me of the Iron Triangle. When flying above the Triangle, you almost never got in the first shot.

I looked over the left bulkhead and saw the observer marking a map with a red grease pencil. As bad a map-reader as I was, I knew that we had crossed the Cambodian border. I sat back and lined up three Willie Peter grenades, just in case.

"Stay sharp, Mason," said Reese through the intercom. I could tell that even the Lieutenant was a little nervous. I would find out, years later, that this mission was one of the first, of many, that covertly crossed the border. The Baby Scouts did it. The 1st Air Cav did it. I'm sure that Black Horse did it. For many years I wondered if our illegal reconnaissance missions were just the tip of the iceberg. I doubted it and could only guess at what other illicit operations went on during my year in-country.

The Cambodian mission fell short of expectations. We found nothing but jungle, snakes, strange looking large rodents, and deer. We met up with another Loach just outside of the Cu Chi perimeter. Lieutenant Reese radioed the warbird that we were going to refuel before joining up to go out on dusk patrol. I wasn't happy about this new development, but relaxed a little when I found out we were going to be the high ship. The shakes subsided and my trigger finger relaxed a little.

Dusk Patrol also turned out to be uneventful. After putting the ship to bed, Lt. Reese asked me, "How do you feel?"

"Ok, sir. I'm a little trigger happy and scared as hell."

"Can you keep this up for the next few weeks?"

"I think so, if I fly with you." Reese said everything would work out. I wasn't so sure, and that very night I became a bunker rat.

My fingers were bloody but I continued to work long into the night. I wouldn't stop until I had finished my own, personal bunker. I cut a large hole in the hootch wall, behind my bunk, and then went outside to build a sandbag bunker around the hole. When finished, two days later, the little bunker house was heavily fortified. It was triple-layered with sandbags and steel revetment plates. The inside was spartan. A blanket covered the dirt floor and there was a pillow and a candle. I still slept in my bunk, but felt safer and slept easier knowing that the little fortress was there.

The other Scouts were wondering what was up with me. I became more distant and didn't fool around with them anymore. When a rocket attack came a few days later, I scurried under my bunk, through the hole, and into my tiny, armored safehouse. Right behind me was Ernie.

"This is better than the troop bunker, Mike."

"Yeah, I think so, and it's closer."

I lit the candle and smiled nervously as he looked at me with that stupid, soul-searching stare of his. His fiery, red hair and freckles seemed to glow in the soft light of the flickering candle. He knew! I saw it on his face. He knew I was scared. Ernie didn't say a word and before the night was over, all the Scouts would know my fear.

Ernie loved to talk. Most of the time it was about himself and his glorious exploits in combat. He loved gossip and soon my fear would be common knowledge in the hootch and the troop. He left after the all-clear was given. I stayed in the little house *that Mike built*. I wouldn't come out until morning.

The rest of the week was busy with search and destroy missions. Most of the time I flew high ship. When a Gunship was my partner, I was low ship. My nerves were frayed and I was close to the breaking point. Paranoia became a constant companion and before it became my friend, I went to see Lieutenant Reese.

"I understand," said the Lieutenant, "especially after all you've been through." He continued and said that I was no longer Flight Line Chief.

Michael W. Mason

He said I could contiue to fly high ship, then asked if I thought Ernie would make a good Chief of Scouts.

"Yeah. He's a brash and in your face kind of guy, but you'll always know where you stand with him. He's also a lot like Buck. I think he'd make a good chief." Reese nodded and I knew that Ernie was now the new Chief of Scouts.

The next few days were spent flying dawn and dusk patrols. The low ship had one kill on the second day. My ship just circled at 500 feet and waited to make a gunrun. A smoke grenade was thrown. Lt. Reese saw it and dived with minigun firing. I fired the M60 as we came in low over the smoke-marked target. I never saw the enemy but continued to lay down cover fire. "Mike, knock it off!" Lt. Reese was yelling at me over the intercom. My trigger finger was frozen on the trigger and the M60 continued firing long after we pulled out of the attack dive.

"Ok, sir." It was a hard thing to do…letting go of the trigger. I gasped for breath and sat back in the jumpseat. Never before had I held my breath while engaged in a firefight. It always came easy to me. I looked up and saw the observer staring at me. My hands went up in the air and I looked at him with an expression that said, "What?" He shook his head and looked away. "Screw him," I thought. "He's a FNG. What does he know?"

On the way back to the corral I felt relieved. The built-up anxiety was gone and I felt somewhat like my old self. I still hated the flying but had discovered that I still relished a good firefight. It wasn't fun, but it was still exhilarating.

Ernie got credit for the kill and would tell some tall-tales that night in the hootch. I would spend the time in my bunker waiting for the night to end, and a new day to begin.

The claxon sounded in the darkness of the early morning hours. I came out of my *rat hole* and put on my flight gear. The siren was screaming the *Scramble Alert* and the hootch became filled with sounds of weapons being loaded and cocked. Lieutenant Reese crashed through the door and yelled the legendary call to battle. "Baby Scouts, assemble!" I strapped on my Colt and chambered a round. On full alert we were allowed to lock and load. I carefully lowered the hammer and holstered the bulky, semi-automatic pistol. Reese said, "Our Slicks were ambushed during a Kit Carson dustoff. There's not a ship left and our guys are pinned down. Let's go, Scouts."

We hit the door running. Every Gunship in the troop was warming up on the flight line. The Baby Scout ships were also warming up, waiting for their flight leader and the crews. I was nervous, but in control. My fear was in-check for the first time in two weeks. Until now, I was one of the walking dead…a frightened soldier who served no one but himself. Now, it was different. The Kit Carson platoon and the crewmen of the downed Slicks waited for their rescue, and a frightened Baby Scout looked for healing and his redemption.

By the time I reached the flight line only one Loach was left. It was the new replacement for #395. I froze when I saw that it was as bare as a Slick. There was no minigun, no M60, and no grenades. The other ships were warmed up and backing out of their bunkers. One after another the gunships and Aeroscouts hovered to the flight line and launched at maximum power. The mighty Hog led the way. In a matter of seconds not a single warship, save my stripped-down Loach, remained on the flight line. Every weapon was armed and primed. No one cared about the perimeter safety rule this night. I stood-by the naked Loach and waited for my pilot.

Lieutenant Kerns approached and I told him the bad news.

"The ship is ready but we got no guns."

"No guns?"

"Yes sir. It's the replacement for #395. It hasn't been fitted yet for combat."

"*Damn*!" he said. "Well, let's go anyway. Maybe we can do dustoff."

"Oh, *hell*!" I thought. "That's worse than hunting without a gunship."

I blew off the fire extinguisher drill and climbed into the observer's seat. Between us, Kerns and I had an M16 and a Colt 45. The odds of us returning were not good.

The turbine ignitor was popping at the same time the last Gunship cleared the maintenance hangar. Slowly, the powerful Cobras would catch up to the swift Loaches and the mighty, lethargic Hog.

Cu Chi tower had shut all air traffic down except for the D Troop Centaurs of the 3/4 Cavalry. All of the other aerial outfits of the 25th Infantry Division were grounded as the Centaurs made their way into the starless night. I sat in the weaponless Loach and watched as D Troop of the 3/4 Cavalry unleashed its entire fleet of aerial destroyers, heavy cruisers, and one big, nasty battleship.

We were the last to line up on the airfield. The Loach had no weapons of any significance and if we were to be of any use, it would be as a mini-Slick. Kerns was as nervous as me but we both wanted to help the Cav. I had forgotten my chicken plate but figured it didn't matter. It would be a miracle if we returned from this mission at all.

As the Lieutenant pulled pitch the radio squawked, "Stand down. Stand down. Centaur alert aborted. All ships except the Hog return to the corral." The Centaurs called in and OPS confirmed the order.

"Centaur one-six to ops."

"Go, one-six."

"Permission to stay and scout the AO." It was Lt. Reese. There was a long pause and when OPS came back on the air it said, "Roger, one-six. You be *damn* careful out there!"

"Roger, OPS. I've got the Hog with me." There was no reply from Operations. Everyone knew that when you had the Hog as your bodyguard, your life expectancy went from seven seconds to maybe a minute.

The scramble was called off and Kerns and I breathed a sigh of relief. It's not that we didn't want to fly; we just knew that it would be a suicide mission. Kerns throttled down the turbine and I popped the clip from his M16. I ejected the chambered round and it went flying through the cockpit and out the pilot's door. Kerns didn't notice and snuffed the turbine fire. He got out and walked back to OPS. I stayed with the Loach and waited for the rotor to stop spinning.

I wondered how the rescue mission was going. The Cobras and the Hog probably got off a few rockets before the scramble was cancelled. It was not uncommon for pilots to disregard orders for the sake of *getting off* just a few rounds of minigun fire or a rocket or two. The pilots knew that the officers in OPS would understand. After all, they were pilots, too.

The Loaches returned as I walked down the flight line. I felt like a Baby Scout again and would talk to Lieutenant Reese in the morning. Flying still scared the hell out of me, but the thrill of fighting was still there. I was drawing and twirling my Colt as I left the dark and noisy airfield.

Casualties from the VC ambush were high. Many were dead but, fortunately, the wounded outnumbered the fatalities. All the Slicks were either heavily damaged or destroyed, and their crews were shot up pretty bad. One of the dead was the troop's clerk. Many times I wondered, "What the hell was he doing on a Kit Carson dustoff?"

George Lamb was a nineteen year old youth who wanted to be a *man of war*. He had flown with me months earlier, before the loss of #395. He wanted to be in the war, I guessed, so he could tell family and friends that he was in combat.

George got permission from the Troop's CO to fly a scout mission and #395 was the designated ship. The *old man* must have figured that his clerk would be taken care of by the Chief of Scouts. What the old man didn't know was that George Lamb was a walking disaster. The troop clerk was a klutz!

I knew that I would have to watch him carefully. He would fly left seat and hold an M16. I looked down at the box of grenades between my feet and thanked God that he wasn't going to fly as gunner. George was the guy who would throw the pin and hold the grenade. I shuddered when I thought of him handling Willie Peter grenades.

The mission was routine and almost dull. I was, nevertheless, relieved when we got back to the corral. The pilot cut the throttle and I got out first. As I removed my helmet and chicken plate, George unbuckled his safety harness and clumsily exited the ship. I walked around to lend him a hand, but was too late. He climbed out with his left hand over his head to balance himself. Unfortunately for #395, he was holding the M16 at the time. The muzzle went up into the spinning rotor blades. My heart missed a beat as the ear-splitting *clang* reverberated through my head.

The pilot wasn't looking but felt an odd vibration in the cyclic stick. He looked up, shook his head, and grinned as he passed me the log book. I was mad but didn't say anything to the pilot or George. He was the CO's boy and it really wasn't his fault. He was just being himself and I was grateful just to be safely on the ground.

I marked a big, red X in the log book, then helped George out of his flight gear. He looked at me and said, "Sorry."

"That's ok, George. It happens." He walked to OPS with the pilot. When the rotor stopped, I reached up and pulled down the flexible, wounded blade. It had a gouge and a long, shallow scratch. I thought it looked superficial. The TI (Technical Inspector), came out to inspect the damage. He agreed that it shouldn't be a problem. I signed off the red X and the TI initialed it. Before he left, he said it might be a good idea to check the rotor blade tracking with the electronic strobe gun.

I later told Lieutenant Reese that I didn't think George Lamb should fly with the Baby Scouts. He was reluctant to agree but had a change of heart when I asked, "Do you really want George playing with a box of Willie Peter and frags?" George Lamb, troop clerk, never flew with the Baby Scouts again.

George did manage to get on a Slick as door gunner. He flew the one mission and died. He died because the brass wouldn't, or couldn't, say no to their eager troop clerk. The boy went home in a shiny, aluminum casket because some officer let him play soldier in a war he wasn't meant to be in. It wasn't the NVA or the VC that killed George Lamb. It was sheer stupidity. Sometimes, officers can be real assholes. As for me, Lieutenant Reese would soon come to a decision. He would have to decide my fate with the Baby Scouts. I was hoping my rebirth as a flying gunner would influence his decision. Eventually, the Baby Scout leader delivered the bittersweet news.

BABY SCOUT

Michael W. Mason

FOURTEEN

THE SEX FACTORY OF CHINA BEACH

Lieutenant Reese met with me in the Baby Scout hootch. "I have no choice," he said. "You have to leave the Scouts." I didn't argue but felt like I was kicked in the stomach.

"You are reassigned to the Gunship platoon and will spend your last month in-country with them." I wanted to tell him that I was *back* and ready to fly. Reese knew, though, that I wasn't the same Chief of Scouts anymore. My nerves were frazzled and he couldn't depend on someone who wasn't a hundred percent. He thought I was a walking time bomb with a short fuse. He couldn't have been more correct.

The Lieutenant said to pack and move into the Gunship hootch within the hour. We shook hands and he added, "Mason, after what you've been through, I'm surprised you lasted this long."

"Thank you, sir. I'll always be a Baby Scout, you know."

"I know, Mike. If it matters, you're not the first to go out this way. I've heard stories that…"

"It's ok, sir. I understand. You don't need to try to cheer me up. I'm not happy about this but I do understand."

"Look, you've done a hell of a job for eleven months. Be proud of that. Besides, the Gunship platoon might be a nice change for you. You might even get to fly on a Cobra, or even the Hog."

"It won't be the Baby Scouts, sir."

"Maybe, but LT picked you to be a Scout. Never forget that."

"Is LT dead, sir?"

"I don't know. I've asked around but no one seems to know what happened to Larry."

"What about Danny?"

"Narvone? He's fine. The wound looked worse than it really was. He's got a few metal pins in his leg now and walks with a slight limp, but he's home with his family and doing fine. I think he's going to retire a Spec-6. He got promoted."

"That's great, sir."

Michael W. Mason

"Look, Mason, Mike, we've been through a lot together. This is tough for me, but I think it's for the best. You still have a month to go and the troop is short on trained crew chiefs. You'll do well with the Gunships."

"I hope so, sir. Uh, what are you going to tell the Scouts?"

"The truth. You did good for eleven months before getting burned out."

"Ok. I guess that's about right."

"Remember what you've been through, Mason. I'm surprised you lasted this long."

"I will, sir, and thanks." We talked for a few more minutes and relived past adventures. Lt. Reese had been through as much as I had.

"Remember the Baby Scouts, Mike. You'll always be one of us."

"I will, Lieutenant, and you remember to always keep the hunt on the starboard side."

"Where else?" he said. We shook hands and the Baby Scout leader walked out the door. With his exit went my membership with the best aeroscout outfit in War Zone C.

While I was packing, Ernie came over and thanked me for recommending him for Chief of Scouts. I told him, "You deserve it."

"Mike, what are you going to do now?"

"Crew with the Gunships."

"*Damn*! Maybe you'll get a ride on a Cobra or even the Hog."

"Maybe. I always did want to fly gunner on the Hog." We faced each other for what seemed like an eternity. Out of the blue came the question that I knew would some day come.

"Mike, are you scared?" What he really asked was, "Mike, are you a coward?" Like Hutch, Ernie was always blunt and in your face.

"Yes, Ernie. I'm scared. Flying scares the hell out of me. When it hits the fan, I'm ok and I forget about being in the air. The fighting helps me forget where I am." Ernie stared at me for a moment before answering.

"I can dig that." He tried to make me feel better and it worked.

"We had some great times, huh, Mike?"

"Yeah, we did." We shook hands and Ernie walked away.

I yelled after him, "Remember Saigon."

He answered, over his shoulder, "*Fucking A!*"

My eyes looked around the cubicle to see if I had forgotten to pack anything. My long string of grenade rings hung from the rafters. Though each ring had a story, I decided to leave them, as well as the wallpaper of *Playboy* centerfolds. I figured that whomever moved into my cubicle would probably appreciate the scenery.

I shouldered my dufflebag and picked up my flight helmet. "Good hunting, Scouts," I whispered. The hootch door slammed behind me with a loud "*Bang!*" It exclaimed my bittersweet departure from the Baby Scouts better than any words ever could.

Right in front of me, ten feet away, was the Gunship hootch. I didn't go in right away. I used the pisser pipe, then played with LT and Smokey. It quickly dawned on me that I would have to find someone to care for them after I went home. LT had become more tempermental. I suspected he was suffering from worms and distemper. Smokey, however, was still the same frisky pooch. The mutts would be good medicine for me during my last weeks in-country. When I played with them my mind was anywhere but in the war. LT was not the most playful of dogs but Smokey loved a good romp. He never failed to bring me out of my frequent, self-induced doldrums.

I filled their water bowls and stepped back over the wire-mesh pen that I had built for them. I picked up the dufflebag and flight helmet and kicked open the hootch door that guarded the dark realm of Gunship country.

It was always dark in the hootch. The sun never seemed to find a way into the musty, dirty, wood building. It was also less decorated than the Baby Scout quarters. There were no chains of grenade rings hanging from the rafters and few centerfolds adorned the walls. The place was almost barren. The only saving grace were the many beer cans that littered the dirty, concrete floor.

The guys were the same, though. They were young, tough, and always eager for a good fight. The Gunship crewmen used drugs often, though it was mostly Marijuana. Overall, they made the Baby Scouts look like young republicans.

One of the guys told me to take the bunk by the door. He was a Spec-5, like myself, and recognized me on sight. I knew him, too. He was the Hog crew chief. He looked at my name tag and said, "Mason, you're with me tomorrow night on a flare drop. I need someone with M60 experience." He, like everyone else, knew of my flying problem.

"Any questions?"

"Nope. Got any beer?" He grinned and offered a hand.

Michael W. Mason

"My name is Jake Parsons. You'll be flying as left gunner. Don't touch anything unless I tell you to. Got it?"

"Yeah, Jake. What about the beer?" He laughed and walked over to a cooler. He threw me a *Bud* and popped one for himself.

"Another thing...get rid of that pop gun. Gunship crewmen don't carry rocks on missions." He walked away before I could reply. I knew he was right, though. The days of playing *John Wayne* were over. I wasn't a gunslinging Baby Scout anymore. What I would become was still in question.

My Baby Scout days in the Air Cavalry were over. On the walk to the supply hootch, I pulled the heavy Colt from its holster and began to twirl it on my finger. The days of up-close fighting and killing were over, too. I stopped outside supply and ejected the ammo clip. The slide came back smoothly and I checked to make sure the chamber was empty. It was. The Colt would be missed. It was my alter-ego. Wearing it always added a spark to my persona, and a spring to my step.

I was going to miss the tree top skirmishes. That was what I liked most about the Baby Scouts. You fought the enemy at close range. Sometimes you looked him in his eyes as you killed him. He, of course, would try to kill me, but I was always faster on the trigger or just plain lucky. It also helped that Charlie was a lousy shot.

Flying on the Gunships would be far different. My M60 would kill from afar and my eyes would rarely see the enemy. Instead of being the hunter, I was now the killer. The Gunship crews thought the Baby Scouts were a brave but crazy lot. They were right on both counts. The Scouts could be courageous or just plain nuts. They were the decoy or bait. Once the little ship drew enemy fire, the Gunship would commence its attack. I would miss the Scouts, but would learn to respect the Gunships and their crews.

I turned in my beloved Colt and was issued an M16 and two bandoliers of ammo clips. For sentimental reasons, I kept my black and silver holster. On the walk back to the hootch I ran into Lt. Kerns. I saluted and then we talked a bit. He had only a few days to go, himself. He wished me luck and, I, him."

After cleaning the M16 and loading the clips, I finished unpacking. I didn't have as much stuff anymore because I had already sent it home. With about a month left in-country, the Army gives you a four by two wood crate. I sent home my stereo, movie projector and camera, pictures, medals, and holster. This box of goodies would soon get me in trouble with the commanding officer of D Troop of the 3/4 Cavalry.

In early Janury, 1969, there was a *fragging* in the Troop. The story was never confirmed but everyone talked about it for days. It seems that a very disgruntled soldier rigged a grenade to the CO's bunk. When the Major went to lie down, he heard the detonator pop. He jumped up and flew through the hootch door, just seconds before the blast obliterated his bunk and peppered the hootch interior with shrapnel. The Major left the Cav soon after. His tour was about up, anyway. Some of the guys thought the fragging was in retaliation for the recent Slick disaster. My guess was that an Aero-Rifleman or a Kit Carson Scout did it.

The next night arrived and I found myself door-gunning on the Hog. Jake had given me some OJT, earlier in the day, so I didn't feel too out of place on the mighty Gunship. It was one in the morning and we were circling the AO, which was only a few miles from Cu Chi. On the rear deck was an open crate of parachute flares. I didn't throw any. That was Jake's responsibility.

My eyes followed every movement as Jake primed and tossed the flares. The miniature suns fell about fifty feet, then ignited and lit up the ground where our infantry was playing hide and seek with Charlie. We stayed on station for an hour and never got a call to make a gunrun. I was really disappointed, and looking forward to firing the M60 as the Hog made its awesome rocket and minigun attack.

When we got back to the corral, I was told to report to OPS. It was three a.m. and the new CO was there, and not in a good mood.

"Sir, Spec-5, Michael W. Mason reporting as ordered."

"At ease, Mason. Put your M16 and flight helmet on the chair."

"Yes, sir." I did so and then turned back to face the CO. He wasn't there.

"Over here, Mason." He was standing next to the table that supported the troop's radio and tele-communication equipment.

"I got a call an hour ago. Guess who it was?"

"Sir?" He had a funny look on his sunburned face.

"Your mother."

"My mother?"

"And your dad. Now, why do you think they'd call Operations, asking for you?"

"Well, uh, I don't know, sir."

"You don't know? Well, let me tell you. They thought you might be dead."

"Dead, sir?" I was shocked. "Why would they think I was dead?"

"Good question. Let me tell you. You told them you were dead."

"What? Sir, I never…"

"Yes, you did, Mason. Although, not in word."

"I don't understand." The CO was still angry but there was a slight smirk on his face while he played *twenty questions* with me.

"Mason, did you send home your crate of personal belongings?"

"Yes, sir. A few weeks ago."

"Was there a Purple Heart medal in the box?"

"Uh, Yes, sir."

"When was the last time you wrote home?"

"Uh, gee, I don't know. Maybe a few weeks."

"Let's try two months, Mason. The last letter you wrote home was two months ago. I tend to believe your mother."

"Sorry, sir. I've been kind of busy and…"

"Can it, Mason. You're never too busy to write your mother. Not in this Army or any Army."

"Yes, sir."

The old man was right. What he said was one of the basic axioms of military service. It was even stressed in boot camp. Always write home! The Army was very adamant about that. It was one of the few *laws* that superceeded military procedures. If you had to go to the bathroom you got to go, even if you were in the middle of something important. If you were on an all-day hike, there were five minute *smoke breaks* for the nicotine-addicted. That one puzzled me, though I never complained. It just seemed odd that the Army worked so hard to get you in shape, then would yell, "Light 'em if you got 'em." Writing momma was probably the most important. Apparently, keeping mom up to date, and happy, also kept the brass happy, and the Army running smoothly.

"Mason, your parents found the Purple Heart. What caused them to call here was the fact that you never let them know about it. They hadn't heard from you in so long, that they assumed the worst. You screwed up big time, Mason."

"Yes, sir. Sorry, sir."

"Sit down at the table, Mason. Let's call mom." He smiled a genuine smile. The anger was gone.

The CO made the call himself. The Military Affiliate Radio System relayed the call to the states and in a few minutes I heard a sweet, familiar voice answering, "Hello?" It was my mom.

"Hi, mom. It's Mike." Dad and my two sisters got on the other two phones in the house. We had a long talk.

I said I was sorry for worrying them and explained about the Purple Heart and my shrapnel wounds. My older sister, Carol, said that they had also found my movie projector and films. She said that the entire family, including uncle, aunt, cousins, and grandma, gathered to watch my home movies from Vietnam. Dad loaded the projector, hit the lights, and started the show.

On the screen appeared a half-naked girl playing with a beach ball. My older sister found it hysterically funny and laughed her butt off at this *promotional film* that a movie company had sent me. Dad and Uncle Tony laughed too, though mom was a little taken back by the bouncing babe, ball, and breasts. Grandma took it quite well, according to my sister. All she said was, "Nice bosoms."

I talked with everyone and assured them, many times, that I was ok. I ended the trans-pacific call saying, "I love you." I hung up and thanked the CO. He said, "Alright, Mason, but don't let this happen again. Get a letter off to your mom tonight."

"Yes, sir. Right away, sir." I walked out of OPS and breathed a sigh of relief. The old man took it easy on me and seemed like a good guy. It also felt good to speak to my family. The CO was right. I was derelict in not writing home.

Once in the Gunship hootch, I grabbed some paper and a pen and lay down on my bunk. A ripe, pungent smell of marijuana was in the air. I ignored it and began to write the long, overdue letter.

As I was writing, lying on my back, something began to crawl up my leg. I dropped the notepad and found myself staring into the glowing, red eyes of a kitten-size rat. The dark-brown rodent stopped in its tracks and stared back. Before I could react, it stood up on its back legs and "squeaked" at me. Not understanding rat language, I ignorantly perceived the *Hello* as a challenge. I was about to swat the vermin when he, or she, scurried back down my leg and jumped to the floor. It ran across the floor and then climbed up the wooden doorframe and into the rafters.

"That's Fred." I turned and saw Jake looking up at Fred the rat. "He's kind of like our mascot," he added. "We've gotten used to having him around and, besides, he's never bitten anyone. I looked up and saw the huge rat looking down at me. He looked almost as big as LT. I hoped Fred had a nicer disposition.

I got used to Fred and accepted him as the Gunship mascot. What I didn't like, though, was wakeing up and finding him asleep on my backside or crotch. For some reason, Fred always picked my bunk to relax on. One day, Fred made a fatal mistake. He gave birth to a litter of baby rats. Fred turned out to be…*Fredericka*."

The brass considered the litter an infestation and declared war on the rodent family. Traps and poison were spread about the hootch. The poison got the babies but Fredericka was smart. She lasted a week before a rat trap with peanut butter snapped her neck. The hootch lost its mascot and her babies. Soon, another mascot would join Fredericka in animal heaven.

I was on the flight line when Ernie came up to me and said, "Mike, I think one of your dogs is dead." My eyes followed his hand that pointed to the road.

"Over there," he said. "A tank got him. Sorry."

On the walk to the road my only thought was, "Which one?"

I followed the wide tread marks for fifty yards. My question was answered. It was LT. The little, pudgy hound was literally flattened like a pancake. Only the tail got spared by the tread of the monstrous tank. I picked LT up by the tail and pulled him out of the indentation in the dirt road.

With sadness, I buried my dog behind the Baby Scout ammo locker. As I walked back to the Gunships I thought, "Well, I've still got Smokey." I would have to make sure that he got taken care of after I left. All the Scouts loved him and having the pooch around was like having a familiar, boyhood friend to play with. Smokey was the family dog.

The days went by slowly. It's true what *they* say…time does pass slowly when you're looking forward to something. Some days, it just seems to stand still. It was one of those days when I got the order to report to a Gunship on the flight line. I picked up my rifle and flight helmet and expected to be soon flying on a search and destroy mission.

The Huey gunship was warming up in the bunker. The co-pilot told me to take the left gunner position. He said we were taking two division brass to Vung Tau. I hopped aboard and nodded to the crew chief and the two senior officers. The M60 was lying on the deck. I picked it up and checked the action. It was rough but usable. It would get a good cleaning later.

We flew at 3,000 feet all the way to the R & R center of South Vietnam. The crew chief and I loaded our weapons, then sat back and enjoyed the trip. He enjoyed it and I was nervous the whole time. The officers, a Bird Colonel and a Light Colonel, kept looking at me and the crew chief. They seemed concerned with our laid-back attitude. The chief, a Spec-5 like myself, was slumped back in his seat and calmly smoking a cigarette. I just sat, M60 on my lap, and tried to ignore the officers and my fears. The brass never said anything, but it was obvious that they wished for a different pair of bodyguards.

We unloaded the machine guns when we crossed over the base perimeter. The pilot sat the Huey down near an OV-1 or Mohawk. The pilot, co-pilot, and brass, walked to headquarters. The crew chief said we had four hours to play around.

"What are you going to do?" I asked.

"Have a few drinks and get laid."

I laughed and said, "I think I'm going to check out the beach."

"What a waste," laughed the Spec-five. "Four hours to play and all you want to do is get a suntan?"

"Well, maybe some girls will be there. Some nurses in bikinis, maybe?"

"Doubt it, Mason. Whatever pulls your chain, though." We walked out the gate together but soon parted. He went down a side street and was set upon by young boys, intent on selling their sisters. I continued toward the salty smell of the sea.

Playtime was off to a disappointing start. The beach was beautiful but almost deserted. Not a nurse in sight, muchless any girls in bikinis. Depressed, I took off my my boots, socks, and shirt. I sat in the clean, white sand and looked out over the calm, blue water. The sea was so dark it looked black.

A few other soldiers were on the beach. One had a pretty Vietnamese girl with him. My mind reeled with thoughts of better times and of a girl I once knew. Before sadness and bitter memories claimed me, my ears were filled with a nostalgic sound from my childhood. Looking around, my eyes focused on the Vietnamese equivalent of a *Good Humor* truck. It was a pineapple vendor, pushing a cart and ringing a chain of little bells. He was selling frozen pineapples...Vietnamese ice cream.

Michael W. Mason

I bought one for a dollar. The little man took a whole fruit from the ice-filled chest and hacked off the top and sides with a machete. He stuck a long, round, pointed stick into it and then passed it to me. I sat down with my cold, refreshing treat. The vendor, with bells ringing, trudged down the beach until he was flagged down by the soldier with the pretty Vietnamese girl.

The pineapple on a stick was a cold, sweet treat. I savored the delicious, exotic, Asian fruit bar as a young child would an ice cream cone. Until this day, I had always thought pineapple was only for garnishing a holiday ham. When finished, I picked my teeth with the pointed stick, then threw it and the fruity husk into a nearby trash can. My hands and mouth were sticky so I washed them in the warm surf of the sea. After wading in the surf for a few minutes I got bored and headed back toward the village.

The further I got from the beach, the more Vung Tau stunk. Everywhere I went in the village, there was the smell of rotting garbage. I turned down the side street that the crew chief had taken. There were a few Vietnamese milling around. A young boy, maybe ten, asked me if I wanted his sister or his mother. I ignored him and walked on.

Just ahead, and out of an alley, came three guys. Two were wearing jungle fatigues. The other, civvies. They looked tired but were conversing loudly.

"Mine had big boobs for an oriental."

"You idiot," said the Sergeant to the man in civilian clothes. "She's Asian. Rugs and vases are oriental."

"You're both idiots," said the third guy, another Sergeant. "You paid too much for too little sex." They all laughed and then looked at me as I walked by. One of the Sergeants winked at me and gestured with his thumb toward a nearby alley. I stopped and watched them turn up the main street. A young boy chased after them hoping to make a sale.

I turned up the alley and saw a large, wooden building. It was like a hootch but much bigger. The structure was painted pink, had no windows, and a pair of red double doors swung open as I walked through.

A woman, about thirty but looking fifty, was talking to a soldier who was at the head of a short line. She wasn't very attractive, wore a dirty, white Ao dai and too much makeup. The Corporal she was talking to gave her some money and she pointed down a long aisle.

The entire length of the brothel was one big latticework of wood spars and white bedsheets. It was cubicle after cubicle running the length of the building and on both sides of the aisle. At the end was a large, red curtain. It spanned the width of the whorehouse from ceiling to floor. The Corporal walked down the aisle looking from side to side. He disappeared into a cubicle. A sheet closed behind him.

It was hot inside the brothel but not as sweltering as I thought it would be. There were ceiling fans and a narrow, screened opening that ran around the top of the walls. The air was pungent and smelled like clothes that had sat in a hamper for too long.

The other soldiers ahead of me went through the same routine as the Corporal. My eyes followed them as they entered their chosen cubicles. I was wondering about the red curtain at the end of the building when the painted woman said, "You next."

She stuck out her hand and I gave her ten dollars. Her finger pointed the way and a raspy voice said, "Any opening." A smile formed on my face but she just stared at me. She either had no sense of humor or didn't realize what she had said.

Tentatively, I walked down the aisle looking left, then right, then left again. My ears picked up the sounds of moaning and colliding bodies. Bed springs creaked and the pungent smell got more intense.

I looked into the openings as I walked by. Naked girls lay on metal-frame beds with thin mattresses. The whores all looked the same...black hair and eyes, brown skin, and dour facial expressions. Many of them were old...thirty or more. As my boots scuffed along, kicking up dust from the dirty, concrete floor, the red curtain parted in the middle and a soldier appeared. He took a step forward, stopped, and buttoned up his fly. The rippling curtain closed behind him. The soldier walked by me, his eyes never swaying from the path ahead of him. His walk was brisk and I thought He'd break into a run at any moment. A few seconds later, swinging doors silently heralded his swift departure.

The red curtain had really piqued my curiosity. My feet had stopped and my eyes were locked on it. I really wanted to see what was behind it. At that moment, a cubicle sheet to the left of me opened and a naked woman was standing before me. She looked at me with vacuous eyes, then turned and walked to a wet, stained mattress.

For no good reason, whatsoever, I followed her. My eyes stared down as she lay on her back. A long, slender finger pointed and in broken English she said, "You close, please." I closed the door of white linen and looked at her. She spread her legs and beckoned, "You come."

Michael W. Mason

My mind reeled with disgust. This wasn't right and it wasn't for me. I feared that even a condom wouldn't be protection-enough to save me from being sent to the dreaded *VD Island*. This place, and the woman, were what the Army VD films were all about. If the horrible legend of *Black Syph* was true, then this was where a young, foolish soldier would get it. Although I never fully-believed the stories about a prison hospital for VD-infected soldiers, my mind never discounted the stories, either. According to legend, infected soldiers, sailors, marines, and even nurses, were sent to an isolated place to die. Wives and relatives were sent a bronze star and a letter that read, "We regret to inform you that *GI Joe* was killed in action." Of all the tall-tales that the Vietnam War gave birth to, VD Island, to me, was the scariest.

"You come. You come, now."

"No. I've changed my mind. Sorry." Her eyes looked into mine. I don't know what she saw, but my eyes saw only a reflection of light and myself.

"No? You say no?" There was still no expression on her tired and baggy-eyed face. At that moment the woman looked much older than I first thought.

"Yes. I mean, no. I need to go." Fear was setting in.

She cracked a smile and showed crooked, yellow, nicotine-stained teeth. "You go," she said. A finger gestured to the sheet-covered wall.

"You go that way, now." The woman got up and opened the aisle sheet as I slipped behind the one that covered the wooden wall of the brothel. She, again, was open for business as I walked down the narrow walkway in the direction of the red curtain. Moans came from the cubicles I passed. All were male voices. There seemed to be no passion in the women. As I slowly made my way down the dark aisle, my eyes witnessed vague silhouettes on the backlit sheets. The distorted, human forms reminded me of *shadow puppets*. Another fond childhood memory was lost to me forever.

The women were doing a repetitive job, nothing more. It was like an assembly line of cheap prostitutes. I was in a *Whore Factory*. I had heard of them before but never thought I'd ever be in one. Feeling sorry for the women, and myself, I made up my mind to get out of this filthy whorehouse as soon as possible.

Before me was the red curtain. Relieved, my hand grasped the cotton fabric and moved it aside. I slipped behind it and instantly froze at what my unbelieving eyes witnessed. In the middle of the large space was a circular, white, porcelain trough. It was similar to a workman's wash basin with an umbrella-like fountain of water cascading down from the middle. Around the trough were soldiers with their pants down, or off, and their genitals hanging out over the dirty water in the basin. The men were washing themselves under the waterfall of dirty, yellow water.

A few women sat on wood folding chairs and watched the men while smoking American cigarettes. Like the women in the cubicles, their faces were devoid of any visual emotion or humanity. They just sat, watching the men who scrubbed their organs with soapy hands. Some of the men had a look of fear in their eyes. They were scared and washed as if they would never get clean.

A tall, large man stood at the fountain with his hands on his hips. Two naked Vietnamese woman did the scrubbing for him. Both whores looked unconcerned, almost bored, as they washed the soldier's flacid penis. The women in the chairs noticed me but only glanced my way for a second. I half-expected one of them to take me to the fountain for a cleansing. "Thank God," I thought. "They're going to leave me alone."

While I stood there, a soldier entered the partitioned area from the opposite wall. He was naked and carrying his civilian clothes in his arms. He dropped them in a pile on a chair and walked up to the fountain. He stood there and waited. One of the *seated women* got up, sighed, and walked over to the waiting client.

She picked up a small sliver of white soap and began to wash the man's genitals. He just looked in the air, with closed eyes, while the woman did her chore with unseeing eyes and an expressionless face. Like the women in the cubicles, they, too, were without passion.

In the pit of my stomach, I was sick. My mind quickly sent a command to my feet. They walked fast and took me to the center of the red drapery. The huge, red curtain parted before me. I fled that evil place of *Philistine* temptation. I walked fast and up the aisle of white, shrouded nightmares. My stomach was turning, and convulsing, as I passed a line of paying customers. Breathing was difficult as I crashed through the doors to the outside world. Once on the street, I bent over and suffered from a bad case of *dry heaves*. My mouth had a rotten taste and if I ever needed a drink, it was now.

I took a deep breath and instantly felt better. The putrid air of Vung Tau smelled a lot better than what I breathed inside the Whore Factory. A few civilians, and soldiers, stared at me and probably thought I was just another drunken soldier on R & R.

My only thought was to get back to the airfield. On the way, I swatted a young boy who tried to sell me his mother. The back of my hand caught him in the nose and he stood in the middle of the street, stunned, with blood pouring out of his nose and down his white, tropical shirt. "*Damn*! That felt good."

The crew chief was sitting in the Huey when I arrived. He eyed me closely as I climbed into my gunner seat.

"Well, what did you do? You look out of breath." There was a grin on his face.

"Went to the beach," I said, rubbing my sore knuckles, "and had a few drinks in a bar."

"You look pale."

"Too much sun and whiskey, I guess. The smell in the village also makes me want to puke."

"Yeah, that's for sure." There was a tired look on the chief's face. I had little doubt about where he had spent his free time. I felt sorry for him.

The pilots and brass returned and soon we were outbound, heading north toward Cu Chi. I lit a cigarette and passed it to the crew chief. I lit one for myself and inhaled the soothing, acrid medicine that I sorely needed.

I spent the next hour, eyes closed, thinking of Su Lei. Consolation came in daydreams of our days together in the hotel, the penthouse, and the park. Going to that sordid Whore Factory made me feel guilty, but I knew that Su Lei would have been pleased that I didn't partake of those passionless women. That brothel was scarier than a midnight rocket attack or even a nightime Loach mission, dodging fiery RPGs. When the Huey landed back in the corral, I walked to the hootch thinking, "*Damn*! I'm still not in a shiny, aluminum, flag-draped box.

The following days were busy ones. I helped with aircraft maintenance, weapons cleaning, and caught up on my letters to mom. I even got a ride on a Cobra. One of the snake drivers asked me if I would like to go on a test flight. It was an offer no one could refuse, even me. Putting my fear of flying in-check, I jumped at the opportunity to fly on the newest, hi-tech, war machine in the Army's aerial fleet.

BABY SCOUT

The Centaur Cobras are painted with snarling shark's teeth. Local villagers have complained more than once that the lethal assault helicopters terrified their children whenever they flew over.

I sat in front where the weapons officer sits. The pilot got in behind me and said, "Don't touch nothing." A crewman stood by with an extinguisher as the pilot ignited the jet turbine. The powerful engine *whooshed* to life, the two massive rotor blades came up to speed, and the ship rocked on its skids. The *rocking chair* effect subsided as the RPM increased.

The pilot pulled collective and the huge, twin blades bit into the air. The Gunship slowly rose and backed out of the bunker. My helmet speakers broadcast the takeoff request.

"Cu Chi tower, Centaur two-three."

"Centaur tower. Go, two-three."

"Centaur two-three for takeoff, corral."

"Roger, two-three. Clear for takeoff. Make left base at the gate."

"Roger, Cu Chi. Centaur two-three is on the go." Before the word *go*, we were already in the air and over the hangar. The power of the Cobra is incredible. You sit in very snug seats and feel the muscle of the beast. The pilot took the gunship to 3,000 feet. He said he was going to do a simulated attack dive to check performance and the flight controls.

"Watch the altimiter, Mason."

"Why, sir?"

"Because, Mason, if I don't pull out by 1500 feet, yell."

"Ok," I said, nervously, and again asked, "Why?"

"Because, Mason, if I don't pull up by the time we reach 1500 feet, we can kiss our butts goodbye. We'll plow this bird right into the ground."

"You're kidding?" The pilot ignored my remark. He pushed the cyclic forward and the simulated attack was underway. I watched the altimiter wind down. It looked like a clock with the minute hand rapidly running backwards. I also noticed the airspeed indicator. It was climbing as the altimiter was falling. My mind silently called out the numbers.

"120, 130, 140, 150 knots. 2800, 2700, 2600 feet." My eyes darted back and forth between the two instruments, finally locking on the altimiter.

I was in a rocket sled and the *G*-forces were building. It was hard to move and my back was pinned to the seat.

Michael W. Mason

"2,000, 1900, 1800, 1700, 1600 feet." My thoughts quickly and frantically became words.

"Pull up, sir." My eyes watched the altimiter needle continue its out of control spinning.

"1500, 1400 feet." I was beginning to think we had bought the proverbial farm.

My back slammed into the seat as I was hit with the heavy G-forces of a Cobra that was pulling out of an attack dive. We cleared the ground with a few feet to spare. I was surprised that I didn't pee in my pants and very happy that I didn't have to *kiss my ass goodbye.*

The math didn't add up. If what the pilot said was true, about pulling out of the dive at 1500 feet, then we should have been at the Pearly Gates by now. I thought, "I've been had." I breathed easier, anyway, and sat back and enjoyed the flight back to the airfield.

The Cobra was cooling down in the bunker and I was standing beside her. The pilot walked up to me and asked, "How you doing, Mason?"

"Fine, sir. When can I go up again?" He was surprised at my answer and laughed.

"I'll let you know." He walked away laughing and shaking his head. I found out later that the pilot pulled an old initiation trick on me. I fell for it but was thankful I didn't freak out. My Cobra ride would be the only one I would ever get. My orders had come in. I was going home.

BABY SCOUT

Michael W. Mason

FIFTEEN

THE SILVER BIRD

    I woke to the slam of a door. The Baby Scouts talked loud as they headed out to the flight line. It was the dawn patrol crew and they were excited about their upcoming adventure. I started thinking about how much I was like them not too long ago. My world, then, was flying and shooting up the countryside. These Scouts were probably pretty green. They were just a little too eager for battle, like I once was.
    A few of the Gunship crewmen were rising from their night's sleep. They grabbed their shower bags and flip-flopped out the door. There was nothing for me to do this morning. It was January 29, 1969. Today, I was going home.
    Jake was dressing for a mission. He put on two bandoliers and grabbed his rifle and flight helmet. Something exciting must be happening if the Hog crew chief was going on a mission this early in the morning.
    The Cobras had made the other Huey gunships obsolete. Not the Hog, though. The powerful, aerial battleship might be old but it still packed the biggest wallop in the fleet. Jake was out the door in a hurry and I remembered how I used to rush off to war. It was duty. It was exciting. It was the adventure of a young man's lifetime.
    The shower hootch was empty. It was nice not having the mamasans around doing their laundry. I shaved, brushed my teeth, and just relaxed under the cool water. My war-sensitive ears heard the dawn patrol buzz overhead. A few minutes later I heard another Loach, followed by the unmistakeable *Whomping* of the mighty Hog.
    My body was glowing with perspiration by the time I got back to the hootch. I put on my jungle fatigues and did some packing. Music from a *reel to reel* tape player played songs by bands that I had never heard of before. For the first time I listened to music that never played on the Armed Forces Radio Network.
    "That's the *Jefferson Airplane*."
    "What?" A Gunship crewman had noticed my interest in the tape player.
    "Grace Slick and the Jefferson Airplane. Where you been, man?"
    "I never heard music like this before."

"Oh," the crewman said, "This is *Led Zeppelin*." The music had an attitude. It was raw, vibrating…electric guitars being played like I had never heard before.

"Where'd you get this stuff?"

"My brother sent the tape to me. He said he's going to send me some *Hendrix* and *Moody Blues* next month."

"Uh, far out." I had no idea what he was talking about. The crewman plugged in his earphones and the *new* music became muted. He lay on his bunk, played *mock* drums with his hands, and mouthed something about a pill, rabbit, and a girl named Alice.

Feeling alone, I set off for the mess tent. Morning chow was the same as ever…powdered eggs, sausage, toast, and Kool-Aid. A few Aero-Rifle guys (infantry), were there, along with some Kit Carson Scouts. One of the South Vietnamese soldiers wore a finger and ear necklace. It was visible behind his unbuttoned shirt. He saw me staring and he smiled. I grinned, nodded, and went back to my breakfast. There was a time when seeing something like that would have disgusted, even frightened me. Now, it was just part of the strange, daily faire served up by the Vietnam War. I was used to it.

On the walk back to the hootch, I turned right instead of left. The door slammed behind me and the ghosts of the Baby Scout hootch came alive. The place hadn't changed much, just the faces. Danny was gone, as were Buck, Hutch, Willie, Tom, and Sergeant Jenkins. The voices were loud in my mind. Hutch was making wisecracks about my Colt and holster. Tom was doing his George Burns impersonation, and thinking of the night he set his shorts on fire put a smile on my face.

The voices. The laughter. Those good times would be imprinted on my mind and would help me keep the bad times in balance. I turned and walked away from a past that would always be a part of my life in the present. The door slammed behind me. It loudly exclaimed the end of an era, when teen warriors ruled the skies and a foolish gunslinger thought glory was dying in a firefight.

I walked to OPS and picked up my travel orders. The OD wished me luck. I didn't know him. He was a young Chief Warrant Officer, maybe twenty years old. My fingers clutched my travel orders tightly as I walked out of the small building and stood on the boardwalk. The sun was blinding and almost brought tears to my eyes. That was one of the constants of the war…the sun. It was my daily companion and kept me tanned, soaked with perspiration, and always in the mood for a cold beer.

Tanks and APCs thundered down the road as I walked back to the hootch. The mechanized horses were my only company on this last, lonely day in the Cav. The flight crews were either on missions or working on the flight line. As I approached the gunship hootch, a small, lone figure, dressed in black pajamas, stood on the boardwalk and blocked my way. Mei, the Baby Scout Babysan, had come to say goodbye.

"My, you go home?" She looked up at me with a forced smile and a single tear running down her cheek.

"Yes, Mei. I'm going home. It's my time."

"You come back?"

"No. I won't come back." She looked down and sat on the boardwalk. I sat down next to her, my shoulder touching hers. She scooted closer to me.

"Mei miss My. You favorite Baby Scout. You funny boy. You go, man." In her own way, she was telling me that I had grown up.

"I'll miss you, Mei. I will always remember you and how you took care of me."

"Mei sad you go. My stay Vietnam, My die Vietnam. Mei let you go home." I laughed and her pouty, tear-stained face managed a smile. I put my arm around her and she let her head drop softly on my shoulder. We sat for minutes, watching the war rumble by on a dusty, dirt road. To this day, solace was never so sweet.

"I have to go, Mei." She looked up at me with wet, glistening eyes. She managed a smile and nodded.

"It good you go, My. Mei happy."

"I'll never forget you, Mei. You took care of me." I slowly rose from the boardwalk and helped Mei up by the hand. She didn't let go.

"My more friend than friend. You no know, but you have Su Lei." I was stunned to hear this. Mei was telling me that she had other feelings for me. She squeezed my hand and then was against my chest. The little babysan stood on her toes and planted a hard, long kiss on my lips. I was surprised but responded willingly. My arms went around her and I hugged her close. She was warm and trembling. I patted her head to calm her. She looked at me, smiled, then slowly backed away.

"My…" That was all she said before she turned and ran away. I watched her run. She didn't stop until she disappeared into the Baby

Michael W. Mason

Scout hootch. All those months I had thought of her as a little sister. Only now had I learned that she had more than just sibling-like feelings for me. Melancholic, I walked to the Gunship hootch. The door closed on a small chapter of my life that never had a chance to be fully understood, or completed.

I changed into Khakis and then played with Smokey for a few minutes. It felt good knowing he would be taken care of. Ernie promised that he would look after him. I filled up Smokey's water dish for the last time and then stepped over the wire-mesh fence. Slowly, I walked to the flight line, dufflebag slung over my shoulder.

A Huey Slick was waiting for me, its only passenger. The start-up procedure was routine and soon we were hovering over the grassy airfield. Most of the aircraft bunkers were empty. The war would continue without me. Soldiers, even gunslingers, arrived every day to replace the fallen, the dead, and the fortunate ones like me.

A Cobra sat in its revetment of steel and sandbags. The fortified bunker protected the sleeping, lethal warbird from the occasional rocket attacks. The snarling, shark-toothed killer looked deadly even at sleep.

The Huey moved down the line and my eyes locked on the familiar, nostalgic sight of Baby Scouts cleaning weapons by the Ammo locker. They were laughing and carrying on like they had not a care in the world. I remembered the feeling. In the air, it was kill or be killed. Death was always an unwanted passenger. On the ground, you reveled in the life you might lose on the next mission.

The Slick aburptly stopped, then slowly spun around. It nosed over slightly and gained speed rapidly. In mere seconds, D Troop of the 3rd Squadron/Fourth Cavalry passed by my searching eyes. The pilot pulled back on the cyclic stick and the Huey *whomped* loudly as its rotor blades sliced through the thick, humid air.

The maintenance hangar passed below for the last time. Then, OPS and the hootches. A tiny figure, dressed in black, ran out of the shower hootch and waved. I waved to Mei and fought hard to keep the lump in my throat from travelling to my heart. My last goodbye was not from an American soldier, but from a young Vietnamese girl. If there was irony there, I didn't recognize it at the time.

The pilot banked the Slick and we crossed the perimeter at the main gate. Cu Chi was soon far behind. Then, the brown scar in a vast meadow of green was gone. The ship climbed to a safe altitude of three thousand feet. I was now just a passenger on someone elses milk run.

Far below, the emerald-green countryside passed in slow-motion. It was impossible to tell that South Vietnam was a nation at war. The door gunners were relaxed, their machine guns resting on their steel mounts. I lit up and stared at the horizon. It appeared motionless and time seemed to stand still. The daydreams came and suddenly I was home with my family. Images of Huntington, Long Island filled my mind, as did memories of good times with family and friends.

The daydreams ended with a vision of Su Lei. I expected it. She was lying on the blanket by the duck pond. Her long, black hair covered most of her slender body. Large, oval eyes were filled with twin reflections of myself, looking back. Her full lips were pouty but blossomed into a beautiful smile. It was a memory that I would carry with me for a long time.

The world had changed and I missed out. There was a new morality, new music, new politics, and something called *Psychedelic*. There were hippies, LSD, Mescaline, Psilocybin, Speed, Uppers, Downers, and *free love*. A bad trip was a *bummer* and being cool was *far out* or *groovy*. A lot was going on that I didn't know anything about. I would try to join this new, great society but would fail miserably in the attempt.

The Slick was banking and losing altitude. Tan Son Nhut Air Base was only a few miles away. The ship was on final approach and the door gunners began to unload their guns. I would be let off where it all began one year earlier. In a few hours I would board another aircraft. It wouldn't be a Huey, or a Loach, but a big, shiny *silver bird*.

The Slick sat down on the tarmac. I jumped off, shouldered my dufflebag, and waved to the crew. They waved back and one of the gunners gave me a thumbs-up. It was hot on the tarmac. Intense heat radiated up from the concrete.

Off in the distance was a big, silver, commercial airliner. It was being attended by ground personnel. I figured it was the silver bird that would carry me home. Next to it was a stack of aluminum boxes. There were, at least, fifty of them. The airfield was a busy place and helicopters were everywhere, even Cobras and Loaches. The warbirds looked new and had no armament on them. I wondered if they were headed for D Troop of the 3/4 Cavalry.

Michael W. Mason

"Hey! Over here." I turned and saw a Sergeant waving at me. Next to him, sitting on dufflebags, were other soldiers, all wearing Khaki uniforms. I turned my back on the future hunters and killers and walked over to the group of soldiers.

As I walked up to the Sergeant, he placed a meaty hand on my shoulder and smiled. The friendly man stirred a distant memory of someone I used to admire. He told us to form up and, as we did, he pointed to the gleaming, sliver plane on the tarmac. He said, "Let's go. The world is waiting for us. We're going home."

THE END

EPILOGUE

I had come full circle and the freedom flight was safely on its way to the world. Many of us slept. Others were just staring out the windows. *Mom* took care of us all. She quieted our fears and lent a sympathetic ear to those who needed to purge their souls of unspeakable horrors and sins.

I stared out the window and saw faces and past events…LT getting shot, Danny Narvone sitting in a pool of thick blood, Willie dying, the wounds, the crashes, and my lovely, lost Su Lei. I thought of her most of all. She brought sanity into my life and started me back on the road to my lost humanity.

I also recalled the lighter moments. Tom lighting his butt on fire, the pisser pipe and the Donut Dollies, the mamasans peeking in the shower, the swimming hole, and the milk runs to Saigon and Vung Tau. And Mei. I would always remember the cute babysan.

The horrors were etched on my mind, too: getting blown out of the sky, the near-drowning after #395 crashed into the Go Dau Ha River, the shooting and sinking of the American soldier, the whore factory, the butchery of the Kit Carson Scouts, and the mystery of the My Lai Massacre. It was a secret I would keep until an enterprising newsman exposed the coverup to an angry and incredulous American people.

The worst nightmare of all came to me as I fell asleep. I was looking into the unseeing eyes of a little girl. She lay dead in an obscure field near an obscure village. Her long, black hair was wrapped around her shattered and bloody body. Her colorless, full lips seemed to be pouting. She talked to me.

"I know you."

"My name is Mike."

"Yes, My. I know." The eyes were lifeless and the voice was without emotion. A conversation ensued and we talked about family, friends, enemies, and lovers.

Her answers were better than mine. She made sense where I made rhetoric. The young girl saw more with her dead, blind eyes than I could ever hope to see and understand. Her last words were ominous.

"Come for me, My. You must promise to come for me." I never had a chance to answer.

"Wake up!" I startled and looked up to see Mom's smiling face.

Michael W. Mason

"We're in Hawaii." She continued down the aisle, waking sleeping soldiers from their dreams and nightmares.

The lay over was only for an hour. We were allowed to leave the plane to stretch our legs. Hawaii was warm and sunny, where Vietnam was hot and bright. A pretty Hawaiian girl put a lei of flowers around my neck. "Welcome home," she said.

The terminal was busy with arriving and departing passengers. Most of them were tourists. Amidst the sea of flowered shirts were the soldiers. I wondered how many of them were on R & R from Vietnam. They would have to return to the hell that I had just left. Aside from people-watching, there wasn't much to see at the airport. I boarded the freedom flight and buckled in.

I unbuckled at San Francisco International Airport. The sky was blue and it was cold.

Mom was at the door of the plane and said, "Goodbye," to each one of us. We were directed to a charter bus that would take us to the Oakland Processing Center. On the walk through the terminal, a few people shouted obscenities at me. They were mostly young and very angry looking. I didn't understand what I did wrong.

That was my first encounter with people who were vehemently against the Vietnam War. After the My Lai Massacre became public knowledge, returnees got ruder welcomings. Some were spat on. Others were splashed with paint or animal blood. It amazed me how so-called *peace fanatics* could be as violent as soldiers at war.

My last eight months in the Army were served at Ft. Hood, Texas. The brass sent me to truck driving school. Go figure! I learned how to drive the big rigs. A lot of former crew chiefs and gunners were sent here. I assumed there wasn't much need for war-hardened, aerial killers.

I bought a 1958 Oldsmobile 98. It had four doors, a ton of shiny chrome, and eight speakers for my *8 track* stereo tape player. I immediately got caught drag racing by the MPs and was given a week of extra duty by the CO. The punishment turned out to be a blessing as I got to watch the *Moon Landing* while mopping the floor in the recreation hall. For the first time, I understood the power of television, and something called a computer.

My three year enlistment was over on September 29, 1969. Uncle Sam sent me to college on the *GI Bill*. I also worked part-time jobs, selling vacuum cleaners and tending bar. I graduated from the University of Georgia with a B.A. in Radio/Television Broadcasting. While there, in

Athens, Georgia, I met the best friend of my life. Her name was Tish. She was 19, had long, straight, blonde hair, and rode a motorcycle. She taught me how to ride and I think it was then, in a vacant, dirt lot, that I fell in love with her.

I bought a 1972 Triumph 500 and we became inseparable. Tish had a boyfriend and so our relationship never went beyond platonic. I suffered unbearably by not having the nerve to tell her how I truly felt. The years passed and we lost contact after graduation.

She married her boyfriend, a nice guy, and raised two sons. Both are students at Georgia colleges. Tish and her husband went their separate ways in the eighties. She and I have found each other again, thanks to the computer, and we email each other on a regular basis. We're friends again, as it should be, and one day we'll both go riding through the backroads of Athens, Georgia. Tish will always be my friend. It was she who kept me from falling into the abyss of Post Vietnam Depression.

My first job was with a tv station in West Palm Beach, Florida. During my long, broadcast news career I've interviewed, or met, many Presidents, future Presidents, Kings, and Dictators. I've also shaken hands with many Hollywood celebrities. I think Alan Alda was probably the nicest and most down to earth star, or person, I ever had the pleasure to meet.

Fifteen years of my career was spent in Miami, Florida…twelve of them at a tv station where I flew as a backseat cameraman. My arms cradled a professional video camera instead of a machine gun. The pilot, also a Vietnam veteran, chided me about having *flashbacks*. I never did have any, but flying over the Everglades was reminiscent of some Vietnam war zones. I still didn't like flying but it was my job. Looking through the camera's viewfinder was similar to looking down a gunsight. As in a firefight, I was at ease when shooting video instead of bullets.

I did, however, come home with one physical dysfunction. I lost the ability to write with my left hand, or to hold anything in it without shaking. After a few years I regained full use of my left hand, except for writing. I trained myself to write with my right hand. My penmanship is equal to that of a fifth grader. A veterans advisor told me that I was eligible for disability benefits. I never bothered to file a claim, though. I didn't think that Uncle Sam owed me anything.

In 1989 I was invited by the U. S. Government to Lovelace Medical Center in Albuquerque, New Mexico. I, along with other vets, was tested

Michael W. Mason

for *Agent Orange* toxification. The physical was the same as the astronauts got. The results were negative and before I left, I signed the clinic's guestbook. My eyes locked on a familiar name. It was Hutch. He was in the group before mine. It was the last time I made a connection, of any kind, with the Baby Scouts.

I have babies of my own now. Sean is 11, and Lara is 8. I'm separated from my lovely wife, Kelly, and still love her dearly. She lives with the kids outside Washington, D.C., and is a terrific mother and provider. I live in Southwest Florida, alone, in a small, one-bedroom apartment. It's a living, though not much of a life. I have my work, though, and Uncle Rusty and Aunt Audrey live only forty minutes away.

I work at a small tv station in Fort Myers, Florida. The people are nice, professional, and we all work hard to put out the best newscast in the region. According to the ratings, we work at the number one tv station in Southwest Florida.

I miss my parents. They died years ago. It would have been nice if they could have met their grandkids. I also miss my wife, and the kids. When they are grown, I hope they will understand what their daddy did in the *Thankless War*, and what it must have been like to be a teenaged gunslinger.

If they ever read this story, I also hope they are understanding and can find a way to forgive their daddy for his wilding, gunslinging adventure. No matter how I'm judged in this lifetime or the next, being a Baby Scout was the thrillride of my life.

EXCERPT FROM THE SEQUEL

BABY SCOUTS ASSEMBLE!
The Rescue of Su Lei

A northerly wind brought a nasty, bone-numbing chill to Tokaruki Island. The ocean waves crested on the volcanic breakers and the winter breeze sprayed the island with a misty smoke of dampness and salt.

"There will be no killing today," thought the black-haired woman as she stood on the dock, looking out on the vast, dark blue expanse of the Pacific Ocean. It was a cold, sunny day and her salt-sequined hair sparkled with a myriad of crystaline colors.

Su Lei was the last woman on the island. Two days earlier the mad samurai, and a rifle squad, escorted Betty out of the compound. Betty was a nurse from China Beach and was already on VD Island when Su Lei arrived. The nurse was about forty, blonde, and very pretty. She and the Vietnamese woman stayed in shape by jogging together and playing basketball with the men.

"*Crack!*" Su Lei remembered the sharp sound of the rifle. She was on the basketball court when the sound reverberated throughout the compound. She had flinched but showed no emotion. Su Lei knew what was going to happen. So did Betty. Most of the prisoners went quietly on their death walks. Human attributes such as fear, shame, humility, and joy, had long since atrophied. Death had no meaning for the *patients*, other than a way off the island. They went solemnly and resigned to their fate.

Su Lei would miss Betty. She had taken care of her and protected her since arriving ten years earlier. Now, the lone woman on the island was nurturing a prisoner. He was a foolish young man who never had a chance to mature and grow into adulthood. They had found each other while doing laundry. He had mentioned the Baby Scouts and said his name was David Reese. The black-haired woman had found a kindred soul and a link to her past. Suddenly, after many empty years, humanity had come knocking. Hope, she reasoned, couldn't be far behind. Su Lei found the strength to transcend the apathy that had captured everyone else. She and Davey found mutual consolation and, together, their salvation.

Su Lei felt the chill through the heavy, olive-green, Army field jacket. Her somber thoughts returned to the present and a shake of her head sent a shower of salt crystals into the gale-force winds. Reality beckoned her and she slowly began the walk to the main building. Her thoughts dwelled on what Major Freeman had told her. "You and Davey must stay alive. Lieutenant Reese will come for you." Su Lei didn't know how the deliverance would happen, or when, but knowing the history of the Baby Scouts, she assumed it would be sudden and violent. She smiled as she walked into the warmth of the main building. "God help me," she thought. "Death has become my friend."

(Sequel Completion Date: January, 2003)

ABOUT THE AUTHOR

Michael W. Mason is a 52-year-old *baby boomer* and was born in San Juan, Puerto Rico in 1948. Being a *military brat*, he moved often with his parents and attended many schools, including three different high schools. He graduated from Walt Whitman H.S. in 1966 and enlisted in the Army. He studied aircraft maintenance and served tours in Germany and Vietnam. During the Vietnam War, he was a helicopter crew chief and gunner. Mason earned the Air Medal, with clusters, and the Purple Heart after being wounded in combat while flying a mission over the infamous Iron Triangle.

After military service, Mason attended C. W. Post College of Long Island University for two years. He transferred to the University of Georgia and majored in Broadcast Journalism. Mason graduated with a B.A. in Journalism. While studying for his Master's Degree in Communications at Marshall University, Huntington, West Virginia, he accepted a job offer with WCIX TV in Miami, Florida. Since 1974, he has been a reporter, assignment editor, Chief Photographer, photojournalist, and a News Director.

Mason's work in Broadcast News has won numerous awards, including two Emmys and several AP awards.

Mason is a full-time Photojournalist and writes at home. His interests include: sailing, tennis, reading historical novels, mythology, and writing *feel good* stories for friends.

Printed in the United States
3840